THE KLONDIKE STAMPEDE

TWO KLONDIKERS

G. Edwards

THE KLONDIKE STAMPEDE

By

TAPPAN ADNEY

SPECIAL CORRESPONDENT OF "HARPER'S WEEKLY"
IN THE KLONDIKE

PROFUSELY ILLUSTRATED

WITH A NEW INTRODUCTION
BY KEN COATES

ORIGINALLY PUBLISHED IN 1900
BY HARPER & BROTHERS PUBLISHERS

UBC PRESS / VANCOUVER

ISBN 0-7748-0490-4

National Library of Canada Cataloguing in Publication Data

Adney, E. Tappan (Edwin Tappan), 1868-1950.
The Klondike stampede

Originally published: New York: Harper, 1899.
ISBN 0-7748-0490-4

1. Adney, E. Tappan (Edwin Tappan), 1868-1950. 2. Klondike
River Valley (Yukon) – Gold discoveries. I. Title.

FC4022.3.A36 1994   971.9'102   C94-910345-4
F1095.K5A36 1994

UBC Press gratefully acknowledges the financial support for our
publishing program of the Government of Canada through the Book
Publishing Industry Development Program (BPIDP), and of the Canada
Council for the Arts, and the British Columbia Arts Council.

UBC Press
The University of British Columbia
2029 West Mall
Vancouver, BC V6T 1Z2
604-822-5959 / Fax: 604-822-6083
www.ubcpress.ca

CONTENTS

___

CONTENTS

CONTENTS

CHAPTER XIII

CHAPTER XIV

CHAPTER XV

CHAPTER XVI

CHAPTER XVII

CHAPTER XVIII

CONTENTS

ILLUSTRATIONS

IX

ILLUSTRATIONS

ILLUSTRATIONS

xi

ILLUSTRATIONS

xii

ILLUSTRATIONS

INTRODUCTION

Ken Coates

The Klondike Gold Rush is one of the best-known episodes in the history of Canada, if not North America. Since the day gold was discovered in Rabbit Creek in August 1896 until the present, the mystery and mystique of the Klondike stampede has scarcely wavered and has been immortalized in the poetry of Robert Service, the novellas of Jack London, Pierre Berton's longtime bestseller, *Klondike: The Last Great Gold Rush*, Charlie Chaplin's silent movie *The Gold Rush*, the popular television series *Sergeant Preston of the Mounted Police*, displays at Disneyland, and in countless other ways.

One of the best illustrations of North America's fascination with the Klondike Gold Rush came from a most unusual source: a cereal promotion in the early 1960s. Quaker Oats wished to promote sales of its puffed wheat product and launched a quirky gimmick. Each bag of puffed wheat included a certificate which could be converted into a bona fide Klondike gold claim. The offer was a modest one, and those submitting the certificates were rewarded with a document confirming ownership of one square inch of a real Klondike claim. Quaker Oats had indeed purchased a Klondike claim; they had not, however, prepared themselves for the deluge that followed the promotion. Tens of thousands of North American consumers sent in their certificates, anxious to lay claim to a small portion of the Klondike excitement. The Quaker Oats promotion was one of the most successful commercial publicity campaigns ever undertaken, and a fine illustration of the staying power of the Klondike legend.

The Klondike Gold Rush, at its height in 1897 and 1898, had all the elements of a great drama: the unalterable appeal of fabulous quantities of gold, there for the taking; the lure of the unknown; an exotic setting in the far northwest of North America, with its vicious climate and stunning topography; and a cast of quixotic characters—the risk-takers and dreamers who inhabited the mining frontier. The fact that the Klondike was on Canadian soil did not, by itself, add to the lustre of the event, for gold miners had long skipped over international boundaries in pursuit of the mother lode. But the presence of the North-West Mounted Police, the quintessential expression of the Canadian ethos, extended the national commitment to "peace, order, and good government" into the far northwest corner of the Dominion, a stark and intriguing contrast to the libertarian, lawless mining frontier of the American West.

The Klondike had one additional element that added to its mystique: the site was all but inaccessible, and so remained shrouded in mystery. This, of course, added to the uncertainty and melodrama, leaving the most famous event in the last decade of the nineteenth century wide open to alternate interpretations, exaggeration, and hyperbole. Information that was both reliable and accurate was difficult to find, both during and after the Klondike Gold Rush.

And so emerged one of the key elements of the Klondike experience—exaggeration and misinformation. Gold was, of course, the big attraction. The notion that massive amounts of gold lay only inches below the surface made the Klondike the object of intractable fascination. The image of rivers filled with gold was, in the uncertain and difficult economic times of the late nineteenth century, a compelling one, sure to attract endless interest among the continent's legions of unemployed and disillusioned. Moreover, the Far North had long held a special place in the North American psyche, seen as alternately frightening and enticing, forbidding and alluring, dangerous and exotic. Promoters had a vested interest in maintaining the excitement and did much to inspire grandiose visions of the richness and potential to be found in the Klondike. Hundreds of businessmen, many shady or wildly optimistic, offered dozens of services and products to the unsuspecting or uniformed.

Newspapers also contributed a great deal to the excitement and ambiguousness of the Klondike message. Anxious to sell their product and to maintain readers' interest, the North American newspapers plugged the Klondike story shamelessly, doing their best to find or create human interest stories. They correctly identified widespread fascination with the Klondike experience and then did their best to sustain the level of appeal. Many newspapers dispatched journalists to the Yukon, and their accounts of the Klondike experience found an enraptured audience.

Separating truth from fiction, reality from self-interested promotion, honest accounts from the hyperbole of adventure stories, proved to be extremely difficult. The exaggerations were often more interesting that the actual situation — although the Klondike experience was suitably intriguing and captivating on its own. Americans, in particular, were quick to project the historical experiences of the American mining frontier on to the Canadian northwest, and assumed that the same pattern of lawlessness and vigilante justice would apply to the Yukon. With hundreds of stories swirling in the press, not to mention the vivid tales told by raconteurs in west coast bars or by those returning from the Klondike, it was almost certain that the truth would remain elusive.

And so it has generally remained. The Klondike experience persists as a resilient, pliable myth, now sustained by the expanding northern tourist trade, which has a vested interest in maintaining the excitement and mystery for southerners. Indeed, Robert Service's doggerel poetry—"The Shooting of Dan McGrew," "The Cremation of Sam McGee," and the like—probably have done more to inform popular understandings of the Klondike experience than all of the historical scholarship combined.

This is not to say that there have not been numerous attempts to bring order to the Klondike story. Pierre Berton's *Klondike* is the best of the available secondary accounts. Readable and reliable, Berton's book highlights the unusual and the quixotic, defining the Klondike experience primarily as a series of individual stories rather than as a sociological experience. Scholarly descriptions are fewer in number and less dramatic in impact, and few visitors to the modern Klondike have so much as a passing acquaintance with the writings of serious academics.

There is, of course, a vast literature on the Klondike of another sort, much of it consisting of reprints of first-hand accounts of the gold rush experience. Dozens of the stampeders wrote accounts of their trip to the far northwest, and for many this was the only financial reward they would reap from their costly and difficult quest for gold. The published diaries, journals, and descriptions, written by a diverse assortment of stampeders and adventurers, government officials, and police officers, range widely in quality and reliability. Most are documents of their age, and reflect a fascination with the Klondike experience, their pages adding to the mystique of the stampede by reinforcing the myths and creating new legends. There were also a number of guidebooks written, many of them thinly veiled rip-offs of government publications, purporting to offer the "truth" about the mysterious Klondike gold fields.

Amidst the gravel and muck of the frenzy to satisfy the

insatiable demand for Klondike material lie a few choice nuggets, one of the best being Tappan Adney's *The Klondike Stampede*. Adney was an unusual man, a gifted writer who was fascinated with northern and aboriginal life. Born in Athens, Ohio, in 1868, Adney developed a strong interest in the arts and natural history, which reinforced the foundations of his journalistic career. He was dispatched to the far northwest in the summer of 1897 by his employer, *Harper's Weekly* and the *London Chronicle*. He was not the only journalist to accompany the stampeders—correspondents from such diverse publications as the *Illustrated London News*, *Scribner's*, and *The Century* joined the migration to Dawson City—but his published account of the Klondike experience is one of the very best. Adney's book was not greeted with an overly generous reception. It was initially released in 1900, after the publication of dozens of competing titles had overwhelmed the market, making it difficult for all but the most discriminating readers to differentiate the useful from the sensational and the reliable from the excessive.

In *The Klondike Stampede*, Tappan Adney brings the seasoned eye of an experienced and competent journalist to the task of recording an extraordinary event. Adney joined the northward migration, participating in the feverish chaos that was the gold rush. As he moved steadily toward the Klondike, gathering provisions in Victoria, British Columbia, sailing up the Inside Passage to Skagway aboard the *Islander*, he chronicled the day-by-day experiences of the would-be miners of 1897. With occasional digressions to update readers on general information—the various routes to the Klondike, the costs of a year's provisions, and the like— Adney moves comfortably among the stampeders, recounting their stories, the sights along the route north, and the words, wisdom, and worries of the many men—and the handful of women—sharing the journey to the gold fields.

Readers will find in these pages excellent descriptions of

the people, places, events, and experiences of the Klondike stampede. Adney's account is based on the important real-ization that the truth is more than sufficiently interesting, and he consequently avoids the temptation, so evident in Klondike literature, to descend into hyperbole. He does a fine job of capturing the chaos, nervousness, and excitement of the those who made the arduous trek across the White and Chilkoot passes; and his description of the crush of stampeders at Lake Bennett, where the would-be gold-min-ers gathered to build their boats and rafts for the journey to Dawson City, is one of the best available. The account of the Klondike gold fields, which includes pragmatic descriptions of mining techniques, cabin-building, and the operation of dog teams, is solid, reliable, and fascinating. Adney, perhaps better than any other Klondike recorder, captures the per-sonal urges which drove thousands to join the frenzied rush to the Klondike, yet he never loses sight of the broader dimensions of the stampede.

Adney was also one of the few Klondike chroniclers who was clearly intrigued by the fact that the gold fields were on Canadian soil. He devotes considerable attention to the nuances of Canadian customs regulations. He is faintly bemused, and somewhat relieved, by the presence of the North-West Mounted Police, the quintessential illustration of Canadian sovereignty in a land swarming with American miners. In addition, he does not hesitate to criticize Canadian authorities, and his description of the role of gov-ernment officials in Dawson City and the Klondike captures very effectively the stampeders' intense frustration with the actions and policies of the distant federal government.

Tappan Adney was a man of the late nineteenth century and, as such, his account carries the perspective and values of that generation. This is particularly the case in his harsh and unflattering descriptions of the native peoples of the far northwest. He describes the facial make-up of the Chilkoot

(Tlingit) as leaving the women with "a hideous, repulsive expression" (p. 94). The Chilkoot packers, who were actually shrewd businessfolk, were to Adney, "not trustworthy, and are wholly unscrupulous" (p. 95). After a difficult trading experience near Little Salmon River, Adney suggested that "these Indians, pilfering thieves that they are, doubtless are only practising on the white men what the Chilcats have taught them" (p. 155).

There are other notable lapses. Adney devotes precious little space to the women — small in number, but nonetheless vital to the Klondike — who participated in the gold rush, thus maintaining a tradition of Klondike writing that has largely relegated women to the margins of northern history. By contrast, he was acutely aware of the plight of animals, particularly the horses used in the climb over the mountain passes from tidewater to Lake Bennett.

Tappan Adney left the Klondike in mid-September 1898, heading downriver by riverboat to St. Michael and, from there, by ocean steamer to Seattle, ending a sixteen-month odyssey of quite exceptional proportions. It was an experience, Adney recounts, "none of us can hope to see repeated in a lifetime. A life of freedom and adventure has a fascination which grows rather than diminishes, and yet the privations that every person who went into Klondike endured taught him better to separate the good from the bad, the essential from the non-essential, and to recognize the real blessings and comforts of civilization" (pp. 455-6). Like the good journalist that he was, Adney did not succumb to overstatement and exaggeration. Instead, he captured, vividly and convincingly, in words and images, one of the more remarkable events of the nineteenth century.

Adney returned to the north in 1900 to report on the Nome, Alaska, gold rush. He later moved to Woodstock, New Brunswick, where he died in 1950. Adney did not share the fame of his contemporary writers, such as Jack

INTRODUCTION

London and Robert Service, as *The Klondike Stampede* arrived too late to attract significant attention. In later years he was better known for his research and writing on canoes and canoe-making than for his work on the Klondike.

The literature on the Klondike stampede continues to grow, and there is no sign that the level of interest will soon abate. In fact, with the 100th anniversary of the discovery at Rabbit Creek approaching, enthusiasm for the Klondike legend is sure to be sustained into the next century. This proliferation of material will, no doubt, add to the complexity, diversity, and nature of Klondike mythology. But readers will need to continue looking for reliable and insightful accounts which will strip away the façade of the Klondike experience and provide a more accurate rendering of the world's greatest gold rush.

It is here, among the small number of timeless books about the Klondike Gold Rush, that Tappan Adney's *The Klondike Stampede* takes its place. Reprinted only once previously (in 1968, by Ye Galleon Press of Fairfield, Washington), Adney's book has rarely received the attention it deserves, although northern specialists have long found much of value in its pages. Its re-publication here will ensure that this valuable book will be read again and that it will serve its vital purpose of helping to demystify this diverse, exciting, and dramatic episode of Canadian history. Do not be deterred by the suggestion that this book is "accurate" and "reliable," and, hence almost by definition, less interesting than the more exaggerated accounts penned by other stampeders. As if to prove the adage that truth is stranger than fiction, Tappan Adney's *The Klondike Stampede* contains more than enough excitement, unusual characters, and dramatic situations to sustain the interest of any person intrigued by the events of the Klondike Gold Rush.

THE KLONDIKE STAMPEDE

CHAPTER I

N the 16th of June, 1897, the steamer *Excelsior*, of the Alaska Commercial Company, steamed into the harbor of San Francisco and came to her dock near the foot of Market Street. She had on board a number of prospectors who had wintered on the Yukon River. As they walked down the gang-plank they staggered under a weight of valises, boxes, and bundles. That night the news went East over the wires, and the following morning the local papers* printed the news of the ar-

* The *Examiner* was practically " scooped " on the first story, giving it only a few lines; the *Chronicle* and *Call*, perceiving its news value, served it in the most sensational manner. The New York *Herald* printed the *Call's* story simultaneously. Mr. Hearst, of the New York *Journal* (and *Examiner*), telegraphed San Francisco to know what was the matter, and the next day the *Examiner* plunged in to make amends for its oversight. This is the gossip in San Francisco.

rival of the *Excelsior* with a party of returned miners and $750,000 in gold-dust, and the sensational story that the richest strike in all American mining history had been made the fall of the year before on Bonanza Creek, a tributary of the Klondike River, a small stream entering the Yukon not far above the boundary-line between American and Canadian territory; that the old diggings were deserted, that the mines had been partially worked that winter, and that millions more were in the ground or awaiting shipment.

On the 17th the *Portland*, of the North American Transportation and Trading Company, arrived at Seattle with some sixty more miners and some $800,000 in gold-dust, confirming the report that the new find surpassed anything ever before found in the world. The Seattle papers, equally alive to the interests of their own city, as the outfitting-point for Alaska, plunged into the story with sensational fury. If the stories of wonderful fortune needed corroboration, there were nuggets and sacks of shining gold displayed in windows of shops and hotels. One hundred and thirty thousand dollars' worth of gold, brought by one man from the new diggings, was displayed in one window in San Francisco.

In an incredibly short space of time the inhabitants of the coast cities were beside themselves with excitement. "Coast Again Gold Crazy," was the Eastern comment. A stampede unequalled in history was on. The East could not understand its significance.

"The news that the telegraph is bringing the past few days of the wonderful things of Klondike, in the land of the midnight sun, has opened the flood-gates, and a stream of humanity is pouring through Seattle and on to the golden Mecca of the north. It is a crowd at once strange, weird, and picturesque. Some say it eclipses anything in the days of '49. The good ship

2

WILLAMETTE LEAVING SEATTLE

EXCITEMENT IN THE EAST

Portland, which recently brought a million and a half of treasure to this port, sails for Alaska to-morrow at noon. She will carry every passenger and every pound of cargo that she has the ability to transport. The *Portland* has booked for this passage fifty first-class and ninety-eight second-class passengers. The names of an ex-Governor and a general are in the list. Fifteen hundred passengers are booked for Alaska for the overland passage. Every available steamer is full. The steamers *Queen, Mexico, City of Topeka, Al-Ki*, in rotation, will sail by August 5th, to be followed by the *Willamette, City of Kingston*, and *City of Seattle*, pressed from service elsewhere."—Seattle despatch of June 21st.

The *Excelsior* was booked to its full capacity of passengers, and ten times that number of passengers were turned away. From the Canadian ports, Victoria and Vancouver, every steamer that could be taken was preparing to deliver passengers at Dyea, where the overland route began.

Within a week from the *Excelsior's* arrival, the excitement reached the East. Every source of information about Alaska, or the route to be traversed in getting there, was besieged by hundreds and thousands. The United States government, overwhelmed by applications for information, which it could not supply, at once despatched a trustworthy man from the Department of Labor to the scene of the new strike. The Canadian government was better supplied. The reports of Mr. William Ogilvie, who was surveying the boundary-line between American and British possessions at the time of the strike, had reached his government the previous winter and spring, and the details of the strike were embodied in an official report dated June 5th. Anticipating the rush that was certain to follow, and with commendable zeal, the Dominion Council had organized a system of government, including a code of mining laws for the new

5

district, which was believed to be underlaid with gold, and, beyond a doubt, was in Canadian territory. A land surveyor, with assistants, was despatched to assume charge of the mines, while customs officers, judges, and other officers of government, including a military governor and a detachment of northwestern mounted police (to reinforce the handful already there), either had started or were to start at an early date.

Every class in the community was affected. Companies were formed and stock offered to the public merely on the strength of starting for the Klondike. Men threw up good positions in banks, and under the government; others, with homes and families, mortgaged their property and started; while those who could not command the one to two thousand dollars considered as the very least necessary to success were grub-staked by friends equally affected by the excitement but unable to go in person. The newspapers were filled with advice, information, stories of hardship and of good fortune; but not one in ten, or a hundred, knew what the journey meant nor heeded the voice of warning. "There are but few sane men," says one, "who would deliberately set out to make an Arctic trip in the fall of the year, yet this is exactly what those who now start for the Klondike are doing." And this:

"TIME TO CALL A HALT

ONLY A FEW WILL BE ABLE TO REACH DAWSON
THIS YEAR"

And another:

"WINTER WILL SOON SET IN THERE

SUFFERING SEEMS INEVITABLE

What Gold-Seekers Must Endure—Their Chief Food in Winter is Bear-Fat, and a Bath or a Change of Clothing is Death."

6

NEWSPAPER ACCOUNT OF KLONDIKE

The following actual newspaper account probably surpasses anything ever written or told of the new country. It is entirely a fabrication of a returned Klondiker, but its wide circulation illustrates the credulity of the gold-crazed public:

"THOUSANDS STARVE IN THE KLONDIKE

ALMOST 2000 GRAVES MADE IN THREE YEARS

Hardships Great to Bear

Steamship Companies Control Food Supply and Allow no Private Importations

"GREAT FALLS, MONTANA, *July* 23.—Frank Moss, an old-timer of this section, who four years ago was one of a party of four Americans first to visit the Klondike country, returned to-day, and tells a story of horrors and starvation seldom equalled even in modern novels.

"He describes Klondike as a placer camp, seven miles long and thirteen miles wide, situated in a sink and walled in by bowlders of rock three thousand feet high.

"Gold, he says, abounds, but no ordinary man can stand the hardships of the uncivilized region. When Moss left here four years ago he was a sturdy fellow more than six feet tall. From hardships and privations he is a cripple for life and badly broken in health. In three years he saw more than two thousand graves made in the Klondike basin, a large majority dying from starvation.

"The steamship companies bring in all the food and allow no private importations; consequently it is not uncommon to go for weeks with but a scant supply, and for days entirely without any food.

"The gold brought in last week to Seattle, Moss says, does not represent the findings of individual shippers, but a large proportion was confiscated from the effects of those two thousand miners who fell a prey to the hardships. At the death of a man possessed of dust his body was buried without a coffin, and the dust divided among those who cared for him. With proper reliefs established by the government, Moss says, gold could be taken out at the rate of $2,000,000 a month.

"The richest strike has been made by a boy twenty-one years old, named George Hornblower, of Indianapolis. In the heart of a barren waste, known as Bowlder Field, he found a nugget for which the transportation companies gave him $5700. He located his claim at the find, and in four months had taken out more than $1,000,000.

"The richest section, he says, is yet undeveloped. It is one hundred miles from Klondike, and is known as the Black Hole of Calcutta. It is inhabited by ex-convicts of Bohemia, and murders and riots take the place of law and order.

"A few months ago, Klondike organized a justice committee, and its laws prevail there now.

"Suffering will be great, with the great crowds preparing to go to the scene now, Moss says; hunger and suffering will be great when added to the other hardships to be overcome by those who survive. Moss returned with $6000 in dust, and will leave here to-morrow for his old home in Dubuque, Iowa, where he will spend the remainder of his years."

The Canadian government published a warning that all who were starting faced starvation, and should wait till spring; that shelters would be built on the way, but food could not be supplied to those going in unprepared.

On the 26th of July the London *Times* gave full particulars of the strike; on the 28th the Colonial Office issued a bulletin advising Englishmen not to start, but to wait till spring.

The tide was too great to turn. One by one the conservative papers of the country, that had treated the first reports as sensational news, fell into line. On the 28th of July the Messrs. Harper & Brothers commissioned a correspondent to proceed to Dawson to furnish news and pictures of the new gold-fields.*

I, the one chosen for this work, spent the next three days getting together that part of a one year's outfit that could not be obtained on the West Coast, including a complete photographic outfit, comprising a 5 × 7 long-focus Premo camera; ten dozen 5 × 7 cut films for use in plate-holders (having the advantage of lightness and unbreakableness); and eight spools of sensitive film, of thirty-two exposures each, for use in a roll-holder, and expressly ordered hermetically sealed in tins; in addition, a small pocket Kodak, taking 1½ × 2-inch pictures, together with a complete developing outfit. Glass plates were not taken, on account of weight and their liability to break in the mail.

On the 30th of July I purchased, at the office of the Canadian Pacific Railway in New York, a through *printed* ticket reading "New York to Dyea," including passage on the steamer *Islander*, scheduled to leave Victoria on the 15th of August, on her second trip.

By this time reports had arrived of an easier pass, only four miles from Dyea, and known as the White Pass, with trail already constructed and parties with pack-horses and outfits going over with ease to the head of navigation on the Yukon, where boats were to be built. At Montreal I secured, by telegraph, space on the *Islander* for six pack-horses. At Winnipeg I hurried to the Hudson's Bay Company's store for winter clothes and furs, but the town was already cleaned out, not a fur robe nor skin coat to be had. Instead—and fearing that

* After my departure arrangement was made by Messrs. Harper & Brothers with the London *Chronicle* for simultaneous publication of the matter to be furnished.

nothing of the kind suitable for the arctic climate would by this time be left on the Coast—I got the regulation *capote* of the employés of the Company, made of the heaviest black *duffel* reaching to the knees and with a hood; also twelve-pound "four-point "*duffel* blankets; a variegated yarn sash, such as is worn by the Northwest *metis*; a red-and-black knit *tuque*; and the best moose-hide moccasins; leaving the rest of my outfit to be purchased in Victoria, which I reached on August 8th.

AUTHOR IN HUDSON'S BAY COSTUME

CHAPTER II

Outfitting in Victoria—Departure—Incidents on the Steamer—Preparations for Landing at Skagway

VICTORIA, B. C., *August* 15, 1897.

THE streets of leisurely Victoria are thronged with strange men, and there is an earnest look on their faces and firmness in their step. When the sealers return each autumn there is another crowd, but not like this. Victoria has never seen this crowd before. They are the kind of men who are the pioneers in every new country; men from every station of life, but all of one mind, actuated by one purpose. They are buying horses, and watching men who in front of stores explain the "diamond hitch"; they are buying thick, warm woollens; belts that go around the waist, with flaps that button down over little compartments; little bags of buckskin, with gathering-strings at the top; heavy, iron-shod shoes, made in the likeness of nothing in the heavens above or the earth beneath, but strong, durable, and suited for the purpose in view; and moccasins of moose-hide, with socks as thick as a man's hand and that reach to the knee.

The crowd is cosmopolitan. It has gathered from remote points. There are Scotch and Irish, French and German, together with plain American. Klondike!—

magic word, that is possessing men so that they think and talk of nothing else. Victoria sells mittens and hats and coats only for Klondike. Flour and bacon, tea and coffee, are sold only for Klondike. Shoes and saddles and boats, shovels and sacks—everything for Klondike. The man who is not going by next boat for the North, or who is not "waiting till spring," or who has not decided reasons for not going at all and why every one else should not go, must be a rarity. He does not exist in this town, so far as I have been able to discover in one week's time. Even in the singsong of the Chinaman the ear will catch the sound "Klondike." Boys who at other times might be impudent, now, with a look of wonder, point and say, "He's going to Klondike!" It's a distinction to be a Klondiker.

Even here the bigness of the undertaking is realized. A dozen men have grasped me by the hand and said : "I wish you success. Any one who has the courage to start there deserves every bit." It may be a business man, an editor, or the man who stands at your back at the hotel table. All are alike interested ; all who could have gone with the first rush, and those who can are going "in the spring." They doubt if one can get in now before it freezes tight ; and they may be right when they say that hundreds, if not thousands, of men with their outfits at the Chilkoot and White passes will camp'there all winter, unable to get across.

Victoria is awakening to the realization of a fact—a blunt, hard, yet agreeable fact. Circle City and Juneau, where the gold has hitherto been mined, are in American territory, and so Seattle has practically monopolized the Alaska outfitting business. But Klondike River is in Canadian territory, and Canadian laws apply to the remotest corner of the Dominion, and every miner's outfit that goes across the boundary - line, no matter where, owes a duty. Why, then, should not Victoria and Vancouver do the business for Klondike, and thereby save the miners the duties? Some wide-awake business men answered the question by at once despatching a

PACK-HORSE AND SLEDGE-DOG WAITING TO BOARD THE STEAMER FOR DYEA

man to Seattle to purchase an outfit and to ascertain the prices.

A miner intending to go to Klondike has the alternative of buying on the American side and paying duty, or of buying here. Government, we are told, has been established, and I am assured by the collector of this port, Mr. Milne, that should miners prefer to bring their outfits across the line they will be accorded precisely the same treatment at Dawson or Tagish Lake (just over the pass — the officers left here two weeks ago) as in Victoria or Montreal. " There is but one law for every part of the Dominion of Canada. We do not want to be severely strict with the miners, but you know how much easier it is to relax than to tighten." It is going hard with those American cities which have hitherto had the whole business of outfitting, but it should be borne in mind that the next news may be of bigger finds on American soil. Events are moving in such rapid succession that it is simply bewildering, and one rubs one's eyes to make sure that it is not all a pleasant dream. Familiar spots and even old friends have the same unreal look.

What does it mean? Some men have been digging with shovels into the earth and filling large pans, and with water washing off the lighter material, leaving some heavy yellow metal which, when gathered in bags and old coats, made a load that several men could not lift. This came down from there three or four weeks ago. Now vessels and men and horses and dogs are set in violent motion in the direction whence it came. Surely, that is a strange power the yellow metal has !

One who has never undertaken to gather all that a man will need for a space of ten or twelve months, so that he shall not have to call on any one else for material assistance, has any idea of the time required. The most important item on the list is good advice—plenty of it. One does not fully comprehend the helplessness of average mankind until he meets some of these men on the streets. Scores of men would never have gotten one inch to the northward of the town of Victoria without the help of others. Two men in three virtually are carried along by the odd man. They are without practical experience; it is pitiful to see them groping like the blind, trying to do this thing or that, having no notion of what it is to plan and to have the ends fit like a dovetail. I asked a Frenchman from Detroit how he meant to get over the pass—was he taking a horse? "Oh no; there would be some way." And yet he knew that every returning steamer is bringing word like this, which is from a recent private letter from Dyea to a large outfitter:

"For Heaven's sake, if you have any influence to prevent it, do not let any one come here without horses; hundreds of people will be encamped here all winter, unable to get across."

Some queer outfits have gone north in the last few days. One man, evidently a person of means as well as leisure, has taken, among other things, one case of thirty-two pairs of moccasins, one case of pipes, one case of shoes, two Irish setters, a bull pup, and a lawn-tennis set, I am told he is not a trader, but going "just for a jolly good time, you know." Another man is taking an enormous ox, and he created a sensation leading it through town with a pack-saddle on its back. He intends to eat it. Wise man! Some say we shall have to eat our horses.

Knock-down boats of every conceivable sort are being taken up since the reports have come down that boat timber is very scarce, as well as high in price.

I have had cut out, from my own plans, the ribs and sides of a lumberman's bateau twenty-three feet long, five feet beam, eighteen inches width on the bottom, five and a half feet overhang in front, and four feet at the stern, the bottom being of three-quarter inch cedar, the sides of five-eighth and one-half inch stuff. It is, in fact, an extreme type of dory, a perfect rough-water boat, its flaring sides preventing the boarding of waves, its narrow bottom enabling it to pass through a narrow channel. It is easily handled with either pole, paddles, or oars. I have roughly calculated that one ton will sink it a foot. Its actual load will be less. But reports are discouraging about boats. The trails up the mountains are reported so narrow and tortuous that long pieces cannot be carried over. In that case I can cut the lumber into sections. It may never get over. Hundreds of boats, it is said, are being left behind. News is contradictory, when it is to be had at all. It is unsafe to leave any precaution untaken. The same rule applies to horses. No one here for a moment says I have too many, though I have more for the amount to be carried than any other outfit that has left Victoria thus far. One outfit of seventy-four horses is going up from here to carry goods for the mounted police.

According to the Coast papers that have correspondents on the scene, hope of getting over *via* Chilkoot is slight. The baggage of over three thousand ahead of us is stranded at Dyea, unable to be handled by the packers, and all who can are starting over White Pass.

Dyea has been made a sub-port of Juneau, for the convenience of foreign vessels; our goods are billed "Dyea," but will go off at Skagway.

THE ROUTES TO-DAY

1. *Via* St. Michael. Ocean steamer to St. Michael, a distance of 2725 miles (from Seattle); transferring to flat-bottomed river-steamers up the Yukon River, a distance to Dawson variously estimated at from 1298 miles to 1600 or 1700 miles; the "easiest" route, but restricted for river navigation to the period from June to September.

2. *Via* Lynn Canal. Two routes, viz., (*a*), the Chilkoot trail.

ROUTES TO KLONDIKE

From Dyea over Chilkoot Pass, 27 miles to Lake Lindeman, head of navigation of Lewes River, a main tributary of the Yukon, and 575 miles to Dawson; the trail used for the past sixteen years by miners entering the Yukon. Freight is carried by hand, but horses are used as far as the foot of the pass, 18 miles from Dyea. Elevation of pass about 3350 feet. (b), The White Pass trail. Discovered by Captain William Moore ten years ago. Starts four miles from Dyea, ascending valley of Skagway River over pass, 2800 feet elevation, and 20 miles distant from salt water. Beyond the summit not really known, but leading to one of two arms of Tagish Lake. Distance said to be not much greater than *via* Chilkoot. Vigorously advertised during the past two weeks as a good horse trail all the way.

3. Dalton's trail. Overland from head of Pyramid Harbor, *via* Chilcat Pass, thence over rolling grassy country to point on Lewes, near Five-Finger Rapids, and to Fort Selkirk, the latter a distance of 350 miles from tide-water, and 175 miles from Dawson. Available for cattle and horses, and for a railroad. Named after its discoverer, John Dalton, a trader.

4. Stikeen route. Starting from Fort Wrangell, thence up the Stikeen River, a distance of about 150 miles to Telegraph City (an old mining camp). From thence overland to head of Lake Teslin, head of Hootalinqua, or Teslinto, River, a tributary of the Lewes; a distance to Teslin of 122 to 160 miles. None of the new maps agree where the trail is, but the route is being pushed by the Canadian government as an all-Canadian route to the Klondike. A company has chartered the only steamer available at Wrangell and is taking over saw-mill machinery, building steamers, and preparing for the spring "rush" that way.

5. *Via* Edmonton. By courtesy designated a "trail." The insane desire of Canada to find an all-Canadian route to her new possessions has led to the suggestion as possible routes those used by the Hudson's Bay Company to reach the Yukon. From Edmonton a wagon-road of 96 miles to Athabasca Landing; thence by small boat, 430 miles, to Lake Athabasca; thence down Slave River, across Great Slave Lake, and down the Mackenzie River, 1376 miles, to the neighborhood of Fort McPherson, near

the mouth of the Mackenzie; thence up Rat River and over an all-water connection at McDougall's Pass into the Porcupine; and thence down the Porcupine to the Yukon, 496 miles—a total distance from Edmonton of 2398 miles (Mr. William Ogilvie's figures). There the would-be Klondiker, 303 miles below Dawson and against a hard current, is practically farther away from his destination than if at Dyea or Skagway.

The other "route" from Edmonton ascends the Athabasca River to Little Slave Lake; thence by portage to Peace River; ascends that river to a point towards its source; thence overland by a ramification of "routes" to the Liard; up that river and thence by another portage to the head of the Pelly, and down that river to Fort Selkirk; an exceedingly difficult trail, abandoned forty years ago by the company that first discovered its existence.

The above briefly describes the "trails" by which the Canadians, the merchants of Edmonton, and the Canadian Pacific Railway propose to start human beings for the Yukon. It has been termed "the Athabasca back-door route." By the same token there are as many other "routes" to the Yukon as there are water-ways in the northwest of Canada between Montreal and the Rocky Mountains.

The horses, alleged to be pack-horses, that are being brought into Victoria for sale amuse every one greatly. There are ambulating bone-yards, the infirm and decrepit, those afflicted with spavin and spring-halt, and many with ribs like the sides of a whiskey-cask and hips to hang hats on. With their drooping heads and listless tails, they are pictures of misery. Yet they are being bought to pack over the hardest kind of trail. Why, some of them at the Hudson's Bay Company's wharf look as if a good feed of oats would either break their backs or make them sag beyond remedy, while their legs seem barely able to support their bodies. They are brought in from all quarters of Vancouver Island and the mainland. Till now they have been without value or price. Twenty-five dollars up is the invariable price asked, and it is ludicrous to see some of their owners, who a month ago would have fainted in their tracks at the sight of five dollars, now, when you ask the price, shift about, swallow once or twice, and say, "Twenty-five dollars." "Thirty dollars" means that the owner has a pretty fair horse, probably an old packer; but "twenty-five" dollars now in Victoria means that much clear profit, and they have plenty of takers. The pack-saddles are five to six dollars, without the lash-ropes, but with the extra cinch. In front of the saddlery-stores groups of intending miners watch some old-timer explaining the mysteries of the "diamond hitch." A man is a tenderfoot out here until he can throw the diamond hitch, the only hitch that will hold the load on a horse's back. The "squaw hitch," however, does for side packs and is simple.

It is rare amusement to a tenderfoot, getting together a pack-train. A little knowledge of horses helps, but I suppose one should not expect too much. As long as one's pack-train looks positively no worse than one's neighbor's he does not mind. Although he may have a spotted cayuse as big as a sheep alongside a fifteen-hand rawboned roan mare, no one is expected to do any better with the time and material at command. Victorians believe that next spring there will be a wholly better lot of horses; they do not believe the present supply of wrecks will last any longer. My packers consist of a black with a bone-spavin which causes him to throw his leg crossways when he trots; his mate is a small bay pony, narrow-chested; then there is a white-faced "pinto," a large roan mare, and a bully little packer nearly two feet lower than the old roan. Her name is Nelly, the only name I could get of any of my horses. The sixth one is a nondescript—just a thin sorrel horse. They make a brave

19

show with their new pack-saddles and coils of new lash-ropes.

How to handle this formidable outfit was a question, until I ran afoul of two fellows bound also for Dawson. I met them on the train over and sized them up. They were with a contingent from Detroit. Jim McCarron had been a trooper in the Seventh United States Cavalry, and young Burghardt was travelling on his ability to cook, being the son of a baker and a baker himself. Jim was used to handling horses, though he did not pretend to know how to pack any more than I did.

Burghardt did claim he could bake bread. I asked him if he thought we were going to live on nothing but bread. These two men were able to take but one horse each. These they bought in Victoria. Then we joined forces for Klondike on the following conditions : they were to take entire charge of my horses, and were to undertake to put my whole outfit across the pass first, so as to leave me as free as possible for my newspaper work. Then, while I put together my boat, and another for them, the lumber for which they were taking up from here, they were to take the whole eight horses and pack their own outfits over. With them was a Dutchman, large, thick, slow, but strong as a horse, and with one eye. He had a horse too, but it was not part of my outfit.

In the way of food supplies, the dealers here have long lists of canned goods, from which all tastes can be suited. But I intend to stick as closely as possible to the merest essentials. Lumbermen know what a man can live and grow fat on out-of-doors, and so does the United States army. There is something about pork, flour, beans, and tea that makes it easy to add the rest. As to clothing, rubber hip-boots and an oil-skin coat are necessary. For the long, cold winter, misapprehension exists. Those best qualified to express an opinion say that there is nothing better than a deer-skin coat with hood—an Eskimo garment, called a *parka*. Then, one should have a fur robe; one good robe is better than any number of blankets, and should be 7 × 8 feet. In the order of preference, arctic hare is first. Next is white rabbit, the skins being

MINERS' SUPPLIES WAITING TO BE LOADED FOR KLONDIKE

cut into strips, then plaited and sewed together. One needs nothing else in the coldest weather, although one can thrust one's fingers through it. Both rabbit and hare robes are scarce and last only a year. Lynx, fox, wolf, marmot, make good robes; bear is almost too heavy for travelling. I was fortunate indeed to pick up even a marmot-skin robe, eight feet long and five wide, lined with a blanket, Indian-made, from somewhere up the coast.

The following are the goods commonly taken in by

miners. The list includes several articles of which it is only necessary to have one in each party :

SUPPLIES FOR ONE MAN FOR ONE YEAR

8 sacks Flour (50 lbs. each).
150 lbs. Bacon.
150 lbs. Split Pease.
100 lbs. Beans.
25 lbs. Evaporated Apples.
25 lbs. Evaporated Peaches.
25 lbs. Apricots.
25 lbs. Butter.
100 lbs. Granulated Sugar.
1½ doz. Condensed Milk.
15 lbs. Coffee.
10 lbs. Tea.
1 lb. Pepper
10 lbs. Salt.
8 lbs. Baking Powder.
40 lbs. Rolled Oats.
2 doz. Yeast Cakes.
½ doz. 4-oz. Beef Extract.
5 bars Castile Soap.
6 bars Tar Soap.
1 tin Matches.
1 gal. Vinegar.
1 box Candles.
25 lbs. Evaporated Potatoes.
25 lbs. Rice.
25 Canvas Sacks.
1 Wash-Basin.
1 Medicine-Chest.
1 Rubber Sheet.
1 set Pack-Straps.
1 Pick.
1 Handle.
1 Drift-Pick.
1 Handle.
1 Shovel.
1 Gold-Pan.
1 Axe.
1 Whip-Saw.

1 Hand-Saw.
1 Jack-Plane.
1 Brace.
4 Bits, assorted, $\frac{3}{16}$ to 1 in.
1 8-in. Mill File.
1 6-in. Mill File.
1 Broad Hatchet.
1 2-qt. Galvanized Coffee-Pot.
1 Fry-Pan.
1 Package Rivets.
1 Draw-Knife.   [Granite.
3 Covered Pails, 4, 6, and 8 qt.,
1 Pie-Plate.
1 Knife and Fork.
1 Granite Cup.
1 each Tea and Table Spoon.
1 14-in. Granite Spoon.
1 Tape-Measure.
1 1½-in. Chisel.
10 lbs. Oakum.
10 lbs. Pitch.
5 lbs. 20d. Nails.
5 lbs. 10d. Nails.
6 lbs. 6d. Nails.
200 feet $\frac{5}{8}$-in. Rope.
1 Single Block.
1 Solder Outfit.
1 14-qt. Galvanized Pail.
1 Granite Saucepan.
3 lbs. Candlewick.
1 Compass.
1 Miner's Candlestick.
6 Towels.
1 Axe-Handle.
1 Axe-Stone.
1 Emery-Stone.
1 Sheet-Iron Stove.
1 Tent.

CLOTHING, SLEDS, AND DOGS

I bought a small two-and-a-half-point white blanket at the Hudson's Bay Company's store here, for cutting up into squares to fold over the feet inside the moccasins or else made into "Siwash" socks. Foot-gear must be loose and plentiful. A miner lately returned from three years on the Yukon told me he kept one large sack for nothing but moccasins and socks.

On the advice of Inspector Harper of the Northwestern Mounted Police, who is taking twenty men to Dawson, I added two suits of fine Balbriggan underwear, to be worn underneath the woollens, and a shirt of buckskin. He also advised the use of loose Lisle-thread gloves inside the mittens, which enables the hand to be comfortably withdrawn from the mitten in very cold weather. For rough work, as handling a raft or using tools, a stouter glove of buckskin, very loose, would wear better. As regards the loose glove inside the mitten, this agrees with Caspar Whitney's experience in the extreme north of Canada, in the Barren Grounds east of the mouth of the Mackenzie River, in winter. Most people buy the complete lumberman's Mackinaw suit, of coat and trousers, to which may be added a heavy Mackinaw shirt, with high collar. The gayer patterns seen in the Eastern lumber-camps are seldom sold here, but even the plainest Mackinaw is positively immodest.

Many are taking in sleds and dogs. Some splendid St. Bernards are going up. Dogs are expensive. None suitable can be had here at any price, while those for the use of the mounted police, brought from eastward, cost nearly as much expressage as a horse would cost to buy. The sleds (said to have originated in the Cassiar Mountains, and thence carried into the Yukon), to one who is accustomed to the Indian toboggan, whether the flat upturned board or the New Brunswick

kind with cedar sides and beech shoes, seem heavy,
but are built by those who understand the needs of the
country. They are 7 feet long, about 16 inches wide,
with a height of 6 inches. The bow is slightly upturned,
and the top, of four longitudinal pine slats, rests upon
four cross-frames of ash, with ash runners shod with
two-inch steel shoes.

The steamer *Bristol*, a large steel collier, was chartered
on a few days' notice, and advertised to sail several days
before our boat. She was hauled into the outer wharf,
and the carpenters went aboard with scantling and converted her entire hold into stalls two feet in width for
horses; and there were stalls on deck, and hay on top of
them. Rough bunks were put in, filling every available
spot on the ship. It was a scene on the dock such as
Victoria had never seen before. Scores of men were at
work building scows, with which to lighter the freight
ashore at Skagway (pronounced Skagway, not Skadg-
way), loading the bags containing the miners' supplies,
and hoisting one by one the five or six hundred horses
aboard. It characterizes the haste with which the crush
has had to be met that, after leaving, the ship returned
to port to adjust her top load, after a delay of four days
beyond the advertised time of sailing, during which time
the poor animals were crowded in close rows, with no
chance to lie down, and, below, not even chance to
breathe. The men were hardly better off than the
horses, two of which are of my outfit, in charge of the
boy Burghardt. I let two horses go on the *Bristol*, as
Burghardt and McCarron had not at that time bought
their own horses, which could now go aboard the *Islander* in the space reserved for mine. On account of
these delays — which culminated in a meeting of indignant passengers on the dock — we who have en-

THE *ISLANDER'S* DEPARTURE

gaged to go on the good steamer *Islander*, Captain John
Irving, will get there as soon as, or sooner than, they.

As I conclude the account of the preliminary work, we
are all aboard the *Islander*. She has left her wharf at
Victoria, to the sound of cheer after cheer from dense
crowds, which have taken possession of every vantage-
ground. The stalwart forms of the mounted police,
truly a fine-looking body of men, take the crowd, and cheer
after cheer goes up for them. There are no more lusty
shouts than those given by thirty-six small boys perched
in a row on the ridge-pole of the wharf overlooking the
water. "Three cheers for the mounted police!" and
"Three cheers for Klondike!"

There are sad faces aboard, and a tear moistens the
eye of more than one hardened miner who is leaving
wife and family behind. But we are glad because of
the cheering crowd, for, as Jim remarks, it would have
seemed pretty blue if there had been nobody here.

STEAMSHIP *ISLANDER*, *August* 19.

As the echoes of the cheers that greet our departure
die away and the city fades from view in the growing
darkness, we go, each of us, about his respective affairs.
Some, worn out by the work and excitement of getting
off, turn in early to bed ; others take a look at the horses,
which are making a regular hubbub on the lower deck.
We find them wedged side by side in a long row along
each side of the ship, with heads towards the engines, and
no chance to lie down. Frightened by the pounding of
the engines and the blasts of the whistle, they are throwing themselves back on their halters and biting and kicking. Jim McCarron, ex-cavalryman, U. S. A., is now in
his element, and I think he wants to show his friends, the
mounted police, that he, too, knows a bit about horses.

Several of our halters are broken, and it looks as if we would have to take alternate watches, but Jim patches up some rope halters. Next day the animals had quieted down, but nearly every horse has a mark from the teeth of his neighbor. Poles should have been put across, separating them.

One man has eight or ten enormous steers aboard, which, with characteristic bovine philosophy, lie down in the road of every one, and will budge neither for threat nor kick. They are being taken in for packing and hauling. We sincerely trust we shall never have to try to eat them when they reach Klondike. It is a good-natured, sober crowd aboard. Several have remarked how undemonstrative it is. One-half are Americans. They are of every degree and of all sorts but dudes. There is a house-builder from Brooklyn, a contractor from Boston, the business manager of a New York paper, and boys that seem not over nineteen.* They have all formed parties or partnerships, some to share every vicissitude of fortune, others only to last until the gold-diggings are reached. Only a few are dressed in the loose, rough clothes of the miner. Several that I know who are going in have kept on their city suits, and it has been amusing to see men unaccustomed to rough garments emerge, one by one, from their state-rooms with their miners' rigs of heavy boots and corduroys. One most picturesque figure is a swarthy man of spare but wiry build who turned out in full buckskin suit, at which some smiled ; but after a talk with him it was impossible not to admit that, while

---

* One of the passengers was Captain (now Lieutenant-Colonel) A. A. Lee, Royal Artillery, going north for the London *Chronicle*, who returned from the passes in time for the Spanish War, during which he accompanied the United States as military attaché of the British army.

the buckskin might "draw" somewhat in wet weather, nevertheless he was as well fixed as any man on board. He is a packer and hunter, and hails from the Black Hills, and has a partner seven feet tall, who is a lawyer.

One noticeable thing is the total absence of oaths or the sort of language one will hear from morn till night among lumbermen. The conversation is pitched in a low key ; men have serious things to talk about — those they have left behind; the pass ahead of them; their outfits, and those of their neighbors. Some are pretty well equipped; indeed, save for a general lack of water - proof sacks, they are well prepared for the rainy

MOUNTED POLICE IN STABLE UNIFORM OF BROWN CANVAS, WITH "HUSKY" DOGS

country which, by the lowering clouds and increasing banks of fog, we seem to be entering.

Of the passengers aboard it may safely be said that each man has half a ton of freight stored away in the hold. Some, representing companies, have more than that. There is a large consignment of sleds aboard, and several boats, all of which are in lengths too long to pack over the pass. One New York party has folding canvas canoes.

During the daytime we lounge about on the bales of hay on deck, some sleeping, others admiring the

TALKING OUTFITS

grand mountain scenery through which we are passing. Others who have rifles to test keep a sharp lookout for ducks. Going through the narrows between Vancouver Island and the mainland we came across numerous small flocks of seaduck, which gave us long shots, in which the excellence of the new " 30-40 smokeless " as long-range guns stood forth unmistakably. " Buckskin Joe," as we have dubbed our mountain man from the Black Hills, has a gun which, like himself, is unique. It is a 30-40 box-magazine Winchester placed side by side on the same stock with a Winchester repeating shot-gun, and there is a telescopic sight between them. It is, however, so put together that it can be taken apart and each gun fitted to a separate stock, which he has with him.

Freight is in utmost confusion ; three parcels of my own that came aboard as my personal baggage went into the hold—result, some valuable photographic chemicals probably crushed, although in heavy boxes. No one knows where to find his oats and hay. Everybody is borrowing from his neighbor. We have three bales of hay and a thousand pounds of oats, and, except for one bale of hay, not a pound of our horse-feed have we been able to get at.

The time passes between boxing-bouts on deck, singing to the accompaniment of the piano, inspecting one another's outfits, and poker, five-cent limit. The second night out, when just out of Seymour Channel, the engine suddenly stopped. All hands rushed on deck, and we saw lights alongside that were reported to be those of a steamer on the rocks. It proved to be the *Danube*, which was returning from Skagway. She was all right, but sent some word aboard to our captain about the customs, and a report was circulated that there was to be trouble ahead for us "Canadians." It was well understood by us that our goods, in consequence of being "in bond" through the strip of American territory this side the passes, could not be touched by us at Skagway. Several of the Canadian officials on

PROSPECTIVE MILLIONAIRES

board expressed the hope, which we all shared, that the American customs officials had been given power to use discretion in view of the exceptional circumstances of this stampede, or, if not yet given such power, that they would use it anyhow. If the United States officers decide that "bulk must remain unbroken"—the technical term used when goods are in bond and under seal—it will be the poor miner who will suffer. He will suffer

by not having access to his food and cooking and camping utensils until after he gets over the pass; and if he
does break bulk, and thus destroys the seal which is
evidence of Canadian purchase, he will be liable to the
Canadians for the duties after he crosses the pass. We
were, therefore, in no small suspense until the afternoon
of the 17th, when we reached Mary Island, in Alaska.
Here the American customs official, Mr. P. A. Smith,
came aboard, and after supper he sent for all the passengers to meet him in the dining-saloon, where he
addressed us in the following words:

"Gentlemen, I have just a few words to say to you,
and I shall speak as loud as I can, but, if I shall not be
able to make myself heard, I hope those who do hear will
tell the others. I suppose that most of you are Canadians,
and I wish to make a few suggestions to you, so that you
may be put to as little trouble as possible in transit. My
advice to you is to get organized, and appoint committees
to look after the landing at Skagway. I was on the
Danube, and I gave its passengers the same advice, and
they appointed a committee of ten, who saw to the separation of the freight and that each man got his own goods.
If you do not do this there will be great confusion, for I
suppose you are aware that the landing is done in scows.
These committees can attend to everything, and you will
have no trouble whatever. The passengers on the *Danube*
had no trouble whatever. I would say another thing to
you. There are persons in Skagway who gather in
things; and your committee can appoint watchers to
keep an eye on your things and to guard the supplies.

"Now, as to food at Skagway. I suppose you know
that, according to the strict letter of the law, goods
bonded through cannot be broken without payment of
duty; but such things as tents and blankets a man must

32

have. Those you will be allowed to use; but I would advise you to stop off at Juneau and to buy there enough food to last you over the pass. It will not cost you any more than at Seattle, and you can get just enough and take it aboard; there will be no charge for freight.

"Now, another thing. The government of the United States is very strict about bringing whiskey into Alaska.

SKAGWAY, TWO WEEKS BEFORE OUR ARRIVAL

Any one found with liquor is liable to a severe fine and imprisonment, and if I should find any of you with liquor I should have to arrest him and take him to Juneau, where he would be punished—"

Just here the seven-foot partner of " Buckskin Joe " jumped to his feet. " Mr. Officer," said he, " I have a flask of whiskey with me, and me and my partner—well, we have a quart flask between us. We don't drink; we are taking it strictly for medicinal purposes. What shall we do ?"

"In such case," replied Mr. Smith, " I may say that it is not the intention of the law to examine a man's flask.

C 33

The purpose of the law is to prevent the sale of whiskey to the Indians, and it is very strictly enforced; but, of course, we do not look into people's flasks. I only caution you. There are unprincipled men who would traffic in liquor, and such as these I desire to warn in time."

This short speech, delivered with quiet dignity, created the most favorable impression, and from all on board I heard nothing but words of praise of the attitude assumed by our government. Jim McCarron could hardly restrain his feelings. "That man's a credit to the country," he whispered. The customs officer was surrounded by an eager crowd asking questions.

"What is the penalty for theft at Skagway?"

"They [the miners] give him twenty-four hours to leave; and if he doesn't leave, he is shot."

Inquiry was made about the attitude of the Canadian officials. The Canadian customs party, in charge of Mr. John Godson, were passengers on the *Danube*. Of course, Mr. Smith had no authority to speak, but he gave the impression that the two governments had reached an understanding, and that no hardship would be inflicted on miners by a strict enforcement of the law.

"We came to this agreement," said he, "because many of the miners who are coming up here, after they have bought their supplies and their horses, will have nothing left over to pay duty, and it would be a needless hardship. Our desire is to get them through as easily as possible."

Of our 160 passengers and 109 horses, every one will start over White Pass, although it seems incredible that an easier pass, which this is reported to be, exists so near the Dyea trail.

The new trail seems to have been cut through by a company formed for the construction of a railway, known as the British Yukon Mining, Trading, and

Transportation Company. The American branch is known as the Alaskan and Northwestern Territories Trading Company. Mr. G. H. Escolme, of Victoria, managing director of the American company, who is aboard the *Islander*, says of White Pass trail :

"We have cut a trail over the summit from Skagway, at a cost of $10,000. We own the town site of Skagway, and are building wharves, etc. We cut the trail mainly to prospect for the railroad. I went over the trail on the 15th of July and came back on the 16th. Then the trail did not go beyond the summit, but we have had men working there right along since. It is a private trail; but we are about the only people who are not taxing the miners, and we don't want to do so at any time. We expect to get a few miles of the railroad built this fall ; but even when the railroad is done there will be many who will go over the trail. It may be that we shall charge a small toll. One of my present purposes is to try to reduce the price of packing, which is now 20 cents a pound, and we mean to see that the miners get supplies at a reasonable cost."

We are now approaching Juneau. We have had, with the exception of a few fog-banks, beautiful clear weather, and the trip has been like a summer excursion. But now, well in Alaska, in the shadow of snow-capped mountains and glaciers, the rain is coming down in a steady drizzle. We have been trying hard to overtake the *Bristol*, which started only a day ahead. At Juneau, Jim goes ashore to buy hardtack, tea, bacon, and sugar to last three days (by which time we expect to be over the summit, when we can open our bonded goods); I, to purchase a new hat and look around.

Juneau, sustained by the great Treadwell quartz mine on Douglas Island nearby, has for many years been the

35

outfitting-point for the upper Yukon, and many of the shopkeepers are old miners who understand thoroughly the wants of those going to the gold-fields. The rush has taken Juneau by surprise, but by spring they expect to have full lines of clothing and supplies to meet any demand.

It was the opinion of all that prices at Juneau were reasonable. Oil-skin coats that sell for $3.50 in Victoria sold for $3 in Juneau; but our Canadian woollens were better value than the American. We found the stores thoroughly drained of snow-shoes, a pair of second-hand worn-out Montreal shoes selling for $3.50. Hair-seal boots, mitts, and low moccasins, as well as fur caps made of marmot (sold as "pup wolf"), of black-fox feet, and of hair-seal, are sold by squaws, who await the arrival of the steamer, squatting in a long row against a building at the wharf, and offer their wares to the passengers. The boots have tops that reach to the knee, and sell for any price down to $2.30. The hair-seal is not to be confused with the fur-seal. The skin is covered with short, glistening, mottled, yellowish hair, is full of oil, and is said to be water-proof.

It was raining a steady drizzle the hour or two we were in Juneau. We seemed to have entered a region of perpetual fogs and rain, and our hearts sank as we thought of Skagway. My greatest apprehension was about photography, on account of the rain and absence of sufficient light for "instantaneous" work.

As we drew near the entrance of Lynn Canal, which branches off to the right from Glacier Bay, we ran into a bank of fog, and the *Islander* came to and dropped anchor.

At 10.30 o'clock a meeting of the passengers was called to act upon the suggestions of the customs officer and to devise plans for the landing of our stuff. The steamship only undertakes to deliver passengers and freight at Skagway Bay. The work of landing the freight must be done by the passengers; the steamship people refuse to assume any responsibility. Accordingly, after a lengthy discussion, during which all the kickers had something to say, it was resolved to appoint a committee of three to devise plans for the unloading of the goods, and with power to add as many as necessary to their number. The following is a copy of the minutes of the committee:

"Minutes of the first meeting of committee, composed of Messrs. Arthur T. Genest, William MacIntosh, and George W. Young, appointed by the passengers to form and execute plans for the landing and protection of the freight held on board the steamship *Islander* on August 19, 1897, at 11 P.M.

"The meeting was called to order by Mr. Genest, who was chosen chairman. Mr. L. B. Garside was made the secretary of the committee. After discussion, the following plan was decided upon:

"Upon arriving at Skagway a representative of the committee will go ashore and select a suitable place on the beach for landing and distributing the goods. This will be enclosed by ropes, and the enclosure will be policed by a committee of fifteen, armed with rifles, and doing police duty in shifts of eight hours each. No goods can be removed from the enclosure except upon a written order of the committee. On board ship, Messrs. S. A. Hall and J. Robinson will check the goods as unloaded and sent ashore, and on shore the goods received will be checked by Messrs. D. Orsonnens and N. B. Forrest. Fifty volunteers will receive goods as landed, and, in conjunction with the subcommittee, distribute and arrange the same. Messrs. William Fuller and Duncan MacDonald will police the boat until freight and baggage are discharged."

Further arrangements consisted in the appointment of Mr. J. W. Beall as Chief of Police in the enclosure, with instructions to appoint his assistants, and the previous plans were modified to the extent of allowing removal of goods upon proper identification and receipt to Mr. Beall.

To-night hardly anything is talked about but plans of landing. Every moment, as we approach our destination, our anxiety increases ; while in Juneau everybody had interviewed somebody, and everybody who was not interviewed volunteered something to say. No two stories agreed, save that all told one story of trouble and hardship past comprehension. Only one man was discovered who said the trail was all right. We came to the conclusion that either there are no liars like those of Alaska, or that the people here are very ignorant. Every one throws up his hands in disgust and says, "We will know what it is like when we get there, and not before."

CHAPTER III

SKAGWAY BAY, *August* 20.

THE sun broke through the dense banks
of clouds that rested on the frowning
hills, the fog lifted a bit, the anchor was
weighed, and we steamed onward.

There was much talk about the *Bristol*, some hoping we had passed her;
but soon those who were on the lookout at the bow reported a vessel ahead
on the right hand in a shallow bight, and as we drew
near we saw other vessels, and beyond them a faint
streak of white sparkling in the fitful sunlight across a
little valley, with the steep hills rising on each side, their
tops lost in the canopy of clouds. Beyond the line of
white were green trees, and far away stretched a narrow,
flat valley, winding among the hills. It is Skagway Bay;
and it is White Pass that lies far away in the blue distance.
As we steamed slowly into the little bay the white streak
resolved itself into tents, a city of tents, stretched across
a plain hardly a quarter of a mile wide, level, and pre-
senting a straight front to the bay.

The *Bristol* had arrived three or four hours ahead of
us. Her rails were black with men, who reported all
well, and after a while the voice of Burghardt shouted

39

over the short interval of water the good news that our horses were all right.

The horses and hay were being unloaded into large scows, which were being towed in by row-boats to the beach, which was also crowded with moving figures. The beach is low, and runs out several hundred yards, and then drops off into deep water. At low tide the whole beach is uncovered, so the steamers lie outside and

PRIMITIVE LANDING FACILITIES
Steamship to Scow; Scow to Wagon; Wagon to Shore

wait for high tide to unload their freight. Our vessel was soon surrounded by a fleet of row-boats and large Siwash canoes, trying to pick up passengers for shore at 25 cents each. In crowds on the deck we stood gazing in wonder at the scene before us. Few of us had the inclination to look at the truly grand scenery with which we were surrounded. Snow and glacier capped mountains, rising thousands of feet from green, sparkling water, burying their lofty heads in soft, cottony clouds, are for other eyes than those of miners excited by the preparation for the real commencement of their journey. The captain goes ashore for a customs officer. I go ashore with two others—and such a scene as meets the eye! It is simply bewildering, it is all so strange. There are great crowds of men rowing in boats to the beach, then clambering out in rubber boots and packing the stuff, and setting it down in little piles out of reach of the tide. Here are little groups of men resting with their outfits. Horses are tethered out singly and in groups. Tents there are of every size and kind, and men cooking over large sheet-iron stoves set up outside. Behind these are more tents and men, and piles of merchandise and hay, bacon smoking, men loading bags and bales of hay upon horses and starting off, leading from one to three animals along a sort of lane—which seems much travelled—in the direction of a grove of small cottonwoods, beyond which lies the trail towards White Pass. Everybody is on the move, excepting those just arrived, and each is intent upon his own business. There are said to be twenty-five hundred people along the road between the bay and the summit, who have come on the *Mexico*, *Willamette*, *Queen*, etc. There are not over one hundred tents at Skagway, and there may be five hundred persons actually in the town.

Rough frame buildings are going up as quickly as men can handle scantling, and as fast as they are finished they are turned into stores or warehouses. There are three or four hotels or restaurants; and a United States flag flying over a tent is evidence of the presence of a United States Court Commissioner—the only representative of government here, save that organized by the miners themselves. A large painted cloth sign indicates the location of the correspondents of enterprising newspapers, and the half-dozen newspaper men here gave us a hearty welcome. Men and horses are travelling to and fro in a never-ending stream. There are a number of women ; such as I met being wives who have accompanied their husbands thus far, and most of whom will return.

It will be several days before the pack-trains can get well under way. If we accompany the mounted police,

MINERS GUARDING OUTFITS JUST LANDED

as we have been courteously invited to do, there will be time to go over to Dyea and to see the Chilkoot Pass. How many of the 140 odd who are starting from this ship will see the summit of White Pass? Or, if fortune favors them and they reach the lakes, how many will reach their journey's end this year, or ever? The thought is in every one's mind. Each new-comer from up the trail is received with the anxious query, "What are the chances of getting over?" The only answer that can be given is, "It depends upon what you are."

SOME ACCOUNTS OF CHILKOOT PASS

At dawn a call of " Get up ; the horses are being taken ashore !" resounds over the ship. A large scow is ranged alongside the vessel, and the horses are walked aboard on a plank and ferried to the beach, where they are dumped ashore into shallow water. We notice that men from the *Bristol* are taking horses part way, then dumping them overboard and swimming them ashore. Jim and the boy yesterday set their tent up in the middle of "town," and after we had waded our horses ashore, each man looking after his own, we got our personal effects ashore in small boats.

It is impossible to find any two men to agree upon any detail about the pass. It is tolerably certain that the road for four miles or so to the "Foot of the Hill" is fairly good ; after that it is only described in words not fit to be heard. It is probable that there are several very bad, steep places this side of the summit. Some who are working there say the way is to take a light load on the pack-train all the way in without a stop. Next moment another, equally to be credited, advises to move the whole outfit gradually, short stages at a time. One says but one horse can be led at a time over these places ; another says three can be handled by one man ; while still another lets the horses pick their own way. One packer told of a remarkable escape at a cliff—and it was corroborated by others—of his horse falling forty feet ; when they got down to him he was eating grass, and the lunch-box on his back was undamaged. The day before, two men and three horses fell over the same place. My informant is seven miles from the top. He says, " I mean to go over if it takes all winter." He added : " We are going right on about our business. We do not come down here to town nights and get up late and tired. We get out

43

early, at four o'clock. We do not come down to these miners' meetings."

A party of two arrived on the *Al-Ki* from Seattle on the 11th without horses, hired five men at $7 a day with feed and blankets, and are near the summit, preferring to pay such wages rather than to pay a pack - train from 25 to 30 cents per pound. Their outfit weighs 1200 pounds each. One of them was a barber.

Discouraged men are coming down from the trail, and they have but one story to tell — of terrible hardship, horses falling right and left, seventeen in one place ; the road, if it can be called a road, in terrible condition ; not one in ten will get over.

I talked with one or two determined fellows who came down to the boat, and who had their pack-trains in on the trail. From these I heard a different story. In all I have talked with five or six good men, but they all agree that there is plenty of trouble.

" The road is good for four or five miles—it is a regular cinch ; after that hell begins."

Some say that not one in ten will get over. These are the alarmists and the excited ones. A more conservative estimate is that four out of ten will get through. One party of two loaded their belongings into a small scow and paddled out to the steamer, where they held a long talk with our men, announcing that they were bound for Dyea and Chilkoot Pass. They asserted that the pass here is blocked, while men are moving over Chilkoot, even if slowly. As they paddled away we admired their pluck and gave them a rousing cheer. They did not look like strong men, but they smoked their pipes bravely. All their stuff was on the scow, sinking it low in the water. There were sacks and boxes and two buggy-wheels, with which to make a narrow push-cart. It is pitiful.

Their last words were, "Well, boys, we will meet you on the other side of the mountains." We wondered if they would.

The news of the blockade up the pass is having a discouraging effect on the men. They are earnestly discussing the situation. The mounted police and their 74 horses are all right, and my 8 horses for the outfit of 3, they say, are all right; and every one says *we* will get over. We have now authentic information from experienced men who are putting their stuff over the trail.

A MINER'S WIFE

I asked them what was the cause of the trouble; and from all whose opinion seemed worth any consideration I received but one reply:

"*It is the inexperience of those who are trying to go over.* They come from desks and counters; they have never packed, and are not even accustomed to hard labor."

One party, now within four miles of the top, took in

45

ten horses. They lost four by overloading; then they reduced the weight to 150 pounds per horse. The roads are said to be shelving, and the horses slip and break their legs, and have to be shot. To-day two horses mired, fell, and smothered before their clumsy owners could get their heads clear. I have traced the conflicting stories to this:

This is an army. Those in front are stubbornly fighting their way; they are moving slowly, but they will get over. Behind these are the stragglers, who in turn become the beaten rabble in the rear of the fight. Those up the pass are cool, experienced men, and they are keeping their heads. One man says: " Why, those who are making the most talk are here yet. They have not been out of Skagway; but they get upon a stump and look around, and think they have seen the whole business."

Men have come without horses, and without money to pay the high price for packing — now 35 cents per pound. They are leaving for Chilkoot, or else selling their outfits for what they can get. Flour in the sack has just been selling for 35 cents per hundredweight, or 17½ cents per sack of fifty pounds—many times less than cost; bacon, only 5 cents per pound. On the other hand, horses, up to yesterday, $200; to-day from $125 to $150, poor ones at that. In four or five days, it is said by those who have been on the ground some time, they will be worth hardly anything. At the summit they are not worth 20 cents. A week ago a man could have cleared from $100 to $150 per horse. There are more ways of making money than by going to Klondike.

During the three-quarters of an hour I spent ashore I saw the following:

A horse in a cart suddenly kicked, ran into a pile of hay, broke loose, and started across town, taking the corners of two or three tents. After galloping about among the frail habitations, he was finally caught and led back. Another horse, tied to a log fifteen feet long and six inches through, began to jerk and jump, and went for a hundred yards cavorting down the main street, dragging another horse that was hitched to the same log. A horse with a load of two small bundles of hay suddenly fell down, lay there a moment, then got up and fell again. This was on level ground with a light load.

Every man is armed—all with revolvers, some with repeating-rifles. One facetious packer who came down to the boat said : " There are more inexperienced men to the square foot than in any place I have ever been to, and more double-action revolvers. They ought to have left them at home. It would be a charity for Mr. Constantine [of the mounted police at Dawson] to take them all away, for they will be shooting themselves."

Even at this short distance it is impossible to learn anything beyond one's eye. There seems to be a general movement towards Dyea, but a few are coming this way. This seems only natural when both routes are confessedly so hard. One man, who had been upon both, expressed himself thus, " Whichever way you go, you will wish you had gone the other."

In pursuance of the plan arranged on board the *Islander*, the committee appointed to superintend the unloading of the goods has detailed a checker to act with the purser aboard the vessel as each piece comes out of the hold, and another checker to mark off each piece as it is received on shore. There is probably a hundred tons of miners' freight. Every man is expected to handle and look out for his own goods. Some bring it out of the hold ; others load it upon the ship's boats, which are then rowed as far in to the beach as the shallow water per-

mits. Then two-horse wagons are driven alongside, and
the goods transferred and delivered, at a cost of a dollar
a load, a distance of several hundred yards up towards
the town. The original plan of roping out a space has
been discarded; instead, the goods are loaded upon a large

LANDING GOODS FROM BOAT TO WAGON

float that lies high and dry well up on the beach. Here
others of the miners handle the goods again, and, as far
as possible, put each man's goods in a separate pile. It
is a busy scene—boats are coming and going from the
ship; half a dozen teams are kept busy hauling; boatmen have come up from Juneau and elsewhere, with all
sorts of rowing and sailing craft, to reap the harvest,
and are shouting for passengers to the vessels in the
harbor, at 25 cents out or 50 cents for the round trip.
They are making from $15 to $20 a day.

We have learned already to place no reliance upon any
person's word. Every one seems to have lost his head,
and cannot observe or state facts. The very horses and
animals partake of the fever and are restless. All is
strange and unaccustomed to both men and animals.
Accidents and runaways are occurring every few mo-

48

ments. Suddenly there is a commotion; a horse starts off with a half-packed load or a cart and cuts a swath over tents up through the town, scattering the people right and left. Then all is quiet again, until a moment later in another part there is another rumpus. This sort of thing is getting to be so common that a fellow only looks to see that the horse is not coming in the direction of his own tent, and then goes on with his work. One man was asleep in his tent, 10 × 14, when a horse galloped through it and carried it off bodily. No one gets hurt, which is amazing. The horses are green; the men are green. Men who have never before handled a horse are trying to put pack-saddles on them. A few have heard of the "diamond hitch," but no one seems to know how to throw it. Now and then a rider, in a loose blue shirt, from up the trail, comes cantering down to the beach, swinging his arm loosely at his side, guiding his horse by a jaunty press of the reins against its neck. Every one recognizes the type of Westerner, and says, "That man there is all right."

A little way back from the beach are piles of driftwood brought there by storms; then there are several scores of tents; and then a rough path which people are following leads towards the grove of cottonwoods, amid which we get glimpses of other tents and of new board shanties, from which the sound of axes and hammers comes upon the ear. The tents here in the open are all we see of Skagway. We are too busy with our affairs to look beyond. No one is permitted to take charge of his goods, to carry them away, until every parcel has been landed and assorted.

There is a rumor that a duty of $30 a head is to be collected on Canadian horses; and that our freight will not be delivered to us until said duty has been paid.

The rumor strikes consternation among us all. We are inclined to discredit it, since horses, like tents and blankets, are to be used on both sides of the line. We remember the pains we were at to secure our transit papers, and the reassuring words of the American customs officer who came on at Mary Island. Surely, if a person has "got to have" blankets and a tent, he has "got to have" horses. What provision is there for the refunding of the duty after the horses with packs have crossed the line into Canada? We are left no longer in doubt. A dapper gentleman in an alpine hat and pointed brown shoes, hailing from Portland, Oregon, has set up on a post a small American flag with the perpendicular stripes of the revenue service, announcing that he is the deputy collector of customs for the port, just arrived, and demands on each and every horse brought from Canada the sum of $30. Says he: "I have my instructions from the collector for Alaska. I don't know anything about tents, blankets, etc., but I must collect $30 on every Canadian horse. You can land the horses, but you must not use them here. You can send them through in charge of an inspector, but you cannot put a pack on their backs; if you do you will have to pay the duty—that's all."

I ask him if I may get upon the back of a horse of my own and ride a little way up the trail, to see if it is possible to get over. "No, sir, you cannot." I remind him that the horses will cross eventually into Canadian territory. "They will be of no use when you get there, and you will turn them loose—or else you will sell them here," he replies.

Here is a strip of territory, a few miles in width, which must be crossed before Canadian territory can again be reached. There are no facilities for the transit of goods in bond. Not one in twenty of those here would will-ingly stop. The privilege of bonding goods through the territory is elsewhere extended by both governments; but here is a trail three weeks old and no facilities for transit. The only means of transfer is the miner him-self and his horse's back. The miner's word is the only bond. Even to lead the horse across empty, the horse

UNITED STATES CUSTOM-HOUSE AND COMMISSIONER'S OFFICE, SKAGWAY

and the man must eat, and the man must carry on his own back the oats for his horse, as well as his own food, according to the ruling of Mr. Jones, United States deputy collector for the sub-port of Dyea. There is nothing to do but step up to the custom-house, look pleasant, and pay the $30 a head on our stock. Some-body sets out to find a high-tariff Republican, but can not find one in the camp—no, I mistake; there is one, who comes out and pays his $30 like a man.

The custom-house is a 12 × 16-foot, one-story, board structure, containing a 12 × 16 at the front, a stove, a desk, and some chairs in the rear. Besides the customs officer, there are two or three other persons of the familiar type of low-grade government officials.

We did not mind the remarks made by some cronies of the officer, that it "serves right those who went to Canada to buy their stuff, instead of buying it in the United States." That is the smoke of the Seattle-Victoria fight, and we very properly joined in the laugh that followed the sally of a thick gentleman, with a very full, red face, in his shirt-sleeves, and his feet on the desk, who remarked that newspaper correspondents especially (referring to myself) should not be let up on, as they would say bad enough things anyhow. But we did mind the hardship which the payment of this duty meant upon most, if not all, of us. Jim and the boy could not afford the duty on their single horse each.

The custom-house is one of the few wooden buildings in town. It is situated on the main street, called, I learn, "Broadway," but which is nothing more than a pair of black, muddy wagon-ruts winding around stumps in a rambling way into the woods. A sign announces the office of the United States commissioner. Government is further represented here by a deputy marshal. Inquiry reveals the fact that properly the office of all three officials is at Dyea, which has been made a sub-port of Juneau; but, since the creation of Dyea as a sub-port, White Pass trail has been opened, the town of Skagway started, and practically all the business attending upon the carrying-on of government has been at Skagway. In order to cover both points effectively, the court is held on a point of rocks, known as Richard's Landing, half-way between the two places. To this place the commissioner goes at stated intervals from Juneau and holds court.

Jim and I each quietly mount a horse and slip off up the trail. Words that I have at command cannot describe what is unfolded to our eyes. Only a glimpse of the real town did we have from the beach. But

MAIN STREET, SKAGWAY

here, where the open leaves off and the trees begin, and at a distance of not more than half a mile from low water, begins the town. Along the main trail or wagon-road town lots have already been staked off and claimed. The underbrush has been cleared away between the cottonwoods and spruce, which are a foot or more in diameter, and a piece of paper on the face of a tree announces that

"This lot, 100 feet along the trail by 50 feet west, located and improved by J. Murphy, August 14, '97. Lot supposed to front

on street running east and west according to plot made and ratified by the citizens, August 13, '97. See my notices on stakes at
N. and E. end of lot.

"(Signed)   J. F. MURPHY."

The "improvement" consists of a few bushes cleared
away to make room for a small "A" tent. The owner
seemed to have moved onward, leaving, however, his "improvement" upon the land.

Another notice reads, in terse language, that "this
claim, 50 by 100, is claimed by J. H. Foot"; and others
add the names of several competent witnesses.

Scattered on both sides of the trail are tents of every
size and one or two wooden buildings. A ceaseless
stream of men and horses is moving up the trail with
loads, and a stream is returning empty. Here at the
left is a big tent with large black letters on the side; it
is the "Pack Train" saloon. Beyond are the "Bonanza"
and "The Grotto," while across the street a great sign
overhead bears the suggestive name of "The Nugget."
A glimpse inside of these, as one rides by, shows a few
boards set up for a bar in one corner, the other corners
being filled with gambling lay-outs, around which are
crowds of men playing or looking on. Then come shops
where groceries and miners' supplies are being bought
and sold. Here a doctor has set up an apothecary shop;
here two young New York boys are selling their outfit and
"waiting till spring." Large painted canvas signs announce eating-houses — the "Rosalie," the "Kitchen" —
but there is not a lodging - house in the place. For a
quarter of a mile into the woods run the rows of tents,
while back from the trail, and next to the river, the
sound of axes indicates that the whole of the flat is being
taken up. Here and there is a log-hut going up.

Some of the new arrivals have brought little carts—

a pair of buggy-wheels on a short axle, having a bed in some cases not more than fifteen inches wide and six to eight feet long, with handles at both ends. They load these carts with five or six hundred pounds of stuff, and two men work them along up the trail ; or, if they have a horse, they load the pack-saddle, then hitch the horse in front and start along, one leading the horse, the other steering and balancing the cart from the rear end.

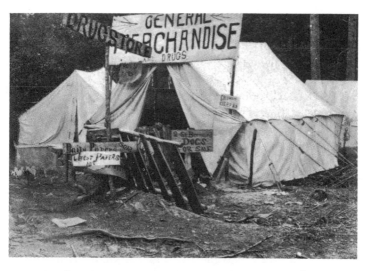

"A DOCTOR HAS SET UP AN APOTHECARY SHOP"

It is an odd sight. One horse, when ready to be loaded beside the scow, became frightened, and started up-town with the cart behind him. He ran into the town, then turned at right angles, crossed a branch of the Skag-way, started, cart and all, up the face of the mountain, turned around, recrossed the river, and came back to the scow, the cart now running right side up ; then, striking a root and bouncing ten feet into the air, it landed upside-down. The cart never ceased for more than a moment to run along, right or wrong side up, on its wheels ; not a man was hurt nor a tent-peg torn up, and it all took place in full view, and the crowd greeted with a shout each time the cart flew up and landed all right. A moment later the incident was forgotten. These little carts cost $30. In a day or two they carry a whole outfit of two or three to the "Foot of the Hill," and then are sold for what they cost. Others pack directly on horses' backs, while the greater portion of the freight is carried by two-horse wagons for 1½ cents a pound. I met two fellows packing on bicycles. They had taken off the pedals, and had rigged a sort of frame on the seat, upon which they packed nearly as much stuff as a horse will carry—viz., 220 to 225 pounds.

Money goes like water through a sieve. It costs a dollar to look a man in the face. Men are like wolves : they literally feed upon one another. Wages for packers— any one who can carry 75 to 100 pounds on his back and work ten hours — are $7.50 a day upward. "Experienced" horse-packers are getting as high as—in one instance—$20 a day. The teamsters are making more than that. One was heard growling because he had only made $50 that day ; they sometimes make $100. Horseshoe-nails are $1 a pound at Skagway; at the "Foot of the Hill," 10 cents apiece ; and a single horseshoe, $2.50. Rubber boots worth $5 sell for $9. A shoemaker, a blacksmith, a watchmaker, also, have set up shop. A constant surprise is the number of women. Some of these are at the dance-house, but the majority are the wives of miners. There is but one child in the whole place. It is a town of grown-up people. The women dress, some of them, in short skirts, with leather leggings or rubber boots, or else in out-and-out men's trousers.

There has been no disorder to speak of. Excepting the gamblers, there are few who might be said to represent a disorderly element. And this, no doubt, is due to the fact that every man here, except those who have come up from the nearby towns of Juneau and Sitka, have had to have the price to get in. This is no country for tramps and loafers.

A LEADING HOTEL

I stop and ask a man what is the name of the main street. "Oh, don't ask me," he replies. "I've been here a week, and I come up here every day, and I get lost." All is movement and action. There is nothing fixed. The tent of yesterday is a wooden building to-day. A smooth spot and some tent-pin holes show where a tent stood yesterday.

The Skagway River is a swift stream of three or

four rods' width at its mouth. It rises far away in the midst of the blue peaks of the Chilkoots, which grow bluer and bluer until they merge into the sky. The sides of the mountains slope at an angle of some forty - five degrees, and against their tops lie eternal glaciers and patches of snow. The river's current is even but forceful, and so swift as anywhere to bear a man off his feet, even though no deeper than to his knees. Its water is milky, from the sediment it bears down from the mountains, and its banks are scarcely more than two or three feet high, extending back perfectly level on either one or both sides to the steep sides of the valley, and covered with a dark loamy soil from the decaying vegetation of centuries and a luxuriant growth of cottonwoods, spruces, hemlocks, and white birches. The trail reminds one of any newly cut road in the forests of the Adirondacks or Canada. At a distance of a mile and a half from low water it crosses the river from the right hand to the left by a log bridge, built by the miners, wide enough for the pack-trains and the hand-carts, but too narrow for the large wagons, which have to unload on the gravelly bank.

Leaving the river, the trail leads on for some two miles. Tents are scattered along the way, and one is never out of sight of men coming or going. About four miles and a sight meets the eye. The space between the tree trunks has been cleared of underbrush, and is filled with tents, side by side, only a few feet apart, on both sides of the trail, and extending back the width of the valley, which is here quite narrow. The men have set up their stoves and hung out hundreds of pounds of bacon to dry, and the air is laden with the savory smell of smoked meat and the camp - fires; for it is evening, and the men are returning from the trail. Weary horses are

ONE METHOD OF PACKING GOODS TO THE "FOOT OF THE HILL"

eating hay and oats alongside tarpaulin-covered piles of goods.

There are fifty or sixty tents in all, and the roadway between is packed smoothly by hundreds of feet. There are more women here—one is baking biscuit and selling them hot for 25 cents a dozen. All are cutting down outfits. The wagon-road stops, and now what seems to be only a foot-path makes a sudden turn to the left and boldly climbs up the steep mountain-side. This is the trail, this the Hill, and the crowds of tents and men make the town at the "Foot of the Hill" the resting-spot before the struggle. We hitch our horses and proceed on foot. To convey an idea of the Hill, one must have recourse to illustration, and I can find none more apt than that used by one who has been over it : "Imagine a mountain of goods-boxes, some of them being bigger than the rest—the size of tents." Imagine them piled in a rough mass, cover them with moss and black loam and trees, with rills of water trickling down among them. The goods-boxes are granite bowlders ; their outer surfaces protrude from the mass, hard and bare, but nature has covered the rest with rich vegetation. The path— if, indeed, it can be called one—twists and turns and worms its way from ledge to ledge and between the masses of bowlders. Here a tree has been cut down, and we clamber over its stump. There a corduroy bridge lifts one over a brook. Men with stout alpenstocks and with packs painfully struggle upward, stopping now and again for rest. It has been comparatively dry for a day, and the trail is said to be not so bad. Between the bowlders it has packed fairly well, and, but for its steepness, would be called a good path. We ascend a distance of several hundred feet—not quite to the top, we are told. On every ledge and bench tents are set up, or piles of sacks, so near the path that one can reach out one's hand and touch them. Men in from the day's work are cooking or reclining beside their goods. Their rifles are in easy reach. Pilfering has been going on, and the men who are lying by their goods will shoot at sight. A string of horses and mules is returning down the Hill, and we see now the difference in horses.

JUSTIFIABLE HESITATION

The lank, big, clumsy horse is in danger at every step. He comes to a drop-off, lifts his head in air, tosses his fore-feet ahead with a groan, and trusts to chance to find a footing. He strikes a sloping rock, flounders for a foothold, and down he goes sideways and rolls over. A string of several dozen went past, but none actually fell. The little cayuse, or Indian pony, however, like the mules, looks where every foot is placed. One cayuse got out of the train and came to a pitch-off of ten or twelve feet; we looked to see it break its neck, but it simply put its head down, slid over the face of the bowlder, and landed squarely and lightly as a goat. Another which we just heard of went down a forty-foot bank, and was back on the trail working next day. We set out down the Hill again. When we are near the bottom we meet a small train coming up in charge of two men.

At the foot of the steep ascent the train stops and one horse goes ahead. He comes to a step-up of over two feet, he gets his fore-feet up, gives a desperate lunge to get his hind-parts up, slips, and falls, his whole weight and that of his load falling on the sharp top of a stump, where he flounders and kicks pitifully. We help the men cut the load off, roll him over on his back off the stump, and help him to his feet, and he gets up with scarcely a scratch. That is one fall, the first we have seen. We are told that fifty horses a day fall here. No one thinks anything about it. The other horses are led up, one by one, the men choosing each step for them. This seems to be the only way to do with horses that are not, like goats, used to looking where a foot goes down. Most of the falls occur where two smooth surfaces of rock come together in a notch, furnishing no foothold. If there is soft mud in the notch, and the sides are wet and slippery, the horse goes down with a smash, and it is lucky if a broken leg does not result.

CHAPTER IV

Pack-horses go to Dyea—Life in Skagway—Experiences of Old-Timers—
Start on the Skagway Trail—Terrors of the Trail—Dead Horses—
Mud and Rocks—Terrible Condition of Men and Horses—A Night
Camp—Trail Closed until Repairs are Made—Return to Skagway

August 21.

TO - DAY a proposition is made by a man by the name of Charles Leadbetter, of San Francisco, who is just over from Dyea, to take all our stuff, not exceeding three thousand pounds when delivered to him at Dyea; to team it thence to the head of canoe navigation; there put it on his pack - train, which will carry it to The Scales, which is at the foot of the summit; there two men will be given us to help us pack our stuff over the summit — a distance of from three - quarters of a mile to a mile to Crater Lake; there we will have to ferry it over the lake, when it will be taken on a burro train to Long Lake, where there is another ferry, and then again on the burros to Lake Lindeman, which is the point of departure. We shall be expected to help with the pack - train, if necessary, and all this he will do in return for our eight horses. It seems a reasonable proposition, except that we are surprised at the time allowed — namely, four or five days — for making the trip through to Lake Lindeman. It is agreeable news that goods are moving right along on the Dyea trail. We still have no doubt of getting through White Pass, but we gladly hail any proposition which will land us quickly and without great trouble at the head of navigation of the Yukon.

The terms do not include our boat lumber. We are advised to cut it into lengths of seven feet, suitable for horse-packing, but it has come thus far in whole lengths, and we desire to keep it so as long as possible. Accordingly, we deliver our horses, with a ton of feed, to the packer, who takes them over on a scow in tow of a tugboat, which makes trips between Dyea and Skagway as often and at such times as the tide permits. The cost for transportation is $10 a head. Our intention is to follow at the earliest date.

There is no shady side to life at Skagway ; everything goes on in broad daylight or candle-light. After supper every tent is lighted up, and the streets are crowded with muddy men in from the trail. The " Pack Train " is filled with people, among whom I recognize several of my friends, who are drawn hither, like myself, by the spectacle. The tent of the biggest saloon in town is thirty by fifty feet. Entering through a single door in front, on the right hand is a rough board bar some ten or twelve feet long, with some shelves against the rear wall, on which are a few glasses and bottles. The bartender, who is evidently new to his business, apologizes for the whiskey, which is very poor and two-thirds water, and sells for 25 cents. Cigars of a two-for-five or five-cent sort, that strain one's suction powers to the limit, are sold for from 15 to 25 cents each. They keep beer also, on tap. After the lecture we received on the steamer from the United States customs officer, we are at a loss to understand how whiskey can be sold openly under the very eyes of the officers. But that is a story by itself. Along each side of the tent are the three-card monte, the rouge-et-noir, and other lay-outs, but not a faro lay-out in the place nor in the town. The gamblers are doing big business.

A big, strapping fellow, in a yellow Mackinaw jacket, trying his luck at craps, is pointed out as having just come

A PROFITABLE ENTERPRISE

in over the trail from Klondike.* Whether he has any dust with him I do not learn, but he is in fine health and spirits. Every man whom I have yet seen from Klondike has a splendid complexion and seems strong and robust. This fellow has a voice like a lion's, deep and resonant. Surely the Yukon cannot be so terrible if it does this to men, or else its tale of death is that of the weak and sickly.

* Ramps Peterson, a well-known Yukon dog-puncher.

Across the street the sound of a piano and the moving figures of men and women seen through the windows remind one that there is a dance to-night, as on every night. This piano is the only one in town, and its arrival is said to have been an event. The four women in the place are not even of the painted sort; paint might have covered up some of the marks of dissipation. Clumsy boots beat time on a dirty floor, but not with much enthusiasm. There is not sport enough to get up as much as a quadrille. The dance-house of a mining-town! Such a thing as shame is not even thought of.

Among the many who are gazing upon the unaccustomed scene, with the same absorbed interest as the youngest of us, are men whom I take to be old-timers. I asked one of these what he thought of it all.

Said he: "I was in the Salmon River mining excitement in Idaho, but I have never seen anything like this. Ten thousand people went in that winter, over a single trail across the mountains; but it was nothing like this. There has never been anything on this coast like it."

Another, who is now the mayor of a town on the Pacific coast not far from the Strait of Fuca, said, in answer to the same question: "I saw the beginning of Leadville, but it was nothing like this; there has been nothing like this."

Still another, a mining engineer from California, said: "I have never seen people act as they do here. They have lost their heads and their senses. I have never seen men behave as they do here. They have no more idea of what they are going to than that horse has. There was one fellow in the tent alongside of mine—I saw him greasing his rubber boots. I said to him, 'What are you doing that for?' 'Why, isn't that all right?' he asked. Another man came along and asked a fellow where his mining-pan was. The fellow said, ' I haven't seen any mining-pan.' Just then the man saw the pan lying along-side the tent, and said, ' Here it is ! Is that a mining-pan ? I didn't know that was a mining-pan.' "

I have talked with many others, some who had been in the Cœur d'Alene excitement on Salmon River, Idaho, and have been miners since '53 and '54. Some, whose fathers were of the old '49's, say the same thing—that the country has gone mad over this Klondike business. And all agree as to the reason—nowadays the news is carried by the telegraph and newspaper to all parts of the world, whereas formerly the excitement was all local, and had died away before word of it reached the rest of the world.

No one pretends to follow the changes that are going on here. Those who have been here a week are old-timers. When the next boat arrives people will ask questions of us in turn.

August 22.

The work of unloading the vessel continues. Most of the hay and the lumber has been loaded upon a scow and hauled inshore, so that the vessel can clear for the south on time. As the quickest way to get the lumber off, six or seven of us take hold of the scow, throw the lumber into the water, and raft it ashore. It is noon before we discover that it is Sunday. Sunday makes no difference in Skagway. All the goods are now landed, and each man is carrying away what belongs to him—also some that doesn't belong to him, if there are any grounds for the vigorous complaints made to the checkers. After the confusion aboard in the hold, the wonder is that any one gets what belongs to him.

It is raining again to-night. None of the weather signs we are accustomed to in the East holds good here. A man who lived six years back of the Chilkoot Mountains says that in this part of Alaska, at this time of the year, it will be clear and cold for four days, and then it will rain four days. It has rained the four days all right, and we are looking for the four sunny ones. This wet weather is discouraging. Every one feels miserable.

August 23.

Day breaks clear. It is full daylight at five or six. The sky is cloudless and the air is warm. Every one is happy.

I engage a man, who hails from Texas, with a thirty-foot dory (which he says came up in pieces from San Francisco to go over the mountain, and which he purchased for a few dollars at the beach), to take all my stuff to Dyea. The wind is piping up Lynn Canal, tossing up the white-caps, and heavy breakers are rolling in on the beach. Our skipper is sure of his boat, so we take my own twelve hundred pounds, with the boat lumber, a ton of hay and oats, and a thousand pounds of baggage belonging to one of my fellow-passengers on the *Islander*, who has seen both trails, and pronounces unhesitatingly in favor of Dyea. He is Monsieur l'Abbé, a lumberman and merchant from Port Arthur, Lake Superior.

Lynn Canal is a long, deep trench between towering mountains, like a great fresh-water lake. The water is only slightly salt to the taste. It is hard to believe that it is the sea. It is as cold as the melting ice from scores of glaciers on the mountain-tops can make it, and a man could not swim twenty yards in such a chill. It is a marvel that any of the horses thrown overboard reached shore.

After a dangerous passage through the heavy seas that nearly swamp us with our top-heavy load, we round the point of rocks, and, with the wind behind us, are driven rapidly towards the mouth of the Dyea pass. We follow the right-hand shore, where the rocks boldly rise perpendicularly from the water, and presently meet a swift current in the mouth of the Dyea River, a stream twice the size of the Skagway, flowing seaward through a broad alluvial plain.

We go a little way, wading and dragging the boat against the current, and land in the midst of a number of

A VIEW OF DYEA

tents and piles of baggage. Leadbetter himself is not here, but his teamster and wagon are, so, leaving word with Monsieur l'Abbé and another that my stuff has arrived, I go back to Skagway. After a desperate tussle against the wind, making almost no headway, we go ashore in a cove, and reach Skagway afoot.

During a temporary absence of Jim and the boy a runaway steer kicked some sparks from a fire against the back of the tent, which had burned out half the end of the tent before neighbors extinguished it. This is the story, but I think the wind blew the sparks from said neighbors' camp-fire. The fire, however, burned the cover and part of the leather off my camera, yet without hurting the camera. It destroyed the tripod cover without touching the tripod; it burned the gun-case without hurting the rifle; it burned some twenty pages of my diary, but took the back, where there was no writing, instead of the front leaves. The actual loss was a few envelopes. Altogether a remarkable escape.

Jim and Burghardt are ready to go to Dyea; so, giving them directions, I take my 5 × 7 camera and start in on the Skagway trail. With the perversity of Alaska weather, it begins to rain by the time the "Foot of the Hill" is reached. There are only a few horses moving in at this time of day. At the summit of the Hill the narrow trail follows the steep bank of a ravine, and here we see the first victim of the trail—a horse lying at the foot of the bank, twenty feet down, beside a small stream. It is dead now, but before it died some stakes were driven around it to keep it out of the water.

Just now we met a man who says that a horse has just tumbled off the trail and down in a hole between two or three immense bowlders, and that only its head is sticking out, and that it is alive. We keep on along comparatively level bowlder-strewn ground, and evidently pass the spot indicated, which is not surprising, as bushes and trees cover every spot and hide the treacherous holes. We are going on firm bottom, with numerous corduroys over muck-holes, but ankle-deep in sloppy, slimy, chocolate-colored mud. It looks perhaps worse than it is. Horses and men, bags and pack-covers, are dyed with this brown stain. Again the trail mounts the slope of the mountain, by a way so rocky that it would seem as if no horse could get up it. The smooth, flat sides of rocks slope inward, affording no foothold to a horse.

We meet a young man on horseback coming down the worst of these places. We step aside and curse under our breath the man who would ride a horse down such a place. We did not know then that he had a broken foot.

PACKING OVER THE HILL

A corduroy bridge, sloping at an angle of fully forty degrees, was soon afterwards put over the whole length of this pitch. The logs give a hold to the shoe-calks that the rocks do not. Where the horses slide and scrape the rocks it looks like the work of chisels.

The trail climbs from terrace to terrace, or follows the brink of perpendicular cliffs, but all is so covered with luxurious vegetation that the heights above and the depths below do not impress one. We come to an empty pack-saddle, and know something has happened here, as down the mountain-side the bushes are bruised, as if some heavy body had rolled down. We need no one to tell us that over the cliff a horse has rolled hundreds of feet, and lies out of sight among the bushes. Again an almost unbearable stench announces an earlier victim.

Every man we meet tells of the trials of the trail. Anxious and weary are they. I saw one half-way up a hill asleep on his pack, with his closed eyes towards the sky and the rain pattering on his face, which was as pale as death. It gave me a start, until I noticed his deep breathing. A little way on three horses lie dead, two of them half buried in the black quagmire, and the horses step over their bodies, without a look, and painfully struggle on. Now (only two miles by survey, but three or four to every one who passes over) the trail begins its steep plunge down the side of Porcupine Ridge, switching back and forth. At the turns it seems as if nothing could prevent a loaded horse from going clean over. The bank goes downward nearly perpendicular several hundred feet, when one lands in the narrow gorge of the Porcupine, a branch of the Skagway. Here are more tents — another breathing-spot. The Porcupine is crossed by a corduroy bridge, and the ascent begins again. The surface of the rocks is now more in evidence, and the trail leads over these, slippery with trampled mud.

Gradually, stage by stage, the trail rises, following the sloping shelves of bare rock, so smooth as to afford no foothold. In one place, for two or three hundred feet, the shelf that the trail follows slopes upward, and at the same time outward. A horse here needs something more than calked shoes to hold on by. No safe trail can be made until steps are cut bodily into these places.

Where there are no rocks there are boggy holes. It is all rocks and mud—rocks and mud.

Suddenly the trail opens out on the mountain-side, and a magnificent view is presented to the eye. Across the valley a rugged mountain, sloping, a mile in height; and down far away to the westward the blue hills and the smoke of Skagway, with Lynn Canal showing a three-cornered patch of lighter color. It is magnificent.

Five or six hundred feet below we can hear the roar of the waters. Another pitch downward and we are again on the Skagway River. Why the trail did not follow the Skagway, without climbing these two terrible ridges, none of us can comprehend. The railway, of course, will follow the river-bed, or else tunnel through the Chilkoot Mountains. Tents and piles of goods are scattered thickly along the trail. No one knows how many people there are. We guess five thousand—there may be more—and two thousand head of horses. Of course there are means of knowing, if one has kept track of arrivals of steamers at Skagway, but no one I know has bothered. A steamer arrives and empties several hundred people and tons of goods into the mouth of the trail, and the trail absorbs them as a sponge drinks up water. They are lost amid the gulches and trees.

Every one is discouraged. Dirty and muddy from head to foot, wet and tired, it is no wonder. Men who have been on the trail two weeks are no farther than this. They tell of parties who have reached even the summit, and there, disheartened, have sold out and come back. Some say boats have been carried as far as the summit and there deserted. Others say boats cannot be taken over at all. The trail is lined from Skagway to the "Foot of the Hill" with boat lumber enough, as one person said, to make a corduroy road the length of the trail.

ON THE "DEAD HORSE" TRAIL

A NIGHT ON SKAGWAY TRAIL

Darkness comes on, and I stop for the night with two old prospectors, alongside a granite bowlder as big as a house. Against its flat side, and partially protected by it, they have piled their stuff, in the very spot I should have chosen for my bed. They have a small fire going, and their three horses are tied to bushes near by, munching their oats. The men are well provided with blankets, which, when supper is over, are spread out on the ground beside the pile of goods, while a rope is stretched to keep the horses from tramping on the bed. They are both old miners. One, a man of fifty-four, had been in former mining excitements, and he had seen bad trails. Now every sort of opinion has been expressed of this trail; and when a man tells me a trail is bad, that counts for nothing until I know what his idea of bad is. I asked this man what he thought of this trail. Said he:

"I have seen worse trails for a short distance—five or six miles or so—but this is the worst I have ever seen for the distance. I went in over the trail when it was first cut through, and I called it then a *good* trail, but I predict that if the rains keep up it will be impossible to get a horse over."

It has stopped raining. We lay our coats under our heads for pillows, and our guns under the coats, and turn in. Of course we cannot take off anything but our coats and boots. We wake up in the middle of the night with the rain in our faces. I put my broad hat over my face, turn over, and go to sleep again.

August 24.

We are up at five o'clock. Half an hour later I am on the trail. There are several others on the trail with their packs. Everybody, no matter how dirty or tired, would give any price for a photograph of himself, "just to send back home to show what I am like." The men imagine

77

their friends would be surprised to see them begrimed and unshaven and muddy under their packs.

We cross the Skagway on another corduroy bridge, where a fine view up and down the valley is to be had. Near here a stream of water comes down the mountain-side out of the clouds, and before it is half-way down it divides into several more streams, which find their way into the Skagway in a dozen places. The dullest or least sentimental man on the trail cannot but stop to admire

CORDUROY BRIDGE ACROSS THE SKAGWAY

this beautiful sight. From this bridge the trail follows the valley of the Skagway, the ground being flat and boggy.

The main summit is still six or seven (estimated) miles distant, and, as it is raining, I put in at the tent of three hardy fellows whom I saw the first day at Skagway, after feed for their two horses. They have been two weeks on the trail. They tell me one of their horses is played out this side of Porcupine.

A HORSE OF LITTLE WORTH

"He fell over a bank forty or fifty feet, and was on the trail next day all right, but he must have been hurt inside. He's all shot to hell now."

Two of them go back to where they left the horse, and return before night. They have a little fun at first by saying they sold the horse for $125 to a man that came along and wanted to buy.

"Of course we told him we couldn't recommend the horse, but it was a *horse !*"

This does not seem unreasonable to us, as any kind of a horse brings whatever one asks for it. At length one of them says : "No; but we did offer it to a man for $10. He said he didn't want it. Then we offered to give it to him. He said he didn't want it even at that price. Then we asked him for a gun to shoot it with, and he lent us a revolver and we shot it."

I saw one of these men afterwards. He told me they had sold their other horse, as they found it was cheaper to pack their goods on their own backs than to carry horse-feed eight or nine miles from Skagway. A few horses are passing along in the rain. One or two large oxen go by loaded with three hundred and more pounds. It is astonishing what they will carry. And then, when they are there, they can be killed and eaten. Doubtless a horse can be eaten also, but most people have preferences.

Every one is downhearted. So near the summit, yet so great has been their struggle that hardly one expects to get over at all, but is seriously discussing the best place to winter. Said one : "I mean to go in if it takes all winter. If a man can hunt and get a caribou, he need not mind it."

None of them feel like going back, but most of them regret having started. All of them blame the misrepresentation about the trail, and there are many anxious inquiries about how it is at Dyea.

The trail along the bed of the river is a continuous mire, knee-deep to men and horses. Here and there is a spot where a spring branch crosses the trail, and in such spots, which are twenty to thirty feet across, there is simply no bottom. One such hole is beside our camp. Of the first train of five horses and three men that I saw go by, three horses and two men got in, and with difficulty got out. After that every horse went in to his tail in the mud, but, after desperate struggles, got upon solid ground. There are worse holes than this. The trail crosses the river by two more bridges, and then continues on to the summit by a road equally bad but no worse than what we have come over. Past the summit no one at present knows anything of the trail, only that a few persons have got through to the Lakes, including two or three women. The trail is all but impassable, yet some are plugging along. These men, it is predicted, will lose their horses in three or four days. Some say that something must be done; they are willing to put in work, but are not willing unless others help.

There is no common interest. The selfish are crowding on, every man for himself. Unless something is done soon the trail will be blocked, and then no one will get through.

"It's no use going *around* these mud-holes," says one of my fellows. "The swamp is all alike. The only thing to do is to make corduroy bridges every foot of the way before there will be a trail. I am willing to start to-morrow and bridge the holes above here."

No wonder they are discouraged. Rain, rain, all the time—no sunshine up in these mountains; tent pitched in a mud-hole, bed made on the stumps of bushes, blank-

AN HOURLY OCCURRENCE

ets and everything else wet and muddy. They are trying to dry out a hair-seal cap and some socks before a
miserable fire. Even the wood is wet, and will only
smoke and smoulder.

August 25.

I remain all night in their tent, and early this morning set out to come back, having seen enough of the
trail to know what the rest is like. I should like to go
on past the summit; but my goods are at Dyea—indeed,
as things go in this country, I cannot be sure that I
have any goods left at all.

I have made careful inquiry about the loss of horses
on the trail. The number at the present time is probably about twenty actually killed, with considerably more
badly hurt or temporarily laid up. Each day now about
four horses are killed. The number is bound to increase
as the trail grows worse (which is nearly impossible)
and the horses grow weak under the strain and from lack
of care. When the sun and rains of summer shall have
melted the snow of the Chilkoots, the White Pass trail
will be paved with the bones of horses, and the ravens
and foxes will have feasted as never until the white man
sought a new way across the great mountain. As many
horses as have come in alive, just so many will bleach
their bones by the pine-trees and in the gulches—for
none will go out.

A little while ago contracts were taken by the packers
at 20 cents, then 25 cents, a pound. Just now $650 was
paid for a thousand pounds, while $1000 for a thousand
pounds was offered and refused.

Yesterday a horse deliberately walked over the face of
Porcupine Hill. Said one of the men who saw it:

"It looked to me, sir, like suicide. I believe a horse
will commit suicide, and this is enough to make them;

83

they don't mind the hills like they do these mud-holes."
He added, "I don't know but that I'd rather commit suicide, too, than be driven by some of the men on this
trail."

This is what one hears all along the trail: "We
brought a boat with us, but we shed it at Skagway. It
cost us $27 in Seattle, and we sold it for $3.50, and were
glad to get rid of it."

Yet two Peterboro canoes are on their way to the summit. I saw them myself, as well as a man poking along

HOW ONE OUTFIT ATTEMPTED TO PACK TIMBER FOR A BOAT OVER
THE TRAIL

in the rain with a load of boat lumber on his shoulder so
long that the wonder is how it ever got around the turns
on Porcupine Ridge.

Word is brought down the trail that one man, so fortunate as to get over and have his boat built and ready
loaded, went to sleep, and in the morning awoke to find
the boat stolen and on its way down the Yukon. Surely
that is hardship, yet only one out of many. The history
of this trail is yet to be written, and will only be heard
by the firesides of old men.

On the way back, squads of men have ceased packing
and are mending the road. There is some talk of closing

the trail. Farther on the rumor is verified. Groups of men in charge of foremen are chopping down trees and building corduroy roads over the worst mud-holes and over the most dangerous portions of the rocks. The manner of building is to take two string-pieces, lay them side by side four feet apart, then lay half-round logs across, and hold these down by two more string-pieces pegged down solidly. They have piled wood over the bodies of dead horses that have become offensive, and these are being consumed by fire.

Between Porcupine and the "Foot of the Hill" the whole road is being systematically and substantially put in order. Not a horse nor a man with a pack is allowed to pass in from the "Foot of the Hill." A rope is stretched across the trail, and several committeemen of the miners stand guard and rigidly enforce the rule that no man with a pack must pass over for the space of three days; by that time, it is believed, the trail will be fixed. One man who attempted to pass got roughly handled. He was threatened with the black spot and all the Irish curses of the boss of the gang. His excuse was that he had a tent up the road and was merely getting back home. There was a miners' meeting last night, at which the trail was declared closed. The town at the "Foot of the Hill" was at the same time officially named "Camp Edgemont."

Two men came through from Dawson a few days ago. No one knew it until after they had left for Seattle except the doctor who keeps the little apothecary-shop at Skagway. He told me about it while measuring out some quinine pills:

"I saw the two boys come by, and I recognized them as from my town, and called them by name, and asked them if they had come down the trail. They said they had, and I asked them in. They came in, and one of them helped the other off with his pack. I noticed it seemed very heavy, so I came right out plump : ' How much dust have you got?' ' Dust?' they said ; 'that's our grub.' ' Oh, now,' said I, ' you might as well tell me how much you've got!' Well, they made me promise not to tell they were there until after they had got away. They opened up, and showed me eighty-five pounds of dust ; the biggest lump was as big as my thumb. They came up by poling-boat to the White Horse Rapids, and afoot the rest of the way. They told me that they threw the sack of dust down fifty times, not caring if they ever picked it up again."

Fifty men might come through and no one would know it. No one knows his neighbor, nor seems to care. Speak to a man once or twice, and every one calls him your "pardner." The better class of men resent this expression ; it is decidedly too familiar and vulgar—about as if a stranger should address you as "Shorty." It is the regular thing here, however, and is no oftener a lie than the expression "my friend."

CHAPTER V

August 26.

THE storm had abated, the tent was gone, and there was nothing to do but follow Jim to Dyea, so I bargained with a Siwash from Wrangel, with a thirty-five-foot single-stick dugout canoe, to be taken over.

At Dyea the tents and goods were gone. I could see nothing of my own. I supposed they had been carried off by the contractor. Among the first I stumbled across was Jim, who, to my astonishment, had just arrived from Skagway, the sea having continued so rough that no one would venture to bring him over. The tents were a quarter of a mile farther on. When I got there I found friends, and to my horror learned that the storm had driven an unusually high tide in upon the beach, flooding all the goods and tents. Wagons had gone to the rescue and saved the most, but some had floated off and had not yet been recovered. A stranger, with a wagon, had rescued my outfit. Looking about, I soon recognized my black waterproof sacks. The stranger proved to be Monsieur l'Abbé ; he had found the goods under a foot of water, and paid a teamster $12 to land them in a place of safety. I did not dare to think of the condition they were in.

Where was Leadbetter? No one knew. His wagoner was there. Would he take my goods now? He had no time to-day. There was no time to discuss the matter with the unwilling teamster. Jim, Burghardt, and the one-eyed Dutchman, who had stuck to the party, and myself hired two Indians with a canoe, and, putting part of our outfit in, and with two more Indians to help, we towed the canoe up the Dyea River for two miles, until we reached the ferry, where the trail crosses the river, and there we found Leadbetter's tent and the tents and goods of a number of parties whom he had contracted to take over.

We pitched our tent among the others in a grove of cottonwoods, and in the morning we brought up the rest of the goods, weighing forty-five hundred pounds. The cost for my share alone was $16. Jim got the stove up inside the tent. Upon opening the clothing - bags, the salt-water had soaked through the carelessly tied ends, as they lay submerged, and every article in three sacks —leather mittens, moccasins, blankets, and furs — were wringing wet ; boxes had come apart, labels off bottles. I was still sure of the photographic outfit, which had been ordered from the Eastman Company's factory in "hermetically" sealed tins. Imagine, then, my feelings as I unwrapped one after another of the dripping tins, and found not one hermetically sealed, but with a common India-rubber band loosely placed around the joint. When opened, water poured out. The cut films, being in pasteboard boxes, were, of course, also destroyed—in all, two hundred and fifty plates—my entire stock, which could not be replaced nearer than Seattle, if there ; and before they could arrive it would be too late to reach

Dawson, and I could not go without them. We closed the tent tight, rigged up lines, wrung the water out of the fabrics, and at the end of two days, during part of which time the sun helped us, we got everything dry. Only a sack or two of flour was damaged—as flour, unless it lies a great while in water, is not saturated more than a quarter to half an inch—and some dried fruit.

The utter hopelessness of that night will never be forgotten. The blame was first my own in not having seen

THE SETTLEMENT AT DYEA

that all my sacks were wrapped and rewrapped at the ends. But that did not relieve the contractor of responsibility, for if he had moved the goods when told the accident never would have happened. The teamster, being in arrears for his pay, was on the verge of mutiny, and consequently in no hurry to remove them.

Leadbetter was up the trail, with a large outfit of horses and burros. He had made various contracts with parties from San Francisco to put them over at a lower rate than that which the Indians had hitherto charged, a quite reasonable undertaking. From some he had taken cash; from others, like myself, horses, and he had agreed to pay the wages of his packmen by transporting a certain quantity of supplies for them. The outfits are moving along slowly, but contracts have run over the time, and there are murmurs of discontent.

I went at once to Skagway. Learning that Wells, Fargo & Company might establish a parcel express service to Dawson during the winter, by arrangement with the carriers of the United States mails, I wrote a telegram to be forwarded from Seattle for five rolls of film, in soldered tins, and to other parties for films for the plate-holders, the agent about-to-be, Mr. Batten, promising to do all that was possible to get the stuff through to Dawson.

The steamer *Danube*, from Victoria, was unloading, and I went aboard to post letters. Mr. Jones, deputy United States customs officer, was in the captain's cabin collecting duty on the horses that were aboard, an interesting development, considering that the duty was not payable until they were landed on American soil.

In a depressed state of mind, I returned to Dyea, although having still the $1\frac{1}{2} \times 2$-inch Kodak and some rolls for the same.

Two months ago there was but one trail commonly known across the Chilkoot Mountains to the head-waters of the Yukon. That trail was known as the Chilkoot Pass route. The new trail, first called the White Pass trail, is now spoken of as the Skagway trail, while the old Chilkoot trail is called the Dyea trail. That the advertising of the Skagway trail as the better route was premature no one pretends to dispute—nay, it is only in terms of unqualified condemnation that it may be mentioned. Those who cut that trail may have honestly believed it to be better, but the effect of rains and of thousands of men and horses tramping to and fro was not foreseen. Some saw the trap in time and pulled out, and are now well over the Dyea trail. In winter there has been but one plan of work heretofore followed: Landing at Dyea by small steamer from Juneau, goods to the extent of from four hundred to five hundred pounds are placed upon the seven-foot sled previously described and hauled up the Dyea River a distance of about nineteen miles to the foot of the summit; thence it is packed, or else hoisted by a long cable, over the forty-degree incline to the summit; thence on sleds again to Lake Lindeman, a distance in all of twenty-seven miles, where the miners wait for the opening of the river, or else sled down the Lakes as far as they choose.

At this time of year it is, of course, wholly different. Indians have been taking packs of from one hundred to two hundred pounds on their backs, either directly at Dyea, or in canoes to what is termed the head of canoe navigation, some six and a half miles from Dyea, and thence on their backs, making the first stop at Sheep Camp, three or four miles this side of the summit, and reaching Lindeman the following day, at a charge of 14 cents per pound. This year, horses and wagons have been put on for part of the way, and white men have come in to share the profitable rates of packing, which have steadily gone up until they are now 40 cents per pound to Lake Lindeman.

The Dyea River is, as I have mentioned before, a stream of nearly twice the volume of the Skagway. As far as the canyon, eleven miles from the mouth, its course is through a level valley of sand, gravel, and bowlders, with groves and patches of cottonwoods and spruce and birch, while along its banks are thickets of alder and a species of willow resembling the red willow of the East. Its swift, milky, ice-cold waters follow mainly the west side of the valley, but at various points little branches roam away from the main stream. The river is filled at this season with salmon, spawning, and with large, fine trout. The woods, to the unobservant, seem devoid of life; but though there is no song of bird, still if one listens he will hear the low chirp of sparrows, while the hoarse croak of the raven is borne to the ear as it flaps lazily overhead. There are also red squirrels, and if those who have hunted in this region can be relied upon, the country abounds in large game as well as small—grizzly bears on the mountain-sides, mountain-goats (miscalled "sheep" here) on the summits that overlook the valley, and numerous small fur-bearing animals.

Dyea is a comparatively old settlement, its principal, it may be said only, house, the store, dwelling, and post-office occupied by the firm of Messrs. Healy & Wilson, having been established as an Indian trading-post thirteen years ago. One of the partners, Captain John J. Healy, six years ago organized in Chicago the North American Transportation and Trading Company, and is now at Dawson as its general manager. Dyea is chiefly an Indian settlement. To the northward of the post-office and close by the bank of the river is the village, composed of small, dirty tents and little wooden cabins crowded close together. There are no totem-poles nor the large houses of more southern Alaska. But for the few permanent cabins, it would seem to be what it largely is, a small settlement where Indians congregate from various quarters, the Chilkats from the westerly arm of Lynn Canal, the Stikeen Indians from down Fort Wrangel, and the Chilkoots, a branch of the Chilkats, who belong here. They are Tlingits, and the men are short, heavy set, powerfully built, broad and thick of chest, large of head, with almost Mongolian eyes and massive jaws. Nearly all have stringy black mustaches that droop at the ends, and some have scant beards

CANOE NAVIGATION

Their color is a light brown. The women are hardly any of them good-looking, and have a habit of painting their faces a jet black or chocolate brown, and I have seen little girls who thus imitated their elder sisters and mothers. The face is rubbed with balsam, then with burned punk, and this is rubbed in with grease. They do this, I am told, for the same reason that their white sisters use paint and powder. They leave enough of their faces untouched about the chin, mouth, and eyes to give them a hideous, repulsive expression. In the spring of the year both men and women blacken themselves thus to protect their eyes from the glare of the sun upon the snow. White men used to do the same thing here, but snow-goggles are now used instead.

The Indian pack-straps consist of two bands of cotton cloth lined with blanket, two inches wide and twenty inches long, having a loop at each end. These loops are fastened to the top and bottom of the load by means of a small rope, and pass around the shoulders in front. A third—"head-strap"—passes over the forehead, the ends being fastened to the load behind. In this way an Indian walks off with twice the load a white man will undertake to carry, and even young boys and women take their seventy-five pounds and accompany the men.

Most arrangements for packing are made with Isaac, "Chief of the Chilkoots," as the sign reads above his cabin. Formerly the Chilkoots monopolized the packing, not allowing other Indians to enjoy the profits, and seriously objecting even to white men packing their own outfits over; but now this monopoly is completely broken.

The Indian men's dress is varied and picturesque. Some wear the gayly colored Mackinaw jacket; others a blue denim garment, half shirt, half coat; still others a loose coat of blanket, the sleeves or a patch across the back being made of the striped ends; and, as the blankets used by these Indians are of the most brilliantly assorted colors, the color effects are distinctly striking. For headgear they wear common little felt hats or bright wool toques or a colored kerchief. All possess rubber hip-boots, but when packing they wear only moccasins outside of "Siwash" or blanket socks, and sometimes an oversock to the knee. Indian fashion, dogs and children, men and women, crowd into their dirty abodes, which smell of spoiled fish. The dogs are not so numerous as I expected, nor yet so quarrelsome and noisy. The Indians train them for sledge-drawing in winter and packing on their backs in summer, and it is not unusual to see an Indian with one or two medium-sized dogs trotting beside him, with a little pack on each side, sagging nearly to the ground, containing his luncheon.

When an Indian is packing he carries his single small blanket tied upon his back under the pack, thereby making a cushion for the pack. A stout stick to balance with and to assist in climbing completes his outfit. Twenty or thirty Indians will take up packs and put a whole outfit over in two days. They are not trustworthy, and are wholly unscrupulous. They do nothing even for each other without a price, and I have carefully noticed that they make no distinction between themselves and whites even for the same service. If one engages them at a certain price and some one offers them more, they lay down their packs and take up the new ones; or if on the trail they hear of a rise in the scale, they stop and strike for the higher wages. Some of them speak good English.

Indians from Sitka say these fellows are wild Indians, and look upon their ignorance of letters with some contempt; but, if ignorant of letters, they are shrewd, hard traders, who are making money fast and saving it. They have a strong predilection for gold, but at the same time, as our silver friends will be pleased to know, silver is in no less favor with them. In fact, it seems to be hard money they want. I knew an Indian to declare solemnly he could not change a five-dollar bill, showing the only two silver dollars he had; but, when a gold five was offered instead, he fished a whole handful of silver out of his pocket, which also proves what barefaced liars they are. They are taking all the small change out of circulation. They come to the traders several times a day, make a trifling purchase to get change, and then store it away. The small-change problem is indeed a serious one. There is not enough small currency to do business with. The gamblers and the Indians are getting it all.

APPROACHING THE CANYON

From the Indian village the road follows the western bank of the river to the ferry, where horses can ford in the early morning. Thence the road continues, crossing and recrossing small branches of the Dyea eight or nine times, to Finnegan's Point (a distance of about five miles from Dyea). The foot-trail makes but two fords in that distance. From Finnegan's Point is a horse-trail one mile to the head of canoe navigation, and thence, over a level waste of sand and loose bowlders, to the mouth of the canyon. From there the winter route follows the bed of the river for two and a half or three miles, between steep forest-clad banks. The summer trail makes boldly up the steep sides of the hill, and, after making several very steep but short ascents and descents, reaching in one place a height of two or three hundred feet above the bed of the river, it drops to the level again at the head of the canyon, and crosses the river on a bridge, the work of private parties, who charge a toll of fifty cents on every loaded horse. The trail thence follows the bed of the stream, which is wide and gravelly, fording again and again, or crossing on logs, to Sheep Camp, fourteen miles from Dyea. The only bad part of the road is in the canyon, but for the most part this has been well corduroyed, so that, no matter how much it rains, there is solid footing. Untrained horses fall here too, but there *is* a trail; at Skagway there is none, unless mud and rocks suffice to make a trail. Healy & Wilson's pack-train of ten or twelve horses, in charge of two men on horseback, runs daily from Dyea to Sheep Camp, carrying two hundred pounds per horse, returning the same night, with hardly ever an accident. Both horses and men know their business. A good many of the miners push their little hand-carts to the end of the wagon-road, and then pack on their backs or by horse; while others build large flat-bottomed scows or skiffs, into which they pile all their goods, and tow them, with much labor, to the head of canoe navigation.

AT THE FERRY, *August* 29.

Still drying out clothes and blankets. We have found one of our horses here, sick from an injury received on the steamer. He falls down with no load and acts as if famished. It is Jim's own horse. Leadbetter has arrived and promises to move us at once by wagon to Finnegan's Point. Our horses are working on the pack-train from Finnegan's Point to Sheep Camp.

Jim and Burghardt are chafing at the delays. So they propose to do their own packing, if I replace the old "skate" with a sound horse—a proposition to which I readily assent by giving him "Nelly," leaving me now with five sound horses and 1400 pounds of stuff, not including the boat lumber. Jim and the boy go to Finnegan's and pick out their horses and start packing.

The Dutchman is to give his horse to an Indian, for packing 200 pounds to the summit, and he has gone with the Indian, his horse, and a pack on his own back.

It is impossible to give one an idea of the slowness with which things are moving. It takes a day to go four or five miles and back; it takes a dollar to do what ten cents would do at home. The blacksmith is either at Skagway, or is drunk, or has left his tools behind. That has been the main trouble with Leadbetter—half his horses are laid off without shoes. A horse loses one or more shoes about every trip. The same story is told by all. They have arrived here with outfits and means of transportation; they have thought their expenses ended, but they have only just begun. Where a party has calculated on getting over in days, it is taking weeks. Yet how much better than at Skagway! Here people *are* moving; there the trail is choked, and no one is getting through.

August 30.

Six burros belonging to the outfit take 800 pounds to Finnegan's Point, and I pay a wagoner to haul the rest to that point.

AT FINNEGAN'S POINT

Twenty tents, including a blacksmith-shop, a saloon, and a restaurant. A tent, a board counter a foot wide and six feet long, a tall man in a Mackinaw coat, and a bottle of whiskey is called a saloon here. At the hotel a full meal of beans and bacon, bread and butter, dried peaches and coffee is served for 6 bits, or 75 cents. It is run by two young women from Seattle. One of them is preparing to start for Sheep Camp with a two-hundred-pound cooking-range. The Indians bring in salmon and trout, and sell them for 2 bits, or 25 cents, each. The salmon weigh from ten to twelve pounds; the trout, two or three pounds.

The Indians fish in a peculiar manner. They go two together in a smallish canoe, one with a paddle, while the other sits facing him in the bow, armed with an iron gaff; and, as the canoe is slowly worked along the pools, the gaffer feels up and down with his gaff until he strikes a fish, when, with a flop, it is landed in the bottom of the canoe. One cannot see a foot in the milky, glacial water, so that spearing is out of the question. Sometimes they surprise the fish in the shallow places. I shot a two-and-a-half-pounder at a ford, grazing and stunning it with a revolver - shot. The Indians do not use a hook and line. There could be no finer place to fish for trout than along this Dyea River; there are deep, narrow pools against the sides of the steep mountains, while on the other side it is open, flat, and gravelly, free from bushes. None, however, have time to try, the ever-present dread that we may never get over weighs on our minds.

The slowness of the pack - trains is disheartening; horses laid off from loss of shoes, no shoes, not even nails to put them on; many are sore, and the poor ones are playing out. The men do not know how to pack. A Montana man says: "Some of these people think that so long as it is a horse, anything is all right. If it was a piece of machinery they would have to take care of it, but they think a horse can stand anything." The packing rate to Sheep Camp is 12 cents per pound. I start the boat lumber for Sheep Camp by two men, who carry the boards each side of them in a sort of rope harness. The lumber weighs 165 pounds, and I pay them $25. My stuff went up to-day on the backs of nine horses, five of which are my own. The packers on their return to-night claim they were threatened with revolvers up the line by men the time of whose contracts had expired; that the pack-train could only take up one more load before moving the others on.

September 2.

Packers have held what they called a "committee" meeting, and the "committee" announce that they are working for wages, and that their only chance to get their own stuff through is to push it through on every available horse to-morrow, disregarding all other claims to precedence. Everybody is excited, and a panic has seized those who are being put over by the train. I try to stand them off, as far as my horses go, but the whole train goes off for Sheep Camp with a ton of stuff belonging to the packers. Leadbetter is up the line with three or four horses, working goods from Sheep Camp to The Scales, gradually and very slowly carrying out the contract. But contracts are contracts, and angry men point to dates on pieces of paper to prove that they are not at The Scales or at Lindeman within the time specified, and they are demanding the return of their horses. Every man is for himself and fears to be left.

RETURN TO SKAGWAY FOR ADVICE

September 3.

I take passage with a party of Indians for Skagway, to consult the United States Commissioner and obtain papers to be served in case parties continue to hold and use the train. To-night the packers hold conclave before a big log-fire. They are sobered a little by this time, and ask me to take charge of the whole train and to run it in the interest of the others, looking after the financial end. There is Glass, a civil engineer of San Francisco; and Simpson, tall, thin, with a scraggy black beard and most disreputable arctic overshoes. He is a butcher from Oakland, and has made a wager to go in and come out on so much money, and has 600 newspapers to sell there. He is a picture of misery. He comes in from the trail soaking wet from rain and mud, but he is the most cheerful man of the lot, and one of the hardest workers. (Simpson privately proposed that I leave my lumber and take his canvas canoe and himself on with his papers. Impossible.) There is Fitzpatrick, jovial and careless, the stowaway who was captured aboard the *Excelsior* as she was leaving San Francisco for St. Michael, and who to-night, in the ruddy glare of the fire, and amid the steam of wet clothes, with his thumbs in the belt of his trousers, tells over, with rich expletives, the story of his capture, and how he had begged and pleaded, even offered money, for passage, but in vain. And there are half a dozen others from all parts of the country, of different professions, but drawn together by common interest, and now trying to work together. I make them a counter-proposition—to take my horses at a low figure and let me do my own packing on from Sheep Camp. The horses are now conceded to be mine.

September 4.

This morning the packers were leaving my horses;

but, rather than keep them idle, I let Simpson take them out, packing one-half for himself and the other half for me at the prevailing rates. I load and help pack 280 pounds for King's party from San Francisco, and at the same time accept an invitation to eat Christmas dinner with them at Stewart River. Turkey, cranberry sauce, plum-pudding, and champagne are promised—a change from pork and beans. During the rest of this morning I had to throw the diamond hitch over the loads of so-called experienced packers, concocting a long story about where I had learned it.

Attended court in the afternoon, according to agreement, at Richard's Landing. There were several cases on—one a quarrel about some mules. The court-house was a ten-by-twelve tent. The commissioner or judge sat on a goods-box with a larger goods-box in front, and the lawyers and defendants and plaintiffs, numbering about a dozen persons, sat on other boxes and discussed the situation informally. After talking awhile inside, all parties would go outside to a large flat rock in front of the tent, and there, with hands in their pockets, talk some more. A settlement was arrived at in each case. There is not much law. Common-sense rules, or tries to; and, if that fails, there is a big United States marshal who sets things straight in about as arbitrary and effective a way as a New York police justice. In my own case there was nothing to do save pay a lawyer $20 for making out the papers, which were placed in the hands of the deputy marshal, to serve in event of trouble.

September 5.

Eight of the packers buy three of my horses at $50 each, the roan mare being disabled by a cut on her foot, and the black somewhere up the trail. They now own a train of ten horses, and have agreed to move in the common interest. With a light pack I start for Sheep Camp. The first thing after entering the canyon trail is a horse down with his pack, and I recognize the old "skate," and Jim and the boy, with Nelly and the "buckskin," and the Dutchman, who is packing on his own back. The old "skate," which we supposed worthless, has been doing really good work on the level ground, and is neither sore nor cut; but this is his first try at the hills. We get him up, and the pack on again. Nelly's back is very sore, and she groans under the pack. Half a mile farther on the pack turns on Nelly, and her back is gone. The pack is taken off and she is led back to the camp, where a revolver-shot puts the poor, patient little beast out of misery. I do not forget the last words of the man who rode her into Victoria, little expecting her to be sold there by her owner. "Poor Nelly! I will never see you again!" Wet blankets, saddles not cinched tight, saddles that do not fit, loads unequally balanced, are doing the sad work. We cannot see until the saddles are off what hundreds of horses are suffering.

Jim is moving along slowly. It is now too late, but if he had waited with me two days longer his outfit would probably have been all at Sheep Camp. I was sorry, for Jim was a good man.

CHAPTER VI

Sheep Camp—Its Population—Mud and Rain—Hotel Palmer—Sheep
Camp to the Foot of Chilkoot—"Stone Houses"—Climbing Chilkoot—
Over the Summit—Delayed by Storms—Lake Lindeman—Boat-Build-
ing—Excitement of Departures—Lake Bennett—Shooting the Rapids
—End of Skagway Trail

SHEEP CAMP is thirteen miles from
Dyea. It is a town of tents, scattered,
to the number of several score, among
spruces, along the bowlder-lined shores
of the Dyea River, here a stream a rod or
two across, and so swift as to be scarcely
fordable. It is a convenient stage before
the climb over the pass, which is four
miles distant. It is also the last place
on the Chilkoot trail where wood can be had for warmth
and cooking. Two pack-trains of ten horses each run
the round trip from Dyea in charge of two men riding
spare horses. There are several hundred horses in all,
and a much larger number of men. The rate of packing to this point is 14 cents a pound. This rate, though
not large on such merchandise as parcels of cigars,
makes oats $16 a sack, and hay not less than $325 a ton.

The population of Sheep Camp may be classified as
follows: those who have packed their own stuff thus far
and are wavering, discouraged by the bad weather; those
moving their goods right through with horses or on their

backs; professional gamblers, and a great swarm of men packing over the summit. These last are mostly hangers-on from Juneau, several being deserters from the revenue-cutters, while others are men who were bound for

THE FORD AT SHEEP CAMP

Dawson, and who had the wit or presence of mind, which few others seemed to show, to recognize a gold-mine when it came before their eyes, even if it was not a Klondike one. They are making great money. The rate to Crater Lake is 12 cents a pound; to Lindeman, 30 cents a pound. Many of them take one pack from here over, and then make one or more short packs over the summit, in this way making as high as $26 a day. It is the hardest kind of work, though, and after a while the feet and ankles get so used up that the men have to give up and go home. It is not always with full pockets that these men are going back, for the crap men and the faro men about a mining-camp seem special creations for the purpose of relieving certain sorts of men from the temptation to spend their hard-earned money in worse ways.

It has been a continual downpour for the past week. My goods are all here, stacked under canvas and rubber covers; but it seems a hopeless task to keep goods dry. Horses have almost no value, just the price of packing for one day; but it costs $10 for a set of shoes. Everything is the color of mud — men, horses, and goods.

Sheep Camp has a hotel. If any one is in doubt on

WEIGHING PACKS AT SHEEP CAMP

that point, a huge cloth sign on the front of the building announcing the fact in letters three feet high is suffi-cient evidence. That the proprietor, a Mr. Palmer, is a modest man is evident in that he has not placed his own name in letters equally large in front of the simple but gigantic word "HOTEL."

It is one of the two wooden buildings in town, built of rough boards, and in dimensions about twenty by forty feet, comprising a single room. A portion is partitioned off at the back by a calico curtain, and here live the proprietor, his wife, and a large family of small children, and here the meals are prepared for several hundred hungry packers three times a day as fast or faster than the pack-train can bring the grub from Dyea. At noon, but more particularly at evening, the floor of the hotel is crowded by a wild, dirty, wet, unkempt crew of men from Chilkoot, who advance in relays to a long table, where the beans, tea, and bacon are thrown into them at 75 cents each, payable strictly in advance. The fare depends greatly on what the pack-train has been able to pick up at Dyea. There is always enough, although sugar or milk may be a bit scarce. The men eat like wolves. "Still, there are some who kick at the price," says Landlord Palmer. "Why, the price they pay hardly pays the packing on what some of them eat."

When supper is over, the floor is thrown open for guests. All who have blankets unroll them and spread them on the floor, take off their socks and shoes and hang them on the rafters, place a coat under their heads, and turn in. By nine o'clock it is practically impossible to walk over the floor, for the bodies. The first night I spent in Sheep Camp I spread my blanket under the table, sharing it with a fellow-traveller who was not so provided. No charge is made for the sleeping privileges of this hotel. In the morning the lavatory arrangements are of an equally simple sort. One simply walks outside to a brook that flows under one corner of the building, and, after ablution in water from a glacier up the mountain-side, lets the water dry on his hands and face. I noticed most of the men did not take even this much trouble.

Observing that I was a photographer, the proprietor mentioned that he had some things belonging to a camera that a photographer had left, and he was at liberty to sell me them if I cared for them, and he brought out —of all things!—three spools of 4 × 5 daylight film! I took them quickly enough. That very day I was going down the trail in Sheep Camp, past a large tent that I had noticed before, when a young man hailed me with, "Say, do you want to buy a camera? I see you are a photographer." A stroke of lightning could not have caused me more astonishment. "I have a camera here, and I guess I don't want it any longer. It's too much trouble." It proved to be the very make of camera that my spools fitted, and, as fortune is said always to run in streaks, he had nine more unused spools, and was willing to part with them for their cost in San Francisco! The young man, Charlie Brannon by name, was one of the lucky men who arrived on the *Portland*, and is now on his way back.

While waiting for the rain to cease I took my remaining black horse down the trail to sell it. It was perfectly sound. No one would make me an offer. At the Ferry an Indian offered $20, to include the halter; but, not having the money, we started together to the village. On the way I met Leadbetter and his former teamster. Leadbetter had just finished saying to him as I approached that I would probably sell for $50. The teamster asked me the price. I said $25, and he jumped at the offer. The horse paid for itself the next day on the pack-train to Sheep Camp. I didn't need to apologize to the Indian, who was looking on at the transaction rather crestfallen. He understood that it was simply his own way of doing business. The blue roan, which only needed a rest, I gave away, rather than shoot it, to a packer, a careful man, who intended wintering his train at Dyea.

September 12.

Three inches of snow reported on the summit, and six inches at Lindeman, but the Indians say the lakes will not freeze for six weeks. Donkeys taken over the pass are starving to death, as there is no grazing. The packers, one by one, are dropping out as the weather grows worse. So the rates keep up. Discouraged, many are trying to sell their outfits, and have set up little stores inside their tents.

The cruelty to horses is past belief; yet it is nothing to the Skagway trail, we hear. There are three thousand horses on the Skagway trail — more to kill, that's about all the difference. Sheep Camp is filling up with broken-down brutes. Their owners have used them and abused them to this point, and are too tender-hearted (?) to put them out of their misery. Their backs are raw from wet and wrinkled blankets, their legs cut and bruised on the rocks, and they are as thin as snakes and starving to death. A Colorado man says to me, "Of all the cruelty to horses—and I've seen a good deal—the worst is on this trail; they are killing them with sticks." They are hobbling about among the tents, tumbling over guy-ropes, breaking into caches, making great nuisances of themselves. No one will take the responsibility of shooting them. Some one may come along and demand $50 for the dead horse perhaps. That settles it. So we drive a batch of them out of town, where the poor creatures may find a little feed.

A wretched, thin, white cayuse came to my tent. He had been driven from four miles above, where his owner deserted him. It was raining a cold rain. He put his head and as much more as he could inside the tent, trying to get next the stove. He stayed there all night and was around all next day, and he had nothing to eat. I am certain he never felt the 44-caliber bullet back of his ear that evening. Thereupon a general killing-off began, until carcasses were lying on all sides.

September 14.

A dozen packers take my outfit across the pass to Crater Lake, but will not touch the boat lumber. Flour is a packer's first choice, lumber last.

One by one my "partners" for each few miles of travel have fallen by the way-side. Several have offered to pay for passage down the river, as boats at Lindeman are bringing prices that are prohibitive to most. Finally I fall in with a young man from Stockton, California, named Al Brown, who started for Dawson with the Leadbetter outfit, and is dumped here by the collapse of the undertaking. He has a good outfit of clothes, no grub, and is determined to reach Dawson, though I tell him I should advise no one to do a thing I should not do myself. He agrees to help me to Dawson, and I agree to pack his goods. Brown has had no experience whatever in the kind of life he has entered upon, but he is an expert oarsman, holding the amateur championship of the Pacific coast. We start for the summit after our outfit, each with packs of stuff that we could not trust to packers, leaving the boat lumber in charge of a trustworthy man, who promises to send it over without delay for $30.

From Sheep Camp the valley is a huge gorge, the mountain-sides rising steep, hard, and bold to a prodig-

AT THE FOOT OF CHILCOOT PASS

ious height. The valley begins to rise rapidly, and the trail is very bad. A mile above Sheep Camp, on the left hand, a huge glacier lies on the side of the mountain, jutting so far over and downward that every moment one expects a great chunk to drop off and tumble into the river. But it does not, and only a small stream of water from its melting forces its way to the bottom. A mile farther on is " Stone House "—a large square rock, crudely resembling a house; it stands on the river's brink. At the base of the mountain is a great mass of slide rock, some of the bowlders being nearly as large as the one by the river. Some of these rocks have piled on top of one another so as to form small caves, which the Indians use for shelter. These also are called " Stone Houses." The valley here makes a sudden turn to the right, and the trail begins to grow steep. The valley is filled with great water-and-ice-worn bowlders. The trail climbs from one to another of these. There is no vegetation, save a few alders here and there, and these cease just above " Stone House."

The trail enters a *cul-de-sac*, climbing higher and higher. The valley seems to end ; a precipitous wall of gray rock, reaching into the sky, seems to head off farther progress, seaming its jagged contour against the sky—a great barrier, uncompromising, forbidding—the Chilkoot Pass.

Horses and men with packs are ahead of and behind us. The sun has broken clear, and shines down on a strange scene. In a pocket under the cliff are some score of tents and huge piles of baggage. The tents are held to the earth by rocks on the guy-ropes. Men are busily at work making up the goods into packs and unloading pack-horses. Adding to the animation the rocks are covered with bright blankets spread out to dry.

The men take up the packs, and this is what happens : They walk to the base of the cliff, with a stout alpenstock in hand. They start to climb a narrow foot-trail that goes up, up, up. The rock and earth are gray. The packers and packs have disappeared. There is nothing but the gray wall of rock and earth. But stop ! Look more closely. The eye catches movement. The mountain is alive. There is a continuous moving train ; they are perceptible only by their movement, just as ants are. The moving train is zigzagging across the towering face of the precipice, up, up, into the sky, even at the very top. See ! they are going against the sky ! They are human beings, but never did men look so small.

Other men are coming back empty, as if dropping back to earth. "The Scales," as the foot of the precipice is called, is one of the most wretched spots on the trail ; there is no wood nearer than four miles, and that is poor. The wind blows cold, and everybody and everything is saturated. "The Scales" gets its name from having been in former years a weighing-place for goods hoisted or packed over.

We start with our packs up the side of the mountain. Chilkoot deceives one in this : it seems to tower directly over one's head, whereas the actual average slope is about forty-five degrees, consisting of a series of benches alternating with slide rock. The trail winds from bench to bench, and there are a number of trails all reaching the crest at about the same place. The general slope of the path is not great, and the labor of climbing so little that when we pause to take breath and look back we find we are half - way up. In several places, however, the trail is very steep ; one must climb on hands and knees from bowlder to bowlder—much, I fancy, as one would go up the pyramids. We overtake horses going up, and an ox. We are astonished to see how so apparently clumsy a creature gets up the steep places. There is one very dangerous place ; it is necessary to attach a rope to the pack-saddle, two or three men go ahead, and when the horse starts up they pull hard on the rope ; otherwise he goes over backward, as one or two horses have done. Once on top, the trail crosses a broken yet comparatively level summit, over one or two dirty glaciers, and then downward three or four hundred feet of easy pitch to the head of a steep glacier, where all at once, if the weather is clear, there breaks into full view Crater Lake, a body of pure green water, of irregular outline, a mile or more in length, lying in a great, rough, crater-like basin of rock. Some were sledding goods on tarpaulins down the glacier, which terminates in a pile of bowlders as big as wash-tubs, and these continue on at a steep angle to the edge of the water. Piled on the bowlders are caches of goods. Some persons have tried to set up tents in this forbidding place. I do not look inside of any to see how they arranged a place flat enough and smooth enough to sleep upon, but infer that sleep is accomplished even under such adverse conditions, as they belong to the boatmen, of whom there are three, ferrying goods to the foot of the lake at 1 cent a pound. Forty dollars a day was paid for the use of one row-boat, but the men are making more than that. They earn their money having to live in such a place, and no wood within miles. One of them tells me he has been there two weeks, and that each morning he has wrung the water out of his clothes before putting them on. We are fortunate in getting our goods taken over at once, while we go around by the trail to the foot of the lake, where in a little notch among the rugged rocks are tons of freight. By the time we unload and pile our stuff it is dark. With tent, blankets, and some grub, Brown and I start for " Happy Camp," where we hear there is wood, but have gone only a few hundred yards when we have hopelessly missed the trail. We hunt for a level place, and at length find one up the hill-side, where by pulling some bunches of moss we make a spot where we can lie. It is a very wretched prospect. Throwing down the tent, we spread our blankets, and then fold the tent over. From being cold, we nearly suffocate. In the morning, we can tell something has happened. Peeping out, we find that we are covered with two inches of snow. We are only a few feet from the trail, and a man goes by with a pack ; but we cannot be seen, for we are like the surrounding rocks—white. Shaking off the snow, we sit there, eating a tin of meat and a piece of hardtack. It is the Californian's first experience with snow, and he enjoys it.

Next morning we follow the water from Crater Lake, a stream of some size, about four miles, past "Happy Camp"—a misnomer, if ever there was one—until we reach the head of a lake, where there is wood and a little grazing for a few wretched horses. The wood is spruce, scrubby and sprawling, some of the trunks being a foot thick, but the trees themselves not over ten or twelve feet in height. There were about fifty tents at the lake, which is known as Long Lake, and is two miles long. We set up our tent on the spot where a party were camped who were just leaving, thereby having a few bare spruce boughs ready laid for our own bed.

Next day it begins to storm adown the valley—such a storm as I never saw before. It blows until it seems as if the tent, which is held down by heavy rocks on the guy-ropes and the edges of the tent, would be taken bodily and thrown into the lake. Goods have to be piled end-ways to the wind or else be blown over.

The storm continues for several days, with wind, snow, and rain, the sun shining clear each morning through the rain. We engage some men to pack our stuff over, doing considerable ourselves. Now we see the need of the heavy shoes ; anything less heavy would have been cut in pieces by the bare, hard rocks.

Having waited several days in vain for the boat to come over the summit, we start back to Sheep Camp, and on the way we hear that Sheep Camp has been washed entirely away, and many persons lost. At " Stone House " the square stone is gone. Several parties camped there tell us the first they heard was a roar, and, looking across the valley, saw a stream of water and bowlders coming off the mountain-top, the bowlders leaping far out in air as they tumbled down, an immense torrent, and it poured into the Dyea River, overwhelming a young man who had gone to the river for water, undermining the big rock, flooding the tents, carrying away several outfits, and speeding towards Sheep Camp, bearing trees and wood with it. Sheep Camp, when we reach there, is a spectacle. The big saloon tents and many small ones are wiped out, and the main street, lately a trail of black mud, shoe-top deep, is as clear and solid as sand can make it. The catastrophe occurred on the 18th, at seven o'clock in the morning, before many were up. Numerous outfits were either buried or have been carried away by the flood. People are digging in the sand, wringing garments and hanging them out on the bushes to dry. Only one life is known to have been lost.

This disaster has decided many who were hanging in the balance. Whether they have lost their outfits or not, it has given them a good excuse to go back. From this time on only the strong-hearted continue on their way. Amid such general destruction I hardly expected to find my boat lumber, but it had been removed to a place of safety by the packer, whose feet had given out ; but we find two men to take it over, and it accompanies us. I found among the wreckage a fine pair of Alaskan snow-shoes, the toe of one broken off, which the owner parted with for $2. It is snowing as we again climb the sum-

LAKE LINDEMAN

mit, making the ascent both difficult and dangerous. The storm still rages at Long Lake. Tents are being blown down or are banging like the jib of a schooner going about in a three-reef breeze. Wondering if this is a per-manent condition of the weather here, we start for Lindeman. The drop of eight hundred feet in elevation from Long Lake to Lindeman puts one into a new and smiling country. There are a hundred and twenty tents at the lake, half that number of boats in process of building, half a dozen saw-pits at work, and a general air of hustle-bustle. In the words of the geography, "Ship-building is the principal industry" of Lindeman.

The ferryman at Long Lake refuses to go out in the storm, so we pay him full price, 1 cent a pound, for his boat, a large double-ender, load our goods in it, rig a small square-sail in the bow, and scud to the other end, leaving the owner to get his boat when the storm eases up. A portage of a few hundred yards to Deep Lake, and another ferryman takes us to the foot, a mile distant, where we set up tent.

The river here drops into a narrow canyon at tremendous speed, falling eight hundred feet in two or three miles. The trail strikes across a spur of the hill, striking the lake near its head. Lindeman is a beautiful lake, four and a half miles long, and narrow. with a towering mountain on the opposite side. At its head, on the left hand, a river enters, and there is timber for boats up this river. Vegetation is now plentiful, but it consists mainly of willows and a dwarf *cornus*, or "bunch-berry," which at this season, with its purple-red leaves covering the whole ground, gives a rich look to the landscape. We pitch tent in a lovely spot, on which we decide to build our boat. We pack our goods over from Deep Lake, and when the lumber arrives we build "horses" and set to work constructing the bateau. We find some burros here of the Leadbetter outfit. Only three, hardly bigger than sheep — and how slow! Dr. Sugden is driving them when we first see them. The little beasts, trained at packing ore in the mountains of

California, know how to go around the trees with their packs, but they are helpless in the muddy places, which alternate with the rocks. We take them for one day; but Brown says he can pack faster on his own back, so we let the next man have them.

Every one is in a rush to get away. Six to ten boats are leaving daily. They are large boats, with a load of five to ten men each. The boats are of several kinds. A fleet of seven large bateaux got off as we arrived, but the favorite and typical boat is a great flat - bottomed skiff, holding two or three tons; in length over all, twenty-two to twenty-five feet; beam, six or seven feet; sides somewhat flare; the stern wide and square; drawing two feet of water when loaded, with six to ten inches freeboard; rigged for four oars, with steering - oar behind. Some of this type were thirty-five feet in length. There are several huge scows. Well forward, a stout mast is stepped, upon which is rigged, sometimes, a sprit-sail, but usually a large square-sail made generally from a large canvas tarpaulin.

A party usually sends two men ahead to build the boats. They must go either five miles up the river just spoken of and raft the logs down here, and construct saw-pits, or else to a patch of timber two miles back, and carry the lumber all that distance on their shoulders. A saw-pit is a sort of elevated platform, ten or twelve feet high. On this the log to be sawn is laid, and a man stands above with the whip-saw, while another works the lower end, and in this way they saw the logs into boards. The boards are small, rarely more than nine or ten inches in width. It is a poor quality of spruce, soft and "punky," and easily broken. There is some pine. The boards are an inch thick, and planed on the edges. After the boat is built the seams are calked with oakum and pitched.

BOAT-BUILDING

The green lumber shrinks before it gets into the water, so that the boats as a rule leak like sieves, but the goods rest upon slabs laid upon the bottom cross-ribs.

Everybody is happy, singing at his work. When a boat is ready to be launched every one turns in to help, for some have to be carried some distance to water. And when a boat departs it is with shouts of good wishes and a fusillade of revolver-shots. Nails are in great demand, bringing $1 or more a pound; likewise pitch, which commands the same. A few days ago, in order to finish a

WHIP-SAWING BOAT LUMBER

boat, a man gave $15 for two pounds of pitch. No one will sell lumber at all.

Many are selling out and going back even after reaching here.

The last of September it snowed six inches, and it continued to snow a little each day after that. We had to work under an awning. At Crater Lake there were said to be snow-drifts twenty feet deep. Still the people were coming, it being estimated that there were a hundred outfits on the trail this side the summit, as compared with two hundred and twenty-five two weeks before.

No one knows where Jim is. Three of my horses have been taken over the summit and are working on this side. The burros are feeding on rolled oats. During the day we had them they dined off flapjacks; but this is very expensive horse-feed. Forty cents a pound packing is added to the price of all commodities here. There are many selling out flour at $20 a pack. L'Abbé here throws up the sponge. The little French baker, Richards by name, from Detroit, true to his determination, is here with goods, having been working from daylight to dark, and even Simpson, with his newspapers. He is putting his canvas canoe together with alder frames.

There are but few of the *Islander* party this far. I see only the Beall and Bowman party. A few are ahead, but the rest are behind or on the Skagway trail.

I was laid up for a week—the constant wet and cold had been too much. Work stopped on our boat. On the 4th of October the snow went off. On October 5th our boat is finished; we had decided to remodel her, giving her six inches more width top and bottom. The last seam is calked to-day, and she is carried down to the lake, and the next day we load the goods into her. She stands 23 feet over all; 6 feet beam; 16 feet by 30 inches bottom; draught, 18 inches with 1500 pounds of cargo.

We start amid a salvo of revolver-shots. The lake is as smooth as glass—what Brown calls an "ash breeze." So he gives her the ash oars until a real breeze springs up, when we hoist a sprit-sail, and in a short while are at the foot of the lake, where several other boats are about to be lined through a nasty thoroughfare into Lake Bennett. It has raised a great load of anxiety from our minds that our little boat carries her load so well; above all, even when loaded she responds to the oars in a way that delights Brown.

While we are unloading, a man leading some horses with packs comes down the bank of the lake. There is something familiar about him. A second glance reveals

OUR BATEAU READY FOR LAUNCHING

John B. Burnham, of *Forest and Stream*, whom I suppose still on the Skagway trail, and tell him so, whereupon I discover that here, at Lindeman, is the end of the Skagway trail! Thirty - one miles from Dyea *via* Chilkoot; forty-five miles from Skagway *via* White Pass!

Burnham's party of five, seeing that all could not get through, have undertaken to put two through with full outfits, and this is the last load. Burnham and another are to undertake the journey in four canvas canoes, two canoes being loaded as freight-boats and taken in tow.

The opening of the White Pass as a summer trail was not a blunder—it was a crime. When the British Yukon Company was advertising the White Pass trail and booming its town-site and railway proposition, the trail was not cut out beyond the summit of the pass. There was at that time no trail, and there has been since no trail, but something that they have called a trail, marked by the dead bodies of three thousand horses, and by the shattered health and the shattered hopes and fortunes of scores—nay, hundreds—of men. Captain Moore, whose alleged town-site rights the British Yukon Company acquired, supposed the trail ought to come out at the Windy Arm of Tagish. The exploration party of the Canadian government, proceeding by the natural course, went by way of Touchi Lake into Taku Arm of Tagish, and, in consequence of their belief that that was the trail, have established the custom-house at the outlet of Tagish.

The story of the Skagway trail will never be written by one person. It is a series of individual experiences, each unique, and there are as many stories as there were men on the trail. How much of the awful destruction of horses was caused by the trail, and how much by the ignorance and cruelty of the packers, will never be known. One outfit killed thirty-seven horses, and there were others that equalled or surpasssed that figure. On the other hand, a Black Hills man, no other than he of the buckskins, at whom some smiled aboard the steamer, packed alone with three horses twenty-four hundred pounds from the "Foot of the Hill" to Bennett in eighteen days. Each night, no matter how tired, he put his horses' feet in a bucket of water, washed the mud off their legs and dried them, and washed their backs with salt water. He came through when the trail was at its worst, and sold the horses at Bennett for a fair sum.

The attempt to blast the rock out of the trail ended in a fizzle. The giant-powder ordered from Juneau went back unused. The only real work was done by the miners themselves in corduroying. Half-way in on the trail goods were actually given away, the unfortunate owners having neither money nor strength to pack them either

A LAUNCHING BEE, LAKE LINDEMAN

ahead or back, and the trail being in such terrible condition that outfits not only had no sale value, but could hardly be accepted even as a gift.

At Lindeman comparatively few boats have been sold, each party generally building its own. At Bennett, however, there is a saw-mill, and boats have been built by contract, the prices ranging from $250 to, in certain instances, as high as $600. Passage to Dawson is $50 light; with small outfit, $125.

Landing our goods and covering them with a canvas, we take tent, grub, and tools over to Bennett, a distance of three-quarters of a mile, along a sandy road through a grove of pines. It is long since I have seen anything so clean as this sand. The air is grateful, and it seems like another country, only the ugly clouds hanging over the distant white mountains remind us of what we have left behind. We set up our tent on a gently sloping, sandy beach, among other tents. Lake Bennett to the north lies like a trench between towering, rugged mountains of great grandeur. Their tops and sides are white down to a line a thousand feet above the lake. Every day now this line is creeping a little lower. Our guest to-night is Mr. Harrington, a powder manufacturer on a "vacation," who has just helped Burnham over with a load. He tells us his experiences since we parted on the *Islander*. He regales us with a description of some very fine horse meat he has had. I didn't suppose any one had come to that. Mr. Harrington assures us that it wasn't his horse. This is how it was: A party he knew had a young horse in good condition that they had to kill, and they had tried the steak and had found it tender. Burnham would testify to its goodness, for he had a big piece that he was taking in with him. I see now that it is merely prejudice about eating horse. Hitherto I had considered it about the last extremity, like crow, and it was hard to feel that friends for whom I had high regard should come to horse, much less insist that it was good! Alas, what two months on the Skagway trail does for a man!

Two months, and just starting! Next morning we

take a look at the thoroughfare between the two lakes. It is a gorge about three-quarters of a mile long, with rocks each side, but with a clear channel, except near the lower end, where the river splits against a large, nearly submerged rock. Three large Yukon boats are being lined down by six men. I tell Brown I think we can run the rapid with the empty boat. So, putting Brown in the bow with a large oar, and taking position in the stern with another, I give the word to push off. A moment later we strike the head of the rapid, taking some seas, and then the banks go rushing by.

A quick turn of the stern oar at the big rock, the double-ender whirls, and soon we are dancing in the quiet chop of the outlet, and come to a landing beside our tent at the head of the lake. This is how another saw it:

" As I came down the sandy hill-side to the lake, I saw at the landing two men unloading a trim-looking double-ender boat of distinct individuality that it needed only a glance to show was vastly superior to the ordinary Yukon type. One of the men was a slender six-footer, with a face wind-tanned the color of sole-leather.

" He wore weather-stained clothes that, judging from the general suggestion, no doubt still carried a little of the smoky smell and balsam aroma from camps in the green woods of New Brunswick. His feet were moccasined, and his black hair straggled from under a red toboggan cap. Not only was his rig suggestive of the aborigine, but his every action proved him to be so thoroughly at home in his untamed environment that it is little wonder that at first glance I took him to be an Indian, and that it required several minutes after his jolly smile and voluble greeting to dispel the illusion.

" Adney was an expert at river navigation ; and his companion, though inexperienced in this kind of work, was a champion oarsman, cool-headed and gritty. On a later occasion I happened to be on the trail near the point referred to, when I heard some men calling out from the top of the canyon-like bank that the HARPER'S WEEKLY man was shooting the rapids. I ran across just in time to see the boat swept by with the speed of a bolt from a crossbow, leaping from wave-crest to wave-crest, and drenching its occupants with sheets of spray. Adney and Brown were standing erect in bow and stern, each wielding a single oar used as a paddle, and from their masterly course it was evident that they had their boat well under control. It was all over in a very small fraction of time. They had avoided by the narrowest margin jagged bowlders that it seemed impossible to pass, and in a slather of foam shot out into the smooth water below."—J. B. BURNHAM, in *Forest and Stream*.

MINERS AT DINNER

CHAPTER VII

October 9.

A GALE is roaring down the gap, kicking up a great sea in the lake ; we dare not wait longer ; Burnham not ready, but says, " Don't wait." There is a lull towards noon. We hoist the sprit-sail ; Brown tends sheet, while I take a big steering-oar in the stern.

In a few moments the white-caps are boarding us ; the sail, having no boom across the foot, begins to flap against the mast, obliging us to run under the lee of a rocky point a mile from the starting-place. Half a dozen big boats, with huge square sails, that started right after us, scud by us at railroad speed. We cut a boom for the sail and pick a few berries, which are very plentiful in patches among the rocks, and then push off again. We square away in great shape. There is so little freeboard amidships that if we should get in the

129

trough of the sea we would swamp instantly. Our mast is tough pine, but when the wind snatches the rag of a sail it bends as if it would break.

Now begins the fight. The little sail, small though it is, keeps pulling us to one side. Sailors know what "yawing" is, and it takes all the strength of one pair of arms on a twelve-foot ash steering-oar to keep her head on. Now and then a big comber comes over the stern, and

SAILING DOWN LAKE BENNETT

we have to bail. Not a cove or shelter in sight, and the sea is getting worse.

A little way on we pass a camp on shore where they are drying goods — a capsize, no doubt. Pretty soon, under the lee of little rocky capes, boats are drawn out on shore and parties are camped, driven in by the storm. The raw wind and the spray stiffen our fingers, but it is impossible to let go an instant to put on mittens. We overhaul some little boats, and pass three or four, but the big ones show us clean heels.

About twelve miles down, the lake narrows to about half a mile, and here the waves are terrific, and the cross-waves break over the tarpaulin covering the goods amidships. In the midst of it all the mast goes overboard with a snap. Brown gathers in the sail, and, still scudding, we drop in behind a point fortunately close at hand. Here we are able to get a new and larger mast. One of the boats we had passed follows us in. It contains a New York party of two. When we start again they will not follow, on account of their heavy boat-load.

At evening we run into a little cove opposite the west arm of Bennett, with a smooth, sandy beach, where there are other boats. A few minutes later a big Peterboro canoe, with two men in yellow Mackinaws, runs in under a small sail. It is the United States mail for Circle City. Around the camp-fire that night eager questions are plied these two men to know just what is going on at Dawson, for they had left Dawson only thirty-odd days before.

The steamers had not all arrived when they left, but flour was $6 a sack.

"Would there be starvation?"

We get this reply, spoken slowly and deliberately: "I have been eleven years in Alaska, and there hasn't been a year yet when everybody wasn't going to starve, but no one has starved yet."

"How cold is it?"

"Cold, but not so cold but that a man can stand it. I spent one winter in a tent."

All of which is comforting. The mail-carriers have no tent, but lie down on a tarpaulin, with another over them, and are off at daylight. They have oars rigged to the canoe, and expect to reach Dawson in six or seven days.

We get under way soon after. The wind has moderated, but a heavy sea is still on. We run along easily; we pass one boat that had an earlier start, and are making every inch of the little sail pull in order to overtake another. The lines of the bateau give it a tremendous advantage over the clumsy whip-sawed boats built at the lakes.

We are running along about a quarter of a mile from the right-hand bank, which rises high and steep into the clouds, when we see on the shelving beach a tent, and some blankets and goods spread out in the sun. There are a black dog and a solitary man, and a smallish boat is drawn out on the shore. As we look, the man runs down to the edge of the water and fires off a gun, and then gets into the boat. We run in closer, and heave to as the man comes out, rowing frantically, and when we get near enough he calls out:

"Brown! Brown!"

At some risk of swamping, we hold the bateau into the wind and wait. When he gets within fifty yards we can see that he is much excited.

"My partners!" says he. "I haven't seen them—it was blowing too hard—and Pete went to take it out—and fell overboard—and McManus went after him!"

It is John, a Russian from San Francisco, who, with another Russian and poor McManus, had worked so hard on the trail. We had seen them all often, but did not know their full names. We gather bit by bit from his incoherent talk that their sail had been nailed fast. The yard would not lower, and, in trying to unstep the mast during the hard blow of two days before, Pete had been carried overboard, and McManus had gone into the icy

water to rescue him. It was nearly or quite dark at
the time of this accident, and they were never seen
again.

How the Russian managed to get ashore is a wonder. He had stopped several parties. They had advised
him to go home, but he is anxious to get to Dawson.
He offers Brown half the outfit to leave me and go
with him. Brown refuses. The outfit consists of 3500
pounds of grub, and there are valuable furs and clothing. Brown knows it, for he was well acquainted with
all three. Finally, being able to do him no good, we turn
on down the lake, and last see him awkwardly trying to
row his ungainly craft ashore. He reported later at the
Canadian custom-house, and it was rumored, though
with what truth we could not determine, that in the endeavor to reach Dawson over the ice his hands and feet
were frozen.

By noon we reach the foot of Bennett, where, in a
gentle current, between low banks a few rods apart, the
green waters of the lake start again on their journey—
Caribou Crossing, so called from its being a crossing-
place for the caribou. About a mile, and the stream
enters a very shallow, muddy lake, two or three miles
long, called Lake Nares, and then through another slack
thoroughfare into Tagish Lake.

Tagish Lake, although a single body of water, is more
like a group of lakes, or long arms, deep-set amid high
mountains. The scenery in these lakes is magnificent.
We put a trolling-line out—a large salmon-troll, such as
is used on Vancouver Island waters—while Brown takes
the oars. As we approach the mouth of Windy Arm,
which enters from the southward, we expect a blow and
a battle with the cross-seas, in consequence of what the
guide-books say. Extraordinary fortune is with us, for

we row across its mouth as on a looking-glass, in which the tall hills are doubled.

There is a tug at the trolling - line, and we pull in a fine large trout, in length about twenty inches; in color the belly is milk white, sides drab gray, with large, irregular, often triangular spots of light; pectoral fins steel blue, ventrals tipped with light yellow—a strikingly handsome fish. We get several bites, but hook only the one. That night, in camp with several other boats, near the end of the lake, past the Taku Arm, one party showed seven trout, weighing two or three pounds apiece. My own trout had a six-inch white-fish inside of it.

Next morning we are later than the others breaking camp, for not only do we have a faculty for late rising, but have to unload and reload the whole outfit on account of the leaking. All the boats are leaking badly, but other parties have more men to do the camp-work. Our boat runs so easily that when we have what Brown facetiously terms a good "ash breeze" we can overtake and pass them all. The other boats are clumsy, and though many have four oars to a boat, the oars, being hewn out of a pine or spruce, are so heavy that they can only take short dips, and with a head-wind make no headway whatever. The lower end of the lake is full of ducks on their southward migration—hundreds of them. Having only a rifle, we miss many opportunities. However, by a lucky shot, one drops while on the wing to the little 30 × 30 — indeed, it is as easy to hit them on the wing as while bobbing up and down in the waves. Soon the lake suddenly narrows, and we find ourselves in a slack current, with flock after flock of ducks getting up; and after drifting about two miles, we see ahead, against a bank of evergreens on the right, the red flag of Britain and some tents, and come to a landing in shallow water at the Canadian customs office. We make camp, and before dark the others drop in and camp. Besides John Godson, the customs officer, and several assistants, there is a squad of Northwestern Mounted Police under Inspector Strickland, who is also postmaster. The police are building a large log barracks, and the scene reminds one of the lumber woods of the East, for we have reached

AMERICAN MINERS PAYING CANADIAN CUSTOMS-DUTIES

a region of small but plentiful timber and varied animal life. It is a pretty spot they have chosen, commanding a view of the river both ways.

Foreign goods entering Canada are liable to duty as follows : hardware, 30 to 35 per cent.; provisions, 15 to 20 per cent.; tobacco, 50 cents per pound. Average about 25 per cent.

To all appearance Mr. Godson is carrying out his instructions to deal leniently. Says he: "I ask them if they have dutiable goods; I take their statement, or they may offer me their bills. I do not look into a man's boat. I try to judge each case, and I recognize that few have any surplus cash when they reach here. In such cases I have taken a day or two's labor whip-sawing, or something else in lieu of cash, holding the same in trust until the duties are forwarded. I ask full duty on tobacco. I have taken flour at $20 a sack—trail price." *

Mr. Godson points out that he could have stationed inspectors at both summits and collected duties on American horses every time they crossed the line; but retaliation by either government would only have ground the innocent miner as between two millstones.

The custom-house, which is also the sleeping-apartment of the customs officers and the inspector, is a small tent, the walls being raised three feet higher by logs and banked around with earth. There is a stove inside.

An old-timer, familiar with the river, who is cooking for the officials, tells us all that he doubts if we get through.

"You will get through Lake Marsh, then the White Horse; and if you get through Lake Labarge before it

---

* There were many complaints after leaving the post of unfair treatment. One party bitterly complained to me that their medicine-chest had been "confiscated." Mr. Godson happened to mention this very case as an instance of attempted evasion. The chest belonged to a physician who had distributed its contents among eleven men to escape duty. As it contained gold-foil and dentist's tools and was not a *bona fide* miner's chest, it was held until the owner arrived later. Blankets and seasonable clothing in actual use, and one hundred pounds of provisions were exempted. On the whole, it is my belief that the collection of duties was made as easy as such a species of tax-levying could be.

freezes, you will make Thirty - Mile River, and possibly Pelly River; and if you get that far you may get down with the mush ice."

"What is the mush ice?"

He urges us all to "Hurry! hurry!" So do all the officers—to start that night, before the wind changed.

Mr. Godson goes around to the camps, and by the light of the fire takes inventory of their goods, so that

CUSTOM-HOUSE AT TAGISH AND THE COLLECTOR, MR. JOHN GODSON

they may not be delayed in the morning. One boat leaves at midnight.

We wait until noon next day for the flotilla of canoes, which do not appear, and then put off again. We think a good deal over Inspector Strickland's words—that for the past three years the Klondike has been frozen tight on the 13th of October. It is now the 12th.

137

Lake Marsh, named in honor of Prof. O. C. Marsh, but sometimes called "Mud" Lake by the miners, is separated from Tagish by a sluggish thoroughfare several miles long, and its length is about nineteen miles, narrow, like the rest, and shallow. The sky is clear, and when darkness sets in the air grows bitterly cold, and we bundle up to keep warm. About nine o'clock we put inshore, and find thin shore ice out twenty feet; but we discover a place where there is dry land, build a big camp-fire, and cook supper. The shore ice, as it rises and falls on the gently undulating surface of the water, creaks and cries for all the world like a hundred frogs in spring-time, and it is indeed a dismal sound that bodes us no good.

"If you get through Lake Labarge before it freezes!"

Lake Marsh is freezing and Labarge is far away.

Waiting only to finish eating, we put out again into the lake, whose shores in the darkness we can dimly make out, and head for a point about two miles off. We are about half-way there when the bow of the boat crashes into thin ice. Thinking we are running ashore, we turn out and clear the ice. Judge our dismay when again we crash into ice! We cut through this, turning still farther out, until we are crosswise of the lake. Again we strike into ice. I am at the oars now We keep on pulling with difficulty, each time cutting the blades into the ice for a hold, and we pass through two or three distinct belts of ice that extend far out into the lake. We are now almost in a panic, for it seems as if the outlet must be frozen up tight. When we get to clear water we head north again, keeping out from the shore, and towards morning we land and spread our blankets on the ground among some small spruces on a low bank, with several inches of snow on the ground. After a short nap it is daylight, and we start again. There are no other boats in sight. It is not a great way to the outlet, which we know by the current that begins to carry us along while yet well within the lake, and we are soon floating down a slack stream several hundred feet wide, with low, wooded banks.

The current is easy, the river winding about among banks of sand some two hundred feet high. Along these are the holes of countless thousands of bank-swallows long since departed south.

We go on thus for about twenty miles, the river growing more and more swift. We lie this night on the ground under a big spruce two feet in diameter, and awake next morning wet with soft snow, which fell during the night. After an hour's run in the swift current we pass a fine boat smashed on a rock in mid-stream. Soon we hear a shout, followed by another, "Look out for the Canyon!" and on the right hand see boats lined up in a large eddy, below which is a wall of dark rock and an insignificant black opening. We pull into the eddy alongside. Some of the men are those we saw at Tagish, and some we never saw before. They have all taken a look at the Canyon, and most of them are unloading part of their goods and packing it around—a distance of three-fifths of a mile. We go up the trail to a spot where we can stand on the brink and look directly down into the seething waters of the gorge.

Miles Canyon, named in honor of General Miles, is about a hundred feet wide and fifty or sixty feet deep, and the whole body of the Lewes River pours through at a high rate of speed between the perpendicular walls of basaltic rock of the hexagonal formation familiar in pictures of the famous Fingal's Cave. Half-way down the Canyon widens, and there is a large eddy, which the boats are told to avoid by keeping to the crest of the waves, and then continuing as before. A boat starts in as we are looking, manned by two men at the side oars, and with a bow and stern steering-oar.

After our trip through Lake Bennett in the storm we feel pretty sure of our boat, so we conclude not to carry

AT THE HEAD OF THE CANYON

any of our stuff around. We tuck the tarpaulin down close and make everything snug, and when Brown has seated himself at the oars, and said, "All ready!" we push off and head for the gateway. I think I notice a slight tightening of Brown's mouth, but that is all, as he dips the oars and begins to make the long stroke ; but perhaps he can retaliate by saying some unkind thing of me at this time. As soon as we are at the very brink we know it is too late to turn back, so when we slide down the first pitch I head her into the seething crest. At the first leap into the soapsuds the spray flies several feet outward from the flaring sides. A dozen or two huge lunges into the crests of the waves, and we know that we shall ride it out. All at once—it must be we are not exactly in the middle—the boat's nose catches in an eddy and we swing around, head up stream. It is a simple matter to turn her nose again into the current, and then we go on again, leaping and jumping with terrific force. Brown, who manages the oars splendidly, keeps dipping them, and in a few moments we emerge from between the narrow walls into an open basin.

There are a number of boats here too, but, having nothing to stop for, we keep on into Squaw Rapids, which some regard as worse than the Canyon; when suddenly remembering that the White Horse Rapids is only one and a half miles below, we drop ashore, just above a turn of the river to the left, and make a landing at a low bank.

A view of the rapids must first be had. After turning to the left the river swings again to the right through a gorge of basalt similar to the Canyon but only twenty to thirty feet high and several times its width. For a quarter of a mile it lashes itself into a perfect fury, and then, with a jumping and tossing, it bursts through a gorge a span wide with banks level with the water, and then spreads out serene, once more the wide, generous river. From a vantage-point on the bank above we watch a boat going through, and we see it emerge into the quiet water and make a landing.

We resolve to take out part of our cargo; so, putting all our personal baggage ashore, leaving an even thousand pounds in the boat, which gives us six inches or more of freeboard, we turn her nose into the current.

Following the roughest water, to avoid rocks, we are

soon in the dancing waves and pitching worse by far
than in the Canyon. As we jump from wave to wave,
it seems positively as if boat and all would keep right
on through to the bottom of the river. The water even
now is pouring in, and it is plain that the boat will
never live through. One thought alone comforts us : the
fearful impetus with which we are moving must surely
take us bodily through and out, and then—we can make
the shore somehow. I count the seconds that will take
us through.

The effect to the eye, as we enter the great white-caps,
is that of a jumping, not only up and down, but from the
sides to the middle.

Now we are in. From sides and ends a sheet of water
pours over, drenching Brown and filling the boat ; the
same instant, it seems, a big side-wave takes the little
craft, spins her like a top, quick as a wink, throws her
into a boiling eddy on the left—and we are through and
safe, with a little more work to get ashore.

Men who were watching us from the bank said that
we disappeared from sight in the trough. Brown is wet
up to his waist. Everything is afloat. We jump out
leg-deep into the water near shore, and, when we have
bailed out some of the water, drop the boat down to
the usual landing-place, a little sandy cove, where
we unload, pitch tent, and, while tripping back for our
five hundred pounds of goods, watch the other boats
come through. They are all big ones, and all get
through without mishap. Our goods are not damaged,
because the sacks were tight and they were wet for so
short a time.

We hear of pilots both here and at the Canyon, but
every man takes his own boat through to-day. The
pilots take boats through the Canyon for from $10 to

RUNNING THE WHITE HORSE RAPIDS

$20 each.*   Those who unload have the worst of it, as the heavy boats go through best.   The double-ender swings so easily that it is hard to steer, and is rather small for the business.

The White Horse is a bit of water I have considerable respect for.   The imperturbable Brown, when asked how he felt—if he were scared—replied, " Why, no. You said it was all right.   I suppose you know—it's your boat and your outfit."   I believe that if a charge of dynamite were to explode under Brown he would not wink an eyelash.

Many say they took more water aboard in the Canyon than in the White Horse, while Squaw Rapids was worse than the Canyon.   Once a dog swam the Canyon.   He tried to follow his master's boat, instead of walking around.   He was a water-spaniel, though; but he must have had more ups and downs than he dreamed of when he started in the quiet water above.

There have been no drownings in the White Horse this year, so far as known.   But probably no fewer than forty drownings are to be credited to this bit of water since the river was first opened to white men.   The trail around the rapids is lined with trees blazed and inscribed with the heroic deeds of those gone before.   They are written on trees, on scraps of paper, on broken oar-blades.   Some are amusing, while all are interesting.

A load of anxiety is off our minds now that we are safely through.   Next morning, before starting, we watch some boats come through.   It is a great sight, as they come dancing into view at the turn ; and as they go flying past we give them each a rousing cheer.

* Two weeks before two partners stopped and made enough to buy an interest in a Bonanza Creek claim.

There are no pilots to-day, for courage, like fear, is catching. Last week it was the other way. A great many of the men had wives, and they all had "promised their wives" that they would not run the rapids. It was surprising how many married men there were.

CHARACTERISTIC VIEW ON UPPER YUKON RIVER

Again in the current. The banks have the same appearance as above the Canyon, and are one to two hundred feet high, of sand, against which the current is continually wearing, building up on the inside what the miners call "bars." This, indeed, is the general character of the upper Yukon—steep, slanting sand or gravel banks on the outcurve, low flats densely timbered with spruce on the inside.

About two hours after leaving the White Horse, we make, as we suppose, a cut-off across a sharp bend to the left, and suddenly find that we are rowing up-stream—the Tahkeena River. Turning about, we come pretty soon to an enormous loop in the river. The map shows a slender cut-off, saving two miles. The other boats are pushing us behind, but the cut-off is so slender when we reach it that we conclude that "the long way around is the shortest way home." We have just got around nicely when the river spreads out between bars and islands, our boat stops with a scrape, and we have to climb out and tow the boat up-stream until we find the channel again. When, after much labor, we get through, we are chagrined to find that the hindmost boats have taken the cut-off and overtaken us. In a little while we get the chop of a strong north wind against the current, and at dark run into a lake. Observing a large camp-fire on the left hand, and taking it to be a miner's camp, we make in that direction, and after a stiff pull suddenly crash into something which prove to be fish-weirs, and, resting, we hear children crying and dogs barking — undoubtedly an Indian village. Not caring to lie awake all night watching our goods if we land here, we turn our bow up shore and land behind a point of trees about a mile distant, on a hard beach, at a pile of drift-wood. Pretty soon another boat with three miners comes along, and they build another fire alongside ours. While we are eating some boiled loon that a lucky shot secured us on the river, two Indian boys appear in the firelight with a bundle, which they throw down on the ground and stand curiously staring at us. We ask them what they want, whereupon they open the bundle and display two small mountain-sheep skins, half a dozen caps of ground-squirrel skins, and one of cross-fox. The biggest boy is about nine, the other seven years of age. They beg for something to eat, and offer a cap for a cupful

147

of black tea (leaves), which our neighbors give. One of the miners shows them a small 32-caliber revolver, rusted and perfectly useless. How their eyes snap ! They look it over carefully, inquiring by signs about ammunition, and at length give all their squirrel caps for the pistol and six cartridges. Just then two Indians walk up into the firelight. One is a very old man in a fox - skin cap, a blanket - circular over his shoulders, close-fitting leather leggings, and moccasins handsomely worked with quills. The other is a young man in store clothes, who has learned a few words of English at Dyea. There is Indian talk between the four. Pretty soon the biggest boy pulls the pistol out of his pocket and hands it to the white man with a sheepish look, saying, "Papa no like." The furs were, of course, re-turned. "Papa," standing erect and uncompromising, dignified and stern, was admirable. The young man has seen just enough of civilization to spoil him ; he fawns, and hands us with evident pride a paper upon which some white man has written that the bearer is "all right, and for white men to be kind to him." We give them each a cup of tea, and after a while they go away. We learned afterwards that we acted wisely in not stopping at their camp, for between pilfering Indians and thieving dogs we should have had a sorry time. It is freezing to-night, but there is no snow on the ground.

Lake Labarge, named in honor of Labarge, an explorer for the long-ago-projected Russo-American telegraph, is about thirty miles long and two miles wide at its narrow-est part. It is rare that a strong wind is not blowing either up or down, so fiercely that the miners are often delayed as at Windy Arm. In the morning, however, there is not a breath of air to disturb the surface of the lake. As Al's good strong arms send the boat along in the good "ash" breeze, the water is so still that it seems as if the boat were suspended in the air. The sight of this mirror-like surface, with bold headlands of rounded gray limestone, patched with groves of small dark spruce, is truly impressive. We try the troll, but it drags so heavy that we soon take it in; but there must be trout in the clear green water along the gray cliffs. After a cup of tea in a pretty sandy cove, the air begins to breathe fitfully upon the smooth surface of the lake. Now it has caught the boats behind us and others along the far shore. We clap on sail, and in three minutes the lake is covered with white-caps. We scud along until dusk; there is not a niche in the frowning wall of rock into which we can run and camp. Darkness falls and we can only steer for the dim outlet, where a twinkling glimmer shows us a miner's camp-fire. In half an hour a point of land suddenly opens up, and we see close at hand a large camp-fire, and, when we are near enough to hail, some men on shore direct us into a sheltered bight alongside two large boats. They prove to be friends from Lindeman, who left there one week before. We lay our blankets on the hard, frozen beach gravel, with the tent over all to keep off dew, and we sleep warm, but the others, who have stoves inside their tents, complain bitterly of the cold. In the morning we are white with frost. Another night like this, with a still lake, and Labarge would close; as it is, there is considerable thin ice along shore. In the spring the ice in Lake Labarge does not break up for a week or more after the river is clear. The miners, when they reach the head of the lake, instead of waiting for the ice to go out, often place their boats on sleds and with the strong south wind behind them glide over the lake, which at that season is as smooth and glare as a bottle.

Leaving our friends to follow, we pull to the outlet,

one mile away, and observe that we ran a grave risk of running upon a reef exactly in the middle of the outlet—a nice predicament for a stormy night. From here to the junction of the Hootalinqua, distant 27.5 miles by survey, the Lewes is called by the miners "Thirty-Mile River." The boat slips along in the swift current as fast as the most eager can wish, rapid after rapid, with rocks here and there popping up, making navigation really dangerous. Just as we are pulling off from our hasty lunch a big boat with four oars turns in, containing the little black French baker from Detroit, who is here, after working like a horse day and night on the trail. But Jim, he says, will not get out of the mountains. As the party intend to stop at Stewart, we take letters to post in Dawson for friends at home. Soon after lunch we dash through a break in the wall of hills, out into a broad valley and a leisurely current—that of the Hootalinqua, or Teslintoo, River, which drains Lake Teslin. Looking up-stream any one would say that the Hootalinqua was the main river valley and a larger stream than the Lewes. But the discharge of the Hootalinqua is considerably less on account of its slower current. The water, no longer clear and limpid, is yellow and muddy, while the whole aspect of the country has become more mild. White birches are seen for the first time; the cottonwoods are larger, the very spruce greener, due to the lower altitude.

But the winter is coming on faster than altitude diminishes. We work hard with both oars and paddle, and overtake more boats, which prove to be of our own crowd of yesterday, who kept on through the lake in the night and got the start of us this morning. One of them has a stove set up, and they do all their cooking aboard, which saves time. As the boat drifts along, with the smoke pouring out of the stove-pipe, it looks, at a little distance, like a diminutive steamboat. At dusk our companions turn in to camp, but we go on. After rowing for several miles without finding a camping-place, we discover a little break in the bank, which turns out to be the mouth of a small creek. It is like a little canal, about ten feet wide. While we are dragging the boat into it, Brown's boot sticks in the mud. and in trying to lift it he falls full length into the water, and I have to build camp while he changes his clothes. The outlook is certainly dreary. Snow on the ground, and little wood to build the fire. Cutting a green spruce for boughs, we lay them on the ground in front of the fire made of half-dead wood, and, rigging the oars and poles into a tepee, throw the tent around them. The thermometer has stood at 29° all day, with a wretched wind from the north. We observe signs of musk-rat and beaver here, so the winters cannot be so terrible. After Brown has turned in under the blankets, the little note-book comes out, and in the glow of the red fire the day's notes are written up. We have lost track of the days. Our appetites are growing bigger. We don't do much cooking, being satisfied with hardtack and rolled-oat mush, made in fifteen minutes, served with condensed milk and sugar, and flapjacks cooked in the frying-pan. Every man on the trail has learned the toss of the wrist and flip of the frying-pan in preparing this staple article of the prospector's diet. In the morning we are off at daybreak ahead of all rivals. Towards noon, as we approach Big Salmon River, which enters on the right, we see something ahead that looks like foam. Running into it, we see that it is masses of fine crystals, loosely held together like lumps of snow. It is the first of the mush ice running out. We jab paddles through it, remembering what the old cook had said, but soon leave it behind us.

Brown prefers rowing to steering, so we agree not to change off. Brown has taken to our rough camps like an old-timer. The other night when we had to lie among some very uneven hummocks and stumps, instead of growling he merely said, " We accommodated ourselves to the lumps first-class."

As we near the Little Salmon River, thirty-six miles below Big Salmon, a boat just ahead is seen to land and take aboard three small Indian boys with shot-guns, evidently a juvenile hunting-party. A mile farther we pass the mouth of Little Salmon on the right, and see ahead smoke from a camp and a group of men on the bank. The men begin waving their arms and shouting to attract our attention, and we run in to shore. It is a large encampment of Indians. They have built a sort of landing-place out of logs, floored with hewn boards, evidently for boats to land. As we make fast the float is crowded with the most dirty, smoky, ragged, ill-looking creatures, and more come running down the bank, all excited, and carrying things evidently for sale. They are old men, young men, boys, children with sore eyes. One man carries a tanned moose hide ; others a dried salmon, a chunk of black smoked moose or caribou meat, a black-bear skin, a grizzly-bear skin, a dog skin, a spoon made of mountain-sheep's horn, a beaver skin, etc. As I step out on the platform first one and then another begins pulling at my arms and clothes, and every way I look an arm clutching something is thrust into my face, with a regular hubbub of voices. To escape the fury of the onslaught, I jump back into the stern of the boat, thinking how fortunate it is that the boat is well covered with canvas. We have a box about a foot long that we keep our kitchen-stuff, candles, etc., in. It happens to be left exposed and they catch sight of it. One seizes a candle, another a bar of tar soap, and they begin offering to buy, calling out, "How muchee?" "How muchee?" They have money—silver dollars and half-dollars.

I can't see what they want with soap, but sell them the cake for half a dollar. We need the spoons and candles ourselves, so I make a sortie and take a lot of things away. They next catch sight of my camera, and one man offers $5 for it. I am too confused and busy seeing that nothing gets away to find out what they think the camera is. Brown is in his element; he has the trader's instinct. He has opened up five or six pounds of tobacco, and is up front, with a crowd of Indians around him, getting rid of it at 4 bits (50 cents) a plug. An old Indian, a gentle-looking old fellow, sees my rifle, which I always keep in reach. I show it to him, explaining the "take down" feature and the Lyman sight. His eyes glisten. He cannot speak a word of English. He says something to a young man beside him with a shock of dirty black hair reaching to his shoulders and a red handkerchief tied around his forehead, and the young man puts his hand in his pocket and pulls out a $20 gold piece and offers it to me, at the same time pointing to the gun. I shake my head. A word from the old man and the young man dives in his pocket again and hands five silver dollars along with the gold piece. I shake my head. Down he goes again, and this time shows five more, making $30 in all. He is going up $5 at a jump, and evidently means to own the gun; but, having no intention of parting with it at any price, I put it away, and convince him that it is positively not for sale.

At this moment there is a hubbub around the boat that picked up the little boys. A sudden outcry, then some run up the bank and others come running down. It is wild for a few minutes, and then the excitement subsides. Plainly, something is up. I ask the fellow with the red handkerchief, who speaks a few words of English. He replies, with a smile, "Oh, just Injun talk."

An old Indian with a blanket offers a pair of mittens trimmed with ermine. I ask, "How much?" "Two dollars" (I thought he said). I hand him two silver dollars, and he hands me the mittens, and stands waiting, repeating "Two dolla"—something. Then I understand he means $2.50. I shake my head. He still repeats, "Four bits." So I hand the mittens back and demand my money, which is still clinched in his fist. He refuses to give it up, and makes signs for me to give him back the mittens. I make signs that I have just given them to him. He says something, shakes his head, and feels all over himself—the old scoundrel. Instantly I jump up, so that the whole boat can be seen, and then lift the cover clear, so it can be seen by all that the mittens are not there. Then I step off the platform and actually have to pry the dollars out of his fist.

After several vain efforts to pull Brown away from his customers, I start to push the boat off, when the last of the Indians clambers out. Just as we push off, the old villain who tried to flimflam me out of $2 came running to the boat, threw aboard the mittens, which I knew very well he had, and holds out his hand for the $2, which I give him.

I never knew until now that so much voice and muscle could be put into the operation of exchanging commodities. The method is to get hold of something they want in the clinched fist, pressed tight against their breast, at the same time shoving what they have to sell into one's face, like a man making passes with boxing-gloves, accompanied by cries and grunts to attract attention. When twenty dirty savages are doing this, the effect can be imagined. A Baxter Street clothing man would be skinned alive, or else, like the cats of Kilkenny, there would be nothing left of either at the end of the trade.

When we camp that night we hear of the trouble.

"One of the Injuns," says one of the men that were in the boat, "handed me a watch he said he had bought. I looked at it and handed it back. It dropped out of his hand and struck on a rock and broke the crystal. He picked it up and looked at it, and then handed it to me. I took it and saw that the crystal was broken. Just then he raised a howl, and all the Injuns came runnin' down, and the fellow said I had broken the watch and he wanted me to buy it for $35 or pay $5 for a new crystal in Dawson. It looked like there was going to be trouble. They had three shot-guns loaded, and our rifles were covered up where we couldn't get at them, and we thought we had better pay the $5 and have no trouble.

"Them little devils we took into our boat—why, they came aboard with guns all cocked. We gathered the guns and let the hammers down, and they just laid back and laughed."

When we take stock from our belongings we find missing a pair of scissors, a bag of tobacco, and a candle out of the "wamgun" box.

These Indians, pilfering thieves that they are, doubtless are only practising on the white men what the Chilcats have taught them; they are only getting even.

Next morning a cold north wind and a heavy mist over the water; camp thirty-eight miles below Little Salmon. Cold night, and heavy mist again in the morning makes it difficult to see where to steer among the islands and bars, which are numerous in this part of the river.

The mist is dissipated by the rising sun, but there is a brisk raw wind in our face, and the boat is leaking badly. Brown to-day, while rowing, keeps his coat on for the first time.

The little "steamboat" with us again. At noon we fasten alongside, and use their stove for making some tea and flapjacks. We pass a log-cabin on an extensive flat on the left bank. Two Indian men and an old squaw beckon for us to stop, but we have had enough of Indians. It proved to be the trading-post occupied by George Carmack just before he went down river and found the gold on Bonanza Creek.

We overhaul a bunch of four boats drifting, the men, with guide-books out, scanning the river ahead. They say Five-Finger Rapids is close at hand, and at every island they make ready to pull ashore, being, it seems to us, unduly apprehensive. But we are not in doubt when, turning suddenly to the right, a great barrier looms up a mile ahead — five great irregular blocks of reddish rock ranging across the river like the piers of a bridge — making two principal channels. That on the left is growling ominously over shallow rocks, so we turn to the right and drop into a small eddy a few hundred feet above the great wall. We climb up and look at the rapid. It seems by no means dangerous. The opening is about one hundred feet wide, with vertical walls, through which the river suddenly drops a couple of feet, the waves rising angrily in a return curl, then dancing on in rapidly diminishing chops until lost in the swift current below.

The other boats, evidently not seeing our eddy, have stopped half a mile above, and are roping down the shore. Without waiting (it being too late in the day for a successful photograph), we turn our prow squarely for the middle of the cleft; a drop, a smash, a few quarts of water over the sides, and we are shot through into the fast current, without even looking back. Soon we hear the roar of Rink Rapids, six miles below that of Five-Finger; but keeping close to the right bank, according to directions, we find them nothing but a bad reef extending half-way across the river, on the left; on the right there is not even a ripple.

We run until dark, camping in four inches of snow, but with plenty of dry wood, some of the spruce being two feet through. The five other boats drop in, and we swap experiences around the fire. One young fellow, a boy of about twenty, tells how he came to be here. "I was in Seattle at the time, and I just wrote home that I was going in with all the rest of the crowd of crazy fools." None of his crew knew anything about river navigation when they started, and they have been spending half their time on bars. Another story is of a man who got into the big eddy in the Canyon and spent three hours rowing round and round, not knowing how to get out. Not one life (that any of us has heard of) has been lost this summer at the White Horse, but there have been several smashes. One party, who roped their boat through instead of running, lost all their pork and flour by the swamping of the boat. Twenty-four other boats that day ran the rapids safely.

The river from now on is very wide, and split up into numerous channels by wooded islands. We run into what looks like a good channel, following the left bank, when all at once the river shoals, and we only get off by wading and dragging. A deeper boat would never have got out of the trap. We are nearing the Pelly, but cannot see the river, though its valley is visible on the right. Swinging to the west and skirting a high, flat bank, we pass a small steamer drawn out of the water, then a cabin, then several more, and finally draw up in front of a cluster of log buildings, where a trodden path leads up the snow-covered bank. There is no human being in sight, but half a dozen wolfish, hungry-looking dogs come bounding down the bank with a volley of barks, which quickly subsides into curiosity mingled with ill-disguised suspicion. They are the native Eskimo-Indian dog, heavy, thick-haired, with powerful legs and neck, a sharp muzzle, slanting eyes, and short, erect, wolf ears. A look at them, and a slight knowledge of their kind, decides us to anchor the boat a little distance from shore by fastening a ten-foot pole to the bow and resting the other end in-shore, the long painter being made fast to a post above.

FACSIMILE OF A RECORD ON A TREE AT THE WHITE HORSE RAPIDS

CHAPTER VIII

Former Hudson's Bay Post—Present Alaska Commercial Company Store—
Talks with the Storekeeper—More about the Shortage of Grub—Start
from Fort Selkirk — Heavy Ice — Below Zero — Miners Hauled Out,
Waiting for River to Clear—Dangers of the Heavy Ice — Stewart River
—Accident in the Sweepers—Sixty-Mile Post—"This is Dawson"

October 22.

FORT SELKIRK lies on the left bank of
the Lewes, a mile below its junction
with the Pelly. These streams are
about equal in size, and together form
the Yukon proper. The first post of
that name was built at the junction
of the two rivers in 1848 by Robert
Campbell, an employé of the Hudson's
Bay Company, who entered the region that year by the
head of the Pelly, and was occupied until 1853, when, on
account of the danger from ice during the spring overflow, it was removed to the present site. That same year
a band of Chilkats, who had been watching with jealous
eyes the encroachments of the company upon their hitherto exclusive trade with the interior, or "Stick," Indians,
raided the post during Campbell's absence and burned
the buildings to the ground. Fort Yukon had been established in 1847, at the junction of the Porcupine and
Yukon, by A. H. Murray, of the same company; but it
was not supposed that the "Pelly" of Campbell and the
Yukon were the same stream until several years later,

159

when Campbell dropped down the river to Fort Yukon and proved them identical. Fort Selkirk had been so difficult to maintain, having been supplied in the last two years of its existence *via* Fort Yukon and the Porcupine and Mackenzie Rivers, that it was never rebuilt. In 1883, Lieutenant Frederick Schwatka noted

TRADING-POST AT FORT SELKIRK LOOKING TOWARDS THE YUKON
FROM THE SITE OF THE OLD HUDSON'S BAY COMPANY'S POST

that two stone chimneys of the old post were then standing; at the present time even these are gone and no monument remains of the splendid fortitude of Robert Campbell and of the enterprise of his great company, except some blackened bits of floor logs and the name which he gave. The site of the old post is still pointed out, a few yards in the rear of the present buildings, which consist of a store and dwelling-house built of logs, and several small log-cabins, belonging to Arthur Harper, an agent of the Alaska Commercial Company. These buildings, and some others in the distance, occupied by Indians and a mission, and a long pile of cord - wood, are all that meet the eye as we scramble on hands and feet up a very steep and slippery path to the top of the bank, followed by such of the dogs as have perceived the hopelessness of raiding our boat.

A little smoke rising out of a pipe in the roof of the nearer building is the only sign of life, except the dogs. A paper tacked to the side of the door reads that no steamer has been up for two years and there are no provisions for sale, except some condensed milk at a dollar a can. Stopping only to glance at this, we walk in and find ourselves in a room about fifteen by eighteen feet, with ceiling of rough boards laid over heavy joists, hardly higher than one's head, with one corner, embracing the doorway, fenced off from the rest by a wide board counter, evidently designed so that the Indians, who resort hither to exchange their furs for white men's goods, may not handle the bolts of white and red cotton cloth, blankets, boxes of tobacco, etc., which scantily cover some rude shelves against the back wall. A small glass show - case on the counter contains an assortment of knives, needles and thread, etc. Hanging from nails in the back wall, and from the ceiling, are black bear-skins, tanned moose-hides (a pile of which also lies on the floor), several bunches of sable-skins, and eleven beautiful silver-gray and black fox-skins. Long, narrow snow-shoes, moose-hide moccasins, and mittens lie on the shelves, floor, and counter, while a ladder at the back leads to a loft overhead. The interior is lighted by two small windows in the front and another in the end, and a globular iron stove in the near corner throws out a heat that accentuates a pervading smell of smoked leather and furs. At a small desk behind the counter stands a little, grave, sober man, with dark, thin beard, the sole person in charge of this, a typical Northwest Indian trading - post, and, as it proves, the only white man in the whole place, the agent, Mr. Harper, having gone "outside." *

After nodding good-day and inquiring if we have made our goods safe from the dogs, the store-keeper, J. J. Pitts by name, patiently answers our inquiries about the conditions at Dawson. Then we put our names down on some sheets of foolscap, which Mr. Pitts says is a register of all who have gone by this summer, save about one-third who have passed without stopping, from which it appears that about 3600 persons have passed in. We prepare to go on, intending to camp in the woods a few miles below, when in the most quiet way possible the grave little man remarks that we had better bring our stuff up and stop in Mr. Harper's cabin—an invitation that does not need pressing. While we are gone for grub - sack, cooking - tools, and blankets, Mr. Pitts has kindled a fire in a small cabin back of the warehouse. After building the fire, he brings in a small kerosene lamp (the only one in the place, we discovered), and then leaves us to cook supper.

Our cabin comprises a single room, about twelve by fourteen feet inside, with an eight - foot wall, a small window at the south end, and another at the north. The furniture consists of a rude board table, the butt of a log for a chair, and an empty bunk, or stationary bed for two persons, in one corner. After supper we repair

---

* Mr. Arthur Harper, concerning whom more will be said, died at Los Angeles, California, the same winter.

to the big house and spend the evening talking over a bottle of Scotch, a rare luxury here.

No one would take Pitts for a miner ; and, if eagerness to sell goods were a qualification in a trader, he would not be considered even a good trader. As a person who had stopped at the post once facetiously remarked, Mr. Pitts "seemed sorry if any one bought anything out of the store." He is a man wrapped in his own thoughts. Sometimes such men are cranks. Every man becomes a crank who stays long in this country. And who but an old-timer would growl and growl, and then give the best in the house? It is an instructive talk for us, his being the first intelligent account of facts and conditions that we had heard.

"So many are coming in unprepared, either with outfits, experience, or common-sense," says he. "They ask me what the price of flour is in Dawson. I tell them it has no price. 'But it must have some price,' they insist. 'It has no price. If the stores will sell it to you, you will pay $6 a sack ; but there has been no time this summer when a man could get a complete outfit from the stores. Last winter flour was freighted from Forty-Mile and sold in Dawson for $40 to $60 a sack. You will see it sell this winter for $100.'

"The boats are stuck and there is a shortage of grub and a stampede out of Dawson. People outside talk as if the steamers on this river run on a schedule ; whereas they are liable to be stuck on a bar and not get off at all and be destroyed by the ice in the spring. The country is not and never has been well supplied. Mr. Harper says that in the twenty-five years that he has been in the Yukon there has not been a year when there has not been a shortage of something. One year it was candles, and the men had to sit in the dark. Another year something else. This year it is flour. The only permanent relief is a railroad. This will have its drawbacks, for we will then be overrun with hoboes and silver cranks. At present we are not troubled with these things," and he smiled faintly.

"This is essentially a prospectors' country; it is no place for the majority of those who are coming in. They are carpenters, clerks, and the like. They may do well, but only for a while. The only ones calculated to succeed are those who understand the hardships and have grit and determination besides. Has the young man who is with you a sufficient outfit?" I told him he had not; that he was strong, and was willing to take the risk of getting something to do and buying grub. "That is a very foolish thing for him to do," he replied. "Many people are short, and more may have to leave before spring. The time was when it would go hard with the man who was responsible for bringing in a person like that."

It is not pleasant to contemplate what our condition may be before spring. There need be no starvation as long as there is grub in camp. There may be, and probably will be, serious trouble. Pitts, therefore, seems justified in saying that to deliberately come unprepared with food is hardly short of a crime against every other man in the camp.

The Indians here occupy about a dozen cabins, and are of true North American Indian, of Tinneh, or Athapaskan stock. Along the Yukon, between Fort Selkirk and the Porcupine River, they occupy a number of small villages, speak one language, and distinguish themselves as "Yukon" Indians. They are a hunting race, subsisting by the chase and fishing, exchanging their furs, moose and caribou hides, meat, and dried fish, for flour, tea, blankets, dry-goods, bacon, ammunition, etc. Formerly the fur trade was large, but now the Indians find it more profitable to hunt and sell meat to the miners.

Next morning, October 23d, it is five degrees below zero at seven o'clock, by the government thermometer—bitterly cold, and a thick fog envelops the river. Pitts advises us not to risk starting in the fog. We go back and stand around the big stove, pawing over skins and furs. Pitts wants to send some moose-hides to Dawson, where they are in great demand for moccasins, mittens, and gold-sacks. After picking out some he hesitates, then says, " No, I won't send them ; I don't think you'll reach Dawson."

About noon the fog, which results from the cold air meeting the warmer water of the river, is dissipated by the heat of the sun, revealing on the far side heavy ice pouring out of Pelly and filling half the river.

By keeping to the left we are able to avoid the ice, which is in lumps of every form from soft slush to round, hard cakes bigger than a wagon-wheel. The ice forms in granules, or crystals, in the little eddies and still places behind pebbles and bowlders in the bottom of the streams. When a considerable mass has formed it detaches itself from the bottom, rises to the surface, and floats away. If the mass is sufficiently large, it may pick up portions of the gravel-bed and carry them off. As it meets other masses, they crowd together, and thus it continues to grow, the top, exposed to the air, freezes hard, and a small ice-floe has begun its existence. Meeting others, and freezing together, the floe keeps increasing in size, and then it commences to rub against other floes and against the bank, making a rounded disk, hard on top, with one or two feet of loose slush below. In this manner the "mush," "slush," or "anchor" ice, as it is variously called, forms in all Northern rivers. But the story that in Klondike the rivers freeze from the bottom up, instead of from the top down (because the ground is colder than the air), is a mistake. As we skirt the belt of moving ice the low *shurr* of the floes as they rub together makes us bend to the oars and paddle.

NEARING DAWSON

The water freezes to the oars, until they become unmanageable and again and again we have to stop and pound the ice off with an axe. Mittens are frozen stiff, mustaches a mass of icicles, and no matter how hard we work we can't keep warm. The current is swift. We have gone, we judge, twenty miles when the setting of the sun and the lowering of the fog warns us to make camp. Drawing the boat close up to the shore, and securing the long painter to a tree, we set up our tepee on a high, flat bank, and a snapping blaze of dry spruce soon makes us forget our discomfort. We eat our flapjacks and beans, drink our tea, and lie back on the blankets before turning in. The ominous *sh-sh* of the ice can be plainly heard—a most unwelcome sound. Suddenly there is a long, dull roar under the bank. Springing across the fire, we gain the edge of the bank just as a floe forty feet long goes by, scraping the boat. Without stopping to decide on the manner of getting down, we throw our stuff out on the bank, and then haul the boat out, safe from harm. Our little boat seems now, from the tension of our minds, more than ever to stand between us and death. Although the boat is really safe, we stand for a long time watching the river. The stillness is broken only by the sound of the ice, and the northern lights, flashing with a pale-green light, make a weird impression. We have abandoned all hope of reaching Dawson. There are hundreds on the river this night feeling as we do. At ten o'clock the thermometer, only six feet from the fire, but shaded by a stick, registers one degree above zero. Before an outdoor fire one side of a person freezes while the other burns.

Next morning the river is filled with ice, grating, chafing, grinding, turning against the shore like great cart-wheels. We lighten the boat by chopping the ice from her sides and bottom, and reload. When the sun has dispelled the mist, we wait for an opening in the ice, push the bow out, and the next moment are among the floes, borne helplessly along in the current. Our first care is to keep from being again thrown against the bank, which has a strong tendency to happen; but we soon discover that the double-ender works easily among the floes, and we can do what larger boats cannot—work our way, pushing into the more open leads, and even aiding the current with the oars. A vague uneasiness possesses us yet. At a narrowing of the river the ice begins to crowd around the boat. There is no longer a bit of blue water as big as one's hand; we are packed solid, and hardly moving. We can only sit here with the canvas around us, not knowing what moment the ice will stop. The bleak mountains, thinly clad with vegetation; the tall, dark spruce, now whitened by the condensation of mist; the dull, gray sky; the thick mist clinging to the water; our little boat drifting along—a picture of loneliness.

As night approaches we see on the bank a boat, with a cache of goods on the shore, and two men hail us to stop and help them with their boat, which has been badly crushed in the ice. Landing a quarter of a mile below, in a sort of eddy where the ice has frozen out thirty feet, we chop a recess just large enough for the boat, and, after removing the goods to a safe place on the bank, we go up to where the men are, and find them in a tent—three men in all. They ask us if we have seen a raft of beef above—which we had, but whether of beef we could not tell, as we passed too far from it. They tell us that the raft belongs to William Perdue, who brought in seventy head of cattle over the Dalton trail, losing twenty on the way in the quicksands, but butchering fifty just below Five-Finger Rapids. One of their party is with the raft, and they tell of a serious misadventure of theirs. Near Five-Finger Rapids they saw a white steer loose on the bank. Thinking it was one that had gone astray from the Dalton trail and was lost, they shot it and dressed the meat. This was hardly finished when a man who proved to be Perdue came along inquiring if they had seen a white steer which he said he was depending on to help him get out logs for a raft.

They owned to having killed such a steer, and, as it was undoubtedly the one that belonged to Perdue, there was no alternative but to express regret at the mistake and pay for the meat, and, further, to turn in and help him get out the logs. The raft having been completed and loaded with meat, they left one of their number with it, and came on until the ice crushed in the side of their boat.

In the morning, however, there is no need for our help, as the shore-ice has frozen out so that they can reach the damaged part and repair it. We have to chop our own boat out of four inches of ice, and go on. Before we leave, the men give us some advice that eventually gave us trouble, through no fault of theirs. They tell us to look out for a beef-raft ahead of us; probably hung upon a bar — in fact, a party coming up afoot had definitely reported that to be the case. They recommend that when we meet the raft we bargain for a quarter of meat, which we can buy at about one-half or one-third its worth in Dawson; and that if the men have deserted the raft, to take the beef, as the owners naturally will be only too glad to have it delivered to them. When we have gone some distance, and are still, as we judge, about twenty miles from White River, a flock of about fifty ravens are seen flying over a spot in the middle of the river, and, floating nearer, we perceive a raft lodged squarely upon the head of a small island or bar, deserted. Taking this for the raft referred to by the men, we contrive to make a landing; and when we get up to the raft we discover mutton instead of beef—about one hundred carcasses, covered with the pelts. The ravens had worked underneath, and were having it all their own way. Mutton suiting us as well as beef, we throw a carcass into the boat and go on. Soon after that we see two men struggling along on the shore-ice, each dragging a loaded sled. In answer to our hail they call out, "There is no grub in Dawson. If you haven't an outfit, for God's sake turn right back where you are!"

Night falling, we make out to get ashore where three prospectors are camped, who belong to the so-called "Christy" party, who came over the Skagway trail. With them, as we saw by the record at the White Horse, was the *New York Times* correspondent, Pelletier. The rest of the party, to the number of about a dozen, including two women, at last account were on an island above in the Yukon, where they had been for three days, since the ice began to run hard, the women wanting to go, but the prudent leader, with a wife at home, not considering it advisable in the state of the river.

We are more than glad to hear this, as they left Bennett a week ahead of us. Again chopping a dock for the boat in the shore-ice, which is widening several feet each night, we make camp with the three prospectors, not putting up the tent, but spreading it over our blankets. It snowed two inches during the night.

October 25.

Before we are ready to start the "Christy" boat passes, and the prospectors start after them. By keeping in the open leads and rowing, in two hours we overtake them in time to see them turn in and land on the right bank, alongside two other boats, whose occupants are eating and at the same time trying with poles to keep the ice-floes from crushing them. We hail, and a man calls out that the ice has jammed at the mouth of White River, just below. If that is the case, there is but one thing for us to do, and that we must do as quick as we can. We gain the shore-ice, planning to drop into an eddy, in a bight of the shore-line; but we are caught in the ice-floe, miss the

170

eddy, and the next moment the boat is grinding against the face of the ice, which by the falling of the river now stands clear of the water by several inches. A particularly heavy floe makes for the boat, and the force of the impact tilts the boat until the outer gunwale is even with the water, when the floe sheers off just when we think boat and goods are gone. We line her rapidly down along the shore-ice until, seeing that heroic measures only will save the little boat, we await an opening in the ice, turn the bow out, and swing clear of the shore; and then, after a hard fight, gain the free ice in mid-river, where we resolve, by all that is fit to swear by, that we will stay, jam or no jam. There are no signs of a jam, and we keep on past White River. Ten miles farther, at Stewart River, and on the right, we see a line of boats drawn out, some tents, and a few cabins, and, starting in time, we work in and make a landing all right; but another boat ahead of us fails to pursue our tactics, and she disappears in the direction of Dawson.

About forty boats have hauled out on the ice. Stewart River is the destination of many parties, who intend to haul their outfits up on the ice and prospect its tributaries in search of other Bonanza Creeks. Others have stopped from fear of the ice; and still others by reason of the disquieting news, brought by parties making their way out, that starvation faces the camp at Dawson and thieving is going on, two men already having been shot for breaking into caches.

We have passed or overtaken twenty-five boats since leaving Tagish Lake.

October 26.

Growing warmer: twenty degrees above zero at 7 A.M.; forty degrees above at noon. Start at 2 P.M. with a light wind and snow in our faces.

The Yukon just below the mouth of the Stewart is a maze of islands, but the channels are now clearly marked by the ice, caught on the heads of islands and shoals. We have gone about five miles, and in the growing darkness it becomes difficult to see. A mass of ice looms up straight ahead, and we keep to the left, when we suddenly discover we are going wrong, and turn the bow for the right-hand channel, Brown throwing his whole strength into the oars. We are just clearing the jam when we wedge between two floes. The ice projects over, and destruction is inevitable. Broadside we strike, and then the cause of the mishap is the means of our salvation. The floe on the lower side crushes, but the resistance is enough to sheer us off, and we skim by. Immediately another danger confronts us. At the opposite bank, some long spruce-trees, undermined, have fallen into the water. The current sets directly towards them. Here, again, fortune is with us, for had we passed clear of the island we should inevitably have been carried in the ice-pack full into the sweepers — from Scylla upon Charybdis — and we should have been raked from stem to stern, if not capsized. As it is, we narrowly miss them, and are glad to land just below, at a huge pile of driftwood.

We have hardly set the tent up when we hear a cry, and, looking up, see the "Christy" boat drifting stern foremost. When they see us they call for us to take a line. As they drop down a rope is thrown ashore and we make it fast. It seems they were hugging the shore, as usual, and went fair into the sweepers, the boat stern on at the time. All hands jumped for a space among the packages of goods, and the sweeper, striking the steering-oar, slid up and swept the boat clear. No one was hurt but the leader, who was caught by a sweeper and rolled over once or twice, and is lying now, it is feared, badly hurt.

We subsequently learn that this is a very bad place, several boats having been caught under the treacherous tree-ends. In all its phases the Yukon is a river that commands respect.

Next day we meet more refugees dragging sleds. One party of three, reluctant to take to sleds, are dragging

TRYING TO LAND AT DAWSON

a Peterborough canoe, the bow of which is sheathed with tin to protect it from the ice. We ask one man why he didn't wait and go out on the "ice," for we still have a notion the river freezes smooth like a mill-pond. He answers that "a man doesn't eat any more grub on the trail than when sitting down waiting."

Presently a white sign with large letters, on the shore, warns to "Keep to the left side of the island," which is all one can do now, as the right-hand channel is packed solid. Then we pass a large log building, formerly Ladue's trading-post, opposite the narrow valley of Sixty-Mile River. In reply to our hail a man calls out, "Fifty-five miles to Dawson! Keep to the right, and look sharp, or you'll be carried past!" Thus far, directions volunteered by others having invariably been misleading, we straightway keep to the left, thereby acting, as subsequent events prove, unwisely.

We camp on the left-hand bank, and next morning go on. Long, low, wooded islands follow one another in quick succession. We are repaid once for the extreme loneliness by sight of a wolf, a quarter of a mile away, trotting towards us on the shore-ice, which is several hundred feet wide. After making sure it is not a native dog, we level with the 30-30; but it is a clean miss, and the wolf starts on the jump for cover, the rifle cracking every six jumps. Then he turns around for a last look, just as a bullet kicks the snow up beneath him; then he is gone into the brush.

Night finds us still inside the islands, just above a sudden bend of the river to the left. Next morning, judging that we have only about ten miles to go, and having found some dry spruce and straight white birch, we resolve to stop for a day and build a sled, and also lighten the boat, which is so weighted with ice that we can no longer make headway or work our way among the floes. The ice is four inches thick on the sides and four or five inches thick in the bottom. Oars, paddles, gunwales, canvas, boxes, and bags are incrusted with ice. When we begin digging, picks and all sorts of things that we have forgotten about come to light. The following morning we reload, and, settling ourselves for what we suppose to be about half a day's work, push off once more in the face of a cutting north wind, striking im-

mediately for the right-hand shore, which was, indeed,
fortunate for us, for just at the turn, a mile from our
camping-place, we see on the bank a great number of
boats, tents, and people.

"How far is it to Dawson?" we call out.

"This is Dawson! If you don't look out you will be
carried past!" We dig our paddles into the ice, and in
a short space of time our boat is safe behind a larger
one. It is the 31st of October, one hundred and eight
days since the *Excelsior's* arrival at San Francisco, and
ninety-two days since we joined the Klondike Stampede.

ROAD-HOUSE, NORTH OF HUNKER CREEK

CHAPTER IX

Klondike " City "—Dawson—First Impressions of the Camp—The Grub
Scare, and Exodus

IMMEDIATELY in front of our boat we discover the tent of the "Christy" party, in charge of Pelletier and two sailors—a chuckle-headed Dutchman and a Swede—who gave us a laugh for hanging up around the corner; but they told us we might pile our goods against the side of their tent where we could guard them better, and then, after several pairs of willing arms helped drag our little boat out on the ice, we began to inspect our new surroundings. Winter had clearly settled down, and snow covered everything.

The bank, which was quite level and stood about twenty feet above the river, was several acres in extent and occupied by thirty or forty log-cabins and tents, together with many curious little boxes, made of poles, or two halves of boats placed one above the other, and set on posts higher than one's head and reached by ladders. These latter, which are almost as numerous as the cabins, are "caches," in which goods are stored out of reach of dogs and water. Behind the flat the bank rises steeply to a high terrace, and on the left this suddenly ends and the Klondike River breaks through from the eastward, and, dividing into two shallow channels, enters the Yukon around a low island covered with small cottonwoods. The aforementioned assemblage of dwellings was not, as we had been led at first to suppose, Dawson proper, but a flourishing suburb, bearing the official name of "Klondike City." This "city" was, until the miners bringing rafts of logs down the Klondike destroyed their

KLONDIKE "CITY"—KLONDIKE RIVER ENTERS ON THE RIGHT

fish-weirs, the seat of the local Indians, or *Trochutin*, as they call themselves. But whether from a knowledge of some things that commonly appertain to Indian villages, or whether a certain half-fish-like emblem which serves as a wind-vane at the top of a high pole on the river-bank, the most conspicuous object in the village, is thought to resemble a certain small creature, it is a fact that it is considered by old-timers the height of affectation to speak of Dawson's suburb otherwise than as "Lousetown."

Lousetown is still the residence of Indians, but only of such as are the wives of old-timers, whose little half-breed children run about in furs, and whose dogs, to the number of four or six, lie around the door of their cabins, in their thick fur oblivious to the cold.

Dawson proper lies on the opposite side of the mouth of the Klondike, upon a flat about two thousand yards in width, extending a mile and a half along the Yukon, and terminating in a narrow point at the base of a mountain conspicuous by reason of a light-gray patch of "slide" upon its side bearing resemblance to a dressed moose-hide in shape and color, which has given to it the name of "Moose-hide" or "Moose-skin" Mountain. The greater part of this flat is nothing more than a swamp, or "mus-keag," consisting in summer of oozy muck, water, and "nigger-heads," with a few stunted spruce, but in winter hard and dry.

The town of Dawson, now just one year old, contains about three hundred cabins and other buildings, half a dozen of which stand on the bank of the Klondike. Beyond these, and facing the Yukon, and separated from the rest of the flat by a slough, is the military reservation, with the barracks of the mounted police. The barracks, where there are now about thirty constables under command of Inspector C. Constantine, are a group of eight or ten log buildings for officers' and men's quarters, offices, store-rooms, post-office, court-room, etc., forming three sides of a square, the fourth side, facing the Yukon, being at present enclosed by nothing more than a brush fence four feet high, with a gate, beside which is a tall pole floating the flag of Great Britain.

Beyond the reservation is a town-site staked by Arthur

Harper in the spring of 1897, and next adjoining is the original town - site of Joe Ladue, staked in September, 1896, the two being known as the "Harper & Ladue Town-site"—a rectangle of over one hundred and sixty acres, extending from river to hill. The first houses were built here, and it is still the centre of the town,

STREET IN DAWSON

which was surveyed by Mr. Ogilvie into streets running parallel with the river, intersected at longer intervals by cross streets. First, or Main, Street, the one skirting the river, sixty-six feet back from high-water, is practically the only one used. Along this street, beginning towards the barracks, the buildings consist, first, of a few small earth-covered log dwellings; then several two-story log buildings designated "hotels," with conspicuous signs in front bearing such names as "Klondike," "Dawson City," "Brewery," with more dwellings between them and caches behind; then more large houses—the "M. & M." saloon and dance-hall, the "Green Tree" hotel, the "Pioneer" or "Moose-horn" and the "Dominion" saloon, the "Palace" saloon and restaurant and the "Opera-House," built tolerably close together, the space between being filled with tents and smaller cabins used as restaurants, mining-brokers' offices, etc. On the river's edge, facing this irregular row, are tents, rough buildings hastily constructed out of slabs, scows with tents built over them and warmed by Yukon stoves, and used as offices and restaurants or residences, etc. — a ragged, motley assemblage. In the middle of the road, and evidently built there before the town was surveyed, stands a cabin with one window, the Ladue cabin, the first built in Dawson, and now used as a bakery, when there is anything to bake.*

Beyond the saloons is the block of the Alaska Commercial Company, consisting of a corner store, a two-story building, forty by eighty feet, well built of sawn logs, beyond which are three long, low warehouses of galvanized corrugated iron, all on Main Street; and, on a side street, another warehouse and the "mess-house"— a commodious two-story log dwelling for the employés. The next block is that of the North American Transportation and Trading Company, comprising a store-house similar to that of the other, three corrugated iron warehouses, and a dwelling-house. Beyond this is a saw-

* This landmark was torn down in the spring of 1898. This portion of town between the "M. & M." and the stores was subsequently much altered, and, later, two destructive fires have wiped it out of existence, thus destroying almost the last of the pioneer buildings.

mill, owned by Harper & Ladue ; then more cabins, and at the farther end, half a mile from the stores, the Catholic church and St. Mary's Hospital, in charge of Father Judge, of the Society of Jesuits, and the Sisters of St. Ann.

This, in brief, was the construction of the town of Dawson on October 2, 1897. As one walked for the first time down the smoothly beaten street, it was an animated scene, and one upon which the new-comer gazed with wonder. The Klondike had been frozen for three weeks. Snow ankle-deep lay on the ground and on the roofs of buildings. Smoke curled upwards from bits of stove-pipe in the roofs of cabins and tents. The saloons and stores and bit of sidewalk were thronged with men, more than half of whom were stamped as late arrivals by their clothes and manner. The new-comers were mostly dressed in Mackinaws with heavy cloth caps, but old-timers were marked usually by coats of deer-skin, or the more typical *parka* of striped or navy-blue twill, with light fur caps of lynx, sable, mink, or beaver, unlike in shape those worn anywhere else, and big blanket-lined or fur-lined moose-hide mittens, with gauntlet tops. Men were coming and going, both with and without packs, and now and then a woman, in deer-skin coat or curiously fashioned squaw's *parka* of mink or squirrel skins—all trotting or walking with an energetic stride, probably begotten no less of the sharp temperature than of the knowledge that the darkness of Arctic winter was fast settling down. Dogs, both native and "outside," lay about the street under every one's feet, sleeping—as if it was furthest from their minds that any one should hurt them — or else in strings of two to ten were dragging prodigious loads of boxes or sacks intended for the mines or for fuel, urged on by energetic dog-punchers,

Prices at which goods were selling were gathered by inquiry and from bits of paper posted on the sides of saloons or the bulletin-board at the Alaska Commercial Company's corner. Entire outfits were for sale at $1 per pound, and not waiting long for takers; but flour, the article of which there was the greatest shortage, sold on the street for from $75 to $120 per sack of 50 pounds. Joe Brandt, or some other equally reliable dog-driver, is to start for Dyea in December with a well-equipped dog-team, and will take letters at $1 each, and a limited number of passengers at from $600 to $1000, which includes the privilege of walking behind the sleigh and helping to make camp; a woman, who must ride, pays $1500. This was almost as cheap as to buy and equip a team. Dogs were almost any price a man asked, $300 being paid for good native dogs. A common Yukon sleigh, worth $7 outside, was $40; a "basket" sleigh, $75. Fur robes, without which it was said no man could reach Dyea, were from $200 to $400 each. The stores were full of men warming themselves by the stoves and appearing to have nothing to do. The stock of goods was of course considerably larger than at Selkirk, but there were whole rows of empty shelves where groceries should have been. The Alaska Commercial Company was selling axe-handles and sugar, that's about all. The North American Transportation Company was doing somewhat better. The warehouses, however, looked full, and men in *parkas* with dog-teams were sledding stuff away from piles marked with their names; but every one else was growling and cursing this or that man whom he thought responsible for the shortage, or was anxiously watching developments. It was certain that between five and six hundred persons had been forced down river, where the nearest supply of grub was said to be; several score had started up river in canoes or along the shore-ice, and no one knew how many were only waiting for the river to close to start up river. To go either way at this time, the old-timers regarded as certain death, by the ice in one direction,

HAULING WATER—SCENE ON THE MAIN STREET, DAWSON

from cold or starvation in the other, unless help reached them on the trail.

The immediate cause of this indeed serious condition was, as before stated, the failure of three steamers, loaded with supplies from St. Michael, to pass the flats of the Yukon, 200 miles and more below Dawson. But that was not all. The strike on Bonanza Creek, which depopulated Circle City and Forty-Mile, occurred so late in the fall that steamers could not land supplies at the new camp, and

183

during the winter which followed the miners lived from hand to mouth on what was hauled by dogs over the ice, a distance respectively of 220 and 55 miles. The spring found 1500 people awaiting the arrival of the boats with an eagerness with which the Yukon was by no means unacquainted. Then, too, the news of the strike had gone outside in January and February, was common property in Juneau, Seattle, Chicago, and San Francisco for several months before the *Excelsior* and *Portland* arrived with the first gold of the wash-up and tangible evidence of the magnitude of the strike, and before the world at large knew of even the existence of Klondike a stream of people were pouring over the passes, and, when the river opened in May, they bore down on Dawson. The influx had been anticipated by the two companies which supply the Yukon by way of St. Michael, and every effort was made to push supplies to the new camp. Of the Alaska Commercial Company's steamers, the *Bella* made four trips to Dawson, the *Alice* three, and the *Margaret* one. Of those of the North American Transportation and Trading Company, the *Portus B. Weare* delivered four loads, the *John J. Healy* two, while the *Hamilton* was expected on her maiden trip. By the middle of September about 800 tons of freight had been landed at Dawson, of which about one-half was food and one-half general merchandise, an amount which, although with none to spare, might have sufficed for the needs of the camp until the next spring had there been no additions to the population. Two hundred passengers reached Dawson on the first steamers up-river, and a few went out. By the 1st of August no fewer than a thousand had come in over the passes. Some of these had complete outfits, but the greater number, which included many women and some children, had insufficient to last until spring.

DISTRIBUTING FOOD

Captain J. E. Hansen, assistant superintendent of the Alaska Commercial Company, arrived from below on the first trip of the *Bella*. Captain John J. Healy, general manager, as well as a member of the firm of the North American Transportation and Trading Company, arrived from Forty - Mile on the first trip of the *Weare*. Both began distributing supplies, Captain Hansen in the old Ladue cabin, Captain Healy on a rough platform in the mud of Front Street, no person, however, receiving more than two weeks' supply at a time. According to custom, lists were posted and orders taken for a year's supplies, accompanied by a deposit of about half the cost. Such individual orders ranged from $500 to $10,000 each, and, although subject to the uncertainty of delivery, were termed "guaranteed." It was the custom, when orders were so placed, for the goods as they arrived to be stacked each man's in a pile by itself in the warehouse, to be called for only as needed (the goods being considered safer there than in their own caches), until snow-fall, when they were more easily removed. The anxiety of the agents and those who had placed orders increased as they saw the incoming horde of new-comers and the water in the Yukon rapidly falling. Navigation would close by the 1st of October. When the middle of September came and the river was still falling, Captain Hansen went down on the *Margaret* to Fort Yukon. On the 26th he returned by poling boat, bringing word that the *Alice*, *Healy*, and *Hamilton* were unable to pass the treacherous shoals in that part of the river, and no more boats would be able to get up. The news was carried to the gulches, and hundreds of men came to town to learn if it were true. The Alaska Commercial Company posted notice that they could fill all orders, except a slight shortage in flour, candles, etc. Captain Healy, who is generally thought to have had the bulk of the orders, advised his customers not to be uneasy, that the boats would arrive. Excited men gathered in groups on the streets and in the saloons, and with gloomy faces discussed the situation. Some proposed seizing the warehouses and dividing the food evenly among all in camp. The police, numbering only about twenty men, under

ALASKA COMMERCIAL COMPANY'S STORE AND WAREHOUSES, WITH THE
NORTH AMERICAN TRANSPORTATION AND TRADING COMPANY'S STORES
IN THE DISTANCE

command of Sergeant-Major Davis (Captain Constantine being at Forty-Mile), were placed at the companies' disposal. Captain Hansen accepted the offer and barricaded his warehouse, but Captain Healy declined. In this crisis—namely, on the 28th of September—the *Weare* arrived with 125 tons of freight, mostly provisions; also reporting 20 tons taken off in a hold-up by the miners at Circle City. The excitement subsided a little at the *Weare's* unexpected arrival, and hundreds who were starting down-river delayed their departure. On the 30th the *Bella* arrived with a light cargo, having left her barge at Fort Yukon, and been further relieved of about 37 tons at Circle City. Captain Constantine arrived on the *Bella*, and on the same day the following notice was posted :

" The undersigned, officials of the Canadian Government, having carefully looked over the present distressing situation in regard to the supply of food for the winter, find that the stock on hand is not sufficient to meet the wants of the people now in the district, and can see but one way out of the difficulty, and that is an immediate move down-river of all those who are now unsupplied to Fort Yukon, where there is a large stock of provisions. In a few days the river will be closed, and the move must be made now, if at all. It is absolutely hazardous to build hopes upon the arrival of other boats. It is almost beyond a possibility that any more food will come into this district. For those who have not laid in a winter's supply to remain here longer is to court death from starvation, or at least a certainty of sickness from scurvy and other troubles. Starvation now stares every one in the face who is hoping and waiting for outside relief. Little effort and trivial cost will place them in comfort and safety within a few days at Fort Yukon, or at other points below where there are now large stocks of food.

" C. CONSTANTINE,

" Inspector Northwestern Mounted Police.

" D. W. DAVIS,

" Collector of Customs.

" THOMAS FAWCETT,

" Gold Commissioner.

" *September* 30, 1897."

The posting of the notice was followed by speeches by the authorities — Sergeant - Major Davis and Mr. Fawcett—urging the people to go. Captain Hansen went about the street speaking in twenty places to as many

187

groups of men, telling them, "Go! go! Flee for your lives!" and to the men on the river-front, "Do you expect to catch grayling all winter?" He was greatly agitated, and the excitement was intense.

A meeting of the miners was held, and the views of the agents of the companies called for. Captain Healy alone vigorously opposed the down-river movement and refused to attend, but sent his views by a committeeman, who delivered them to the meeting. He stated that there was plenty of food for all in the camp until the boats got up in the spring. If they felt they must go, they should not go to Fort Yukon, where there was very little, but outside, where there was sure to be enough. In any event, there would be no trouble before spring; they should wait and see, and it would be easier and safer to go out later than to go to Fort Yukon now.*

* Captain Healy, whose attitude towards the miners has been misunderstood when not maliciously misrepresented, subsequently made to me this statement: "I sent for Captain Hansen, and I said to him—for he was very well supplied with flour, more than he needed; he had a quantity in the warehouse, and the *Bella* brought thirteen hundred gunnies [a gunny holds two fifty-pound sacks of flour]—I said to him: 'I have everything but flour. If you will let me have flour, I can let you have bacon, sugar, everything else. Now I have one-year orders for from $500 to $10,-000; you have the same. My proposition is this, to fill every man's order as nearly as possible, but to cut them down from twelve to eight months. That will last them till June. But you must let me have flour. There will be no starvation. Some may go hungry, but no one will starve. If there *is* starvation, it will not be till spring. It is not a question of quantity, it is a question of *distribution*. If there is trouble, as you say there will be, before any one starves those who have none will take it from those who have. My proposition is that you let me have flour enough to fill my orders and that we both cut down our orders from twelve months to eight; for if there is going to be trouble at all, it is better that we take the matter into our own hands right now.'"

The reply of Captain Hansen was, according to Captain Healy, "I must fill my orders."

PEOPLE URGED TO LEAVE DAWSON

The authorities proposed deporting the "non-pro-ducers," rounders, and crooks, which Captain Healy again emphatically opposed, saying that the crooks should be kept where the police could watch them, instead of being turned loose in a defenceless country to pillage and rob.

On the 20th of October fifty or more men left for Fort Yukon in small boats and scows. The *Weare* un-loaded with all haste and took as many as she could find accommodation for, charging $50 for passage. On the 21st of October the *Bella* was advertised to depart, and passage was offered free, by arrangement with the au-thorities. At ten o'clock that morning there was a mass-meeting in front of the Alaska Commercial Company's store; addresses were made urging the people to go. For all who wanted to go on the *Bella* an agreement had been prepared for them to sign, as follows:

"DAWSON, NORTHWEST TERRITORY, *October* 1, 1897.

"The officials of the Government of the Dominion of Canada have arranged to have all persons not provided with food for the winter carried free of charge to Fort Yukon on the steamer *Bella*, on the following conditions: That the steamer *Bella's* officers or owners are not to be held responsible for any delays or possible non-arrival at destination of any passengers or property carried; that all persons carried agree to cut wood, or in any other manner aid in furthering said steamer's voyage, as they may be called upon to do by the captain; that the undersigned specially agree that if the ice runs so thick as to endanger the steamer, and she goes into harbor between Dawson, Northwest Territory, and Fort Yu-kon, Alaska, they will leave the steamer at the request of the master, E. D. Dixon."

One hundred and sixty persons took advantage of this offer and signed the paper, and received food for five days.

Both the *Weare* and the *Bella*, the latter after a most perilous trip, we subsequently learned, reached Circle City, where the captains refused to go farther, on account of the dangers of the ice. Eighty of the *Weare's* passengers kept on in small boats, but were caught in an ice-jam, and, after being for three days without food, reached Fort Yukon afoot. Contrary to the statements of the authorities that there was sufficient food at Fort Yukon, there was not; and if all whom the authorities would have persuaded to go to Fort Yukon had reached there, the condition there would have been much more serious than at Dawson. In all several hundred destitute men reached Fort Yukon, and a few continued on to the next post, Fort Hamlin. It had been represented at Dawson that work would be supplied at Fort Yukon. The agents of the Alaska Commercial Company were doling out ten-day outfits, and the men were cutting wood for pay, when seventy or eighty of them, chafing at the thought of practically losing the winter, made request for a seven-months' outfit so they could prospect neighboring streams, and were about to enforce their demand. Captain P. H. Ray and Lieutenant Richardson, United States Army, happened to be at Fort Yukon upon a military reconnaissance, having arrived on the *Healy*. Lieutenant Richardson was at the Alaska Commercial Company's cache, where the miners were assembled. A committee of one was sent by the miners to Captain Ray, to learn, as the miners expressed it, whether Captain Ray was "representing a government that would care for its people in need, or represented the companies." The committee met Captain Ray on his way from the North American Transportation Company's store (which is two miles from the other), and as a result of this interview Captain Ray returned, gathered a posse, and started back.

"HOLD-UP" AT CIRCLE CITY

Lieutenant Richardson was then "holding the fort," with a revolver in each hand. Captain Ray was met part way by the body of miners, who drew a dead-line in the snow across the path and ordered him to halt. A big fellow belonging to the posse (a Canadian from Victoria, named Todd) stepped across the line, when the miners levelled their guns and the man stepped back. The posse had at first been ordered to arm, but the order had been rescinded, so they had no alternative but to agree to the miners' terms. A committee of seven was appointed to pass upon the claims of destitutes. Their methods, however, proving too lax, Captain Ray took charge, hoisted the United States flag, and issued seven-months' outfits to destitutes, taking their notes for one year, the government guaranteeing payment to the companies. Some went prospecting, others continued to chop wood. There may have been some rough men in the crowd, and it has even been reported that they were simply a mob trying to loot and steal, because it was shown that one of the leaders was not wholly destitute ; but it was certainly not true of them, as a whole, and they acted as any other men would have acted under the same circumstances.

The "hold-up" of the steamers at Circle City took place as follows : The companies, in their endeavors to supply Dawson, had left Circle City, eighty-three miles from Fort Yukon, unsupplied. The miners, incensed at this arbitrary action of the companies, took an inventory of the goods in the two stores and a census of those without outfits, made a list of supplies needed, and appointed a committee to demand that goods as per list be left off the next steamer that arrived. When the *Weare* arrived, the committee, armed with Winchester rifles, demanded a certain quantity of goods, and they were taken out of the hold and placed in warehouse, the miners appointing a checker on the steamer, another at the warehouse, and guards along the way, and, further, placed guards on the steamer to prevent disorder. When the *Bella* arrived, the same thing was repeated. The miners placed their orders at the store in the usual way, paid their money, and received their outfits from the agents of the companies. This, too, was an orderly procedure, although it was not done without a vigorous protest from Captain Ray, who was on the *Bella*, and in an impassioned speech warned the miners that it was both wrong and dangerous to thus hold up the steamer ; first, because it was needed worse at Dawson than at Circle City, and, second, there were, no doubt, rough men in the camp, who, when they saw how easy it was to hold up a steamer with food consigned to Dawson, would hold up the same steamer when returning with gold consigned to Seattle.

Of all who started for Dawson by St. Michael after the gold arrived outside, a number estimated at 1800, exactly 43 reached Dawson, and of these upwards of 35, having no outfits, were compelled to return on the *Bella* and *Weare*. The rest of the unfortunates, such as reached St. Michael, were scattered at various points along the Yukon, with both the regular and specially chartered steamers, only one of which latter, the *St. Michael*, purchased at St. Michael by 60 North American Trading and Transportation Company's passengers, reached even Circle City. The majority, numbering about 500, settled for the winter at Rampart City, near Minook Creek, about 1200 miles from St. Michael.

CHAPTER X

Choosing a Cabin-Site — The River Closes — Narrow Escapes in the
Ice—A Typical Miner's Cabin—House-Building in Zero Weather—
How Cold will it be ?—The Bonanza Trail

N ineffectual attempt to find the
owner of the mutton raft (we
found his assistant at the North
American Transportation Company's
store selling the cargo of an earlier
and more fortunate raft at $1.50 per
pound), and an equally fruitless inquiry for letters at the
post-office, together with such impressions of the new
place as we absorbed on the way thither, on the morning after our arrival at Klondike City, comprised our experience in Dawson for several days, during which we
gave ourselves over to the serious business of finding
shelter for the winter. Cabins in Dawson were worth
from $500 to $1000, and wood for fuel—an important item
—was $30 to $40 a cord. Even had the cost been less, we
should not have thought of buying a house, when timber
with which we could build one of our own was to be found
so near to town ; but my companion, whose resolution thus
far had been to die sooner than to return home, certainly
could not remain long in the face of starvation. In this
juncture, Pelletier proposed that we build together, and
next morning we set off to look for a cabin-site up a beaten
path that we were told led to the mines, it being agreed in

the meantime that Brown should remain a while longer, in the hope of something turning up to relieve his distressful condition.

The Klondike River is a shallow, very swift stream, in summer averaging in width about forty yards; but the valley is much wider, varying, in the first mile from its mouth, from an eighth to a third of a mile, then increasing to a mile in width, with broad, low banks and numer-

THE KLONDIKE IN SUMMER, LOOKING UP FROM THE YUKON

ous islands, the banks rising first at forty-five degrees, then swinging back a mile or more to the crests of the hills and ridges, the bottoms being covered densely with spruces, cottonwoods, and white birches, all above the level being covered with stunted growth of spruce and cottonwoods, the highest peaks being nearly or quite bare. Two miles from the mouth the valley is cut by a V-shaped trench from the southward—the valley of Bonanza Creek. The trail, worn smooth as glass by many sleds, follows the frozen surface of the river, past a little nest of cabins on the right known as the Portland Addition, past a small steam saw-mill just ready for winter work, for two miles, when it leaves the river and crosses the level flat, through an extensive thicket of beautiful white birches, striking at a distance of half a mile the bed of the creek, a shallow, narrow depression winding from side to side of a wooded valley five to eight hundred feet across, and then continues on towards the heart of the mines, a distance of about twelve miles. Where trail and creek meet, in a sheltered spot where spruces and birches grew thicker than usual, we chose the site of our cabin.

A blaze on a tree, bearing the number 97 A, written in pencil, and the formal statement that one Max Newberry claimed five hundred feet for mining purposes, was indication that, as claims are measured on this creek, we were about ninety-seven claims, of about five hundred feet each, below the original discovery claim.

Returning to the Yukon, we found our cache rifled of the mutton, with the knowledge, as was frankly admitted, of the Swede and Dutchman, aided and abetted by a man in a yellow sheepskin cap living in a boat on the riverbank; the statement being soberly made and maintained that the owner of the mutton-raft had been making inquiries about boats with mutton aboard, and they, becoming alarmed, had thrown my mutton into the river! A likely story—disproved sometime after by the owner himself, whose only regret was that we hadn't brought it all down, and by the confession of one of the two custodians, that it was taken by our friend in the boat, who had been left in a pitiable condition by his partners, the boat and contents being subsequently lost when the river closed.

Mr. W. F. Courtney, known in the camp as the "mutton man," charged, as we expected, only half the market price —namely, 75 cents per pound, but this act of a man facing starvation left us, with the winter before us, without fresh meat nor a dollar in our pockets for some time to come.

During the next three or four days we sledded our stuff to Bonanza Creek, but slept each night in the tent by the river. On the 4th of October, Simpson and his 600 pounds of newspapers, now considerably out of date, arrived, the canvas canoe, incrusted with ice, being towed behind a Yukon boat. A few more boats got in, fighting their way in the ice. On the night of the 6th a diversion was created at 2 A.M., when a meat-raft went by, the men calling loudly and offering a thousand dollars for a line, but they went on in the darkness, to certain destruction, it seemed, in the gorge below town. Next day two men, arriving on foot from above, reported at the barracks that they had gone ashore from the raft with the line to "snub" to a tree, and the line had parted. On the 7th, in front of Dawson, where the river is narrowest, the ice began to jam. The floes piled up, and the water backed behind as far as Klondike City; then it broke loose and continued to run again for several hours, when it jammed again and did not move. The Yukon was closed, but remained open below the jam all winter. Blocks of ice lay at all angles, with boats crushed, sideways and endways, useless except for lumber. The last men in had the time of their lives. Messrs. Coe and Racer, of Seattle, picked up at Sixty-Mile post three others, Black, Atkinson, and Adams, whose party had divided there, fearing the ice. All went well until they approached Klondike City. The river had just jammed for the second time. Black and Atkinson went ashore on a shelf of shore-ice on the right hand, at the foot of a precipitous bank. Black reached the cabins, but the rising water drove Atkinson to the bank, where he managed to cling, with one foot in a small spruce, until twenty men with ropes hauled him up. The boat went on, very slowly now. It was in the small hours of night when they reached Dawson, and stopped. They called out their names, but no help could reach them until daylight, when the police put planks over the ice and brought them ashore. This was but one of many miraculous escapes. Near Little Salmon, the boats of incoming government officials were caught; three boats went under the ice, and one man was drowned, the rest getting ashore on snow - shoes. The meat-raft, which was William Perdue's, turned up safe, fourteen miles below, and he lost only the cost of freighting (25 cents a pound). It was said that an arm grasping an oar was seen going slowly by in the ice, but it was not generally believed.

The Yukon miner's cabin is from about 10 by 12 ft. square, to 14 by 18 ft., averaging perhaps 12 by 14 feet. The logs are eight or nine inches thick, and the sides are nine or ten logs high, which, with six inches' elevation for the floor, allows ample head-room. The roof is rather flat, a raise of more than two feet at the ridge being uncommon, and it extends four to six feet in front and is frequently enclosed for a store-room. The roof is made of small poles, covered first with moss, and then, to a thickness of six inches or more, with dirt, which in time is covered with weeds and grass, causing some one to observe that one of the duties of a householder in the Yukon was mowing the hay on his house-top! There is one door in front, and at least one window on the sunny side, fitted whenever possible with a sash of from four to six panes, the better cabins having double sashes, to prevent frosting. As a sash, whenever it is to be had at all, is worth $20, many cabins have only a white flour-sack nailed over the opening. A much better window, and a really decorative one, is made of a dozen or more white ginger-ale bottles, set vertically in an opening the thickness of a log. The floor is either of lumber or poles hewn flat on top. Many cabins, especially on new creeks, dispense with a floor. The cabin is warmed with an ordinary sheet-iron Yukon stove, set on four posts, the stove-pipe passing through a square oil-can in the roof, the space around the pipe being usually filled in with clay. The logs are chinked with moss, which is usually laid on as the walls go up. Properly chinked and roofed, the temperature even in the coldest weather can be raised to an uncomfortable pitch. To avoid ill effects from overheating and likewise poor ventilation, a small box is placed in the roof, with a door which can be opened and closed. Some of the camps have a "Russian furnace"—an oven made of three thick sides of baked clay covered with a large sheet of iron, the open end being fitted with a sliding iron door. A Yukon stove, made by a tinsmith in Dawson, with a drum for baking and three joints of pipe, costs $65. An open fireplace is no use in the coldest weather.

The bunks are simply rough platforms wide enough for two persons, usually built of poles and boards, and covered with spruce boughs, upon which are spread the blankets and robes, a flour-sack containing socks or moccasins often serving for a pillow. If there is a woman about, a bit of curtain shows at the window, and the walls and ceiling are often covered with cheap calico, but even with these touches the air is far from being one of luxury.

The miner's light is pre-eminently the candle, which is used in a special candlestick of steel, with a point to thrust into the face of a bank of earth, and a hook for

FRONT VIEW OF A TYPICAL MINER'S CABIN (IN SUMMER), SHOWING OVERHANGING FRONT AND CACHE

hanging to a nail in the wall. Candles have always been so scarce in the Yukon, and ordinary lamps and oil even more so, that nearly every cabin has what is called a "bitch"—a milk or meat can, with a loose wick at one side, burning bacon grease. The original "bitch" was a piece of fat bacon stuck into the split end of a stick.

We built our cabin fourteen by sixteen feet. But though we did not have to go over one hundred feet for a single stick of timber, we did not fully realize, when we began, the actual suffering of handling logs in a temperature already much below zero and steadily falling. Brown reconsidered his intention of leaving, and stayed on, but even with his assistance, after three weeks of brutal labor, we still had no floor, no dirt on the roof, and neither door nor window nor furniture. The walls, too, were rather low (for a very "swell" cabin), a deficiency which my partner Pelletier, who is a small man, used to explain by saying that we put the roof on as soon as the cabin reached a height where he could stand under the side wall and I could stand under the middle. We built a window of celluloid plates that was the wonder of the gulch, a door of goods-boxes, a table of the same, three rough stools and two bunks in the end, and we covered half of the extension roof, enclosing it with poles, an addition, however, more ornamental than useful.

During all this time we lived in the tent, which was strung by a rope between two trees. The thermometer fell to 39° below zero, but it was astonishing how warm a stove made the tent; as soon as the fire went down, however, it was as cold as out-of-doors. Between us we had thirteen pairs of blankets, thin and thick, and in the midst of these we slept; even then, with all our clothes on and lying close together, we were never really warm; but in time we grew accustomed to what we could not avoid. A great annoyance was caused by the steam of our breath and from our bodies condensing and freezing, until the white frost about our heads looked like that around a bear's den in winter. The breakfast fire would quickly melt the frost; but we never dried out. Each succeeding night there was more frost and more water. The steam from the kettles condensed and froze at the top of the tent, returning in streams of ice down the inside of the tent. This disagreeable feature is observed also in new cabins of green logs, or when the roof is thin and the snow melts through. These "glaciers," as the miners call them, often fill one corner or half the side of a cabin, even when the air inside is, from a Yukon stand-point, comfortable.

In the warmest Yukon cabin nails and other iron-work that extend through from outside are white with frost, no matter how hot the fire in the stove. Out-doors frost collects on eyelashes, eyebrows, mustache, and beard, producing a change in well-known features that is startling. But it causes no harm—only inconvenience, which cannot be wholly avoided by any amount of muffling up. For that reason most of the old - timers are smooth-shaven. All the new-comers had been cultivating luxuriant beards for three months, in the belief that they would afford protection to the face, but the first cold weather showed them that their additional warmth did not compensate for their inconvenience as frost-gatherers.

One day while we were digging in the snow for moss, alongside the trail, a man with four dogs stopped for a chat, by a fire we had built to warm our hands and shovels. We knew him to be an old-timer by his blue drill *parka* and *mukluks*. We remarked that it was pretty cold. "Oh no," said he, "it isn't cold yet. They were saying down-town it was 35° below zero, but it isn't more than 22 or 23." We told him we were living in a tent. "That's right. Stay where you are; when it gets cold you will be ready to move into the cabin."

A LUMBER TEAM ON BONANZA CREEK

It grew steadily colder—no thermometer was needed to show that. Our own was a cheap affair of the familiar summer veranda style, but it had been conscientiously graded to register 60° below zero, although mercury freezes at −40°. It kept shortening until it showed −50°, but when it suddenly landed in the bulb at, at least, −65° we threw the thing away. Old-timers measure the temperature by the following system (obtained by comparison with the standard spirit thermometer): Mercury freezes at −40°; coal-oil (kerosene) freezes at from $-35°$ to $-55°$, according to grade ; "pain-killer" freezes at $-72°$; "St. Jacob's Oil" freezes at $-75°$; best Hudson's Bay rum freezes at $-80°$. This last temperature was authoritatively recorded at Fort Reliance, six miles below Dawson;* but such low temperatures were rarely observed and did not last more than a few days at a time, during which the old-timer simply stayed in-doors and kept warm. No dog-freighter travels when the mercury, which he carries in a small bottle tied to the sled, goes hard like lead. We obtained water through a hole in the ice of the creek, but by the first of December, when that left us, we would gather a sackful of ice and melt it in a large tin can which was continually kept on the stove for that purpose. Bacon we chopped off with an axe; salt was as hard as a grind-stone, and the ice rang like flint-glass.

Our cabin, being near the trail, proved conveniently situated for studying the types of people; it became a regular stopping-place for hand-warming, or for a drink of water, or as a place of deposit when a sled broke down. It was a diversion to watch the throng of men and dogs.

From half-past nine in the morning until the pink-tinged light in the sky died out behind the southwestern hills, during the five or six hours of diffused light that constituted day, the trail before our door was a moving panorama of life, color, and sound. The trees bent under their increasing weight of snow, which there was not a breath of air to dislodge. The sharp "*Mahsh!*" of the dog-freighter, mingled with other language not fit to hear, would be echoed by the dismal howl of a poor "Malamut" dog refusing to *mahsh*. Now a bunch of

* *United States Geological Survey*, 1899, "Maps and Descriptions of Routes of Exploration in Alaska," p. 134.

stampeders, with packs on their backs, would swing along at a half-trot, bound for the scene of the latest-reported strike. Now a man with a sled-rope around his patient neck, and "gee-pole" in hand, dragging an exceedingly heavy load of supplies to his camp, sometimes with one dog, just in front of him, pulling for every pound in him.

Now a string of five heavy-set "Malamuts," drawing two sleds loaded high with boxes and sacks, with a strapping young man with a smooth, red face, a sable-skin cap, striped drill *parka, mukluks*, and moose - skin mittens. The dogs are down in the traces, every mother's son

PROSPECTOR, WITH OUTFIT AND SLED, IN FRONT OF OUR CABIN

pulling his three hundred pounds, the driver helping them over the little hills with a quick step and a cut to his words as he orders his team, that mark him as the trained Yukon dog - puncher, good for his sixty miles a day on a good trail. Scarcely have the freight-sleds

passed when there is a tinkle of little bells, and down the
trail comes seven "Malamuts" with heads up and tails
curled, dancing along with a basket-sleigh, in which,

ON THE BONANZA TRAIL

bundled almost out of sight in lynx robes and *parka*
hoods, are a woman and a little child. A middle-aged, tall
man, in spotted deer-skin coat, white deer-skin *mukluks*,
and fur-trimmed mittens, runs along with his hands on
the sleigh handles, shouting a word of encouragement to
his well-trained dogs—an outfit from Eldorado. Now a

206

train of mixed dogs—St. Bernards, spaniels, and New-
foundlands—goes by.

All day long they come and go, bright spots of life and
color, the more grateful in contrast with its sombre setting of twilight, snow, and dark evergreen-trees. After
the glow of the setting sun has died away, and the night
wood has been stacked beside the stove, and the birch-
bark kindling is ready for the morning's fire, and the
candle burns low, the intense stillness of the winter
forest is broken only by the occasional distant wail of a
dog, or the "*Mahsh*" of some belated driver. Even that
ceases, and there is no sound but the crackling of the
fire in the stove, or a mouse gnawing in a dark corner of
the cabin. There is nothing to do but sleep. Fortunately, it is little trouble to do that. All who speak of it
confess that they never slept so long or so soundly in
their lives.

FREIGHTER

CHAPTER XI

Dogs and Dog-driving—The Typical "Malamut"—A Dog-team Equipment—The Finest Dog-team in the Klondike

IN every part of the world the dog is the companion and helper of man, but nowhere is he so essentially a part of the life of the people as in the northern part of this continent, from Greenland to Behring Sea. The reindeer, as in Lapland and Siberia, may in time supplant him in the Yukon, and horses to some extent do now perform the heavier work; but the dog will hold his place as the inseparable companion of the miner, hunter, and traveller for a long time to come.

The best type of the Yukon dog is the true Eskimo, known by the miners as "Malamut," from a tribe of Eskimo of that name at the mouth of the Yukon. It stands about as high as the Scotch collie, which it resembles a little; but with its thick, short neck, sharp muzzle, oblique eyes, short, pointed ears, dense, coarse hair, which protects it from the severest cold, it is more wolf-like than any other variety of dog. With its bushy tail carried tightly curled over its back, with head and ears erect, and with its broad chest, it is the expression of energy, vitality, and self-reliance. In color it varies from a dirty white through black and white to jet black; but there is also another sort, a grizzled gray, which suggests an admixture of gray wolf, with which it is known to mate. Indeed, these wolf-colored dogs so closely resemble a wolf that if the two were placed side by side a little distance off it would be difficult to distinguish them, but at a nearer view the dog lacks somewhat the hard, sinister expression of his wild relative. The best type of dog is still to be found among the Eskimos. as well as among the Indian tribes of the interior,

A TYPICAL "MALAMUT"

but these latter, known as "Siwash" dogs, are frequently inferior in size, though very tough. The pure type has undergone further change by an admixture of "outside" dog, such as St. Bernard, Newfoundland, and mongrel, that the miners have brought in. The "inside" dog, as the native dog is called by the miners, endures hunger and cold better than the "outside," and is therefore preferred for long journeys over the snow, where speed is desired and food is scarce or hard to carry or procure. For short-distance, heavy freighting the large St. Bernard or mastiff is unsurpassed, but it eats more. In Dawson this winter there is an average of one dog to every three or four of the population—probably fifteen hundred dogs in all—and out of all that number there are but one bull-terrier, one pug, and one or two lapdogs, which, the other day when I was in town, seemed to have organized a little society of their own, comprising the whole small-dog population. Somebodies' pets they, but sadly out of place here, where neither dogs nor men have much time for play. In the whole place there is not another domestic animal but dogs, except nine or ten horses—not a cat, cow, goat, sheep, or fowl.

The load a strong dog can pull is surprising. With the driver at the "gee-pole" of the sled to help over inequalities, a dog will drag three or four hundred pounds along a good trail as fast as a man walks; while with the weight of a man he switches along all day at a lively trot. They are put to the same use as a horse: in winter hauling lumber, cord-wood, logs, and supplies, and in summer packing small loads on their backs. I have seen a team of five native dogs in Bonanza Creek hauling 700 feet of green spruce lumber, weighing 1600 pounds.

It has been said that the native dog does not manifest affection for its master; but that is not always the case. It depends upon what has been his early training—like master, like dog. As a rule, he is stolid and indifferent, deigning to notice a human only in sharp barks and howls, the most dismal sound in nature, but he hardly ever snaps, and after the first surprise at an act of kindness has worn off he shows himself capable of marked affection.

In a community of dogs, as with wolves, there is one

who is master, a supremacy attained only after fierce
and often bloody encounters. I say *often* bloody, for
although actual hostilities are accompanied by an up-
roarious medley of snarls and other expressions of dog
wrath, blood rarely flows, nor is actual pain inflicted,
unless a keen fang has found lodgment in a leg; for the

DOG-TEAM ON THE YUKON (THESE DOGS ARE JUST COMPLETING A
500-MILE JOURNEY)

beast is protected by fur so dense that the most violent
shakings have little effect. The frequent encounters,
therefore, sound and look a great deal worse than they
really are, a fact apparently well understood by the dogs
themselves, for a Malamut dog is the biggest bluffer on
earth, as well as the coolest.

I was watching two dogs one day in the middle of the street. One fine gray fellow was sitting quietly minding his own business. Suddenly, for no reason that I could see, another of equal size put its countenance close to that of the first, lifted its lips from a double row of hideous ivory fangs, braced forward on its fore-feet, and drew its breath in with a *sh* between its teeth. I never saw a more malignant expression. He stood thus for a whole minute, at each breath throwing more and more intensity into the threat, for such it evidently was, until it was perfectly evident that no limit was set to his rage short of chewing the other dog into small particles. The other dog? Why, he never so much as turned a hair, but sat there with the look that only a Malamut can assume. When the other had lashed himself into a fury, he turned his head the other way, saying as plainly as words could say it, "Oh, you bore me very much!"

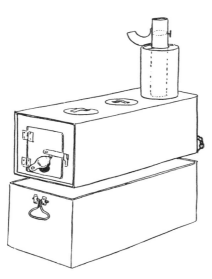

YUKON STOVE RIGGED FOR SLEDGE JOURNEY

Another time I saw what well illustrates their wolfish nature. About thirty dogs of different sizes and values were contending for lord-and-mastership of Main Street, Dawson. The fight, a series of fierce encounters, resolved itself after some hours into a combat between three grizzled black dogs of great strength and another even larger, but evidently a mixture of Malamut and "out-side" dog, having the cut of the Malamut, but with much longer hair, which was of the appearance and color of an old red floor-rug. In every encounter against the three individually the old "door-mat" was successful. Finally the three, during a breathing-spell, turned side by side, faced the other, and gave him "the curse" with ferocious gleam of the eye and lip-lifting. The next moment three dogs were on top of the red one, and then three miners (a crowd was following) pulled three pro-testing dogs away by the scuff of the neck or they would have killed him. A general separation was then begun, dogs being too valuable to lose. The red dog was no sooner released than he got up, looked around defiantly, bleeding from cuts, but still master of the situation. Woe to the under dog in an impromptu mêlée; he has no friend.

A Malamut makes a poor watch-dog, being a natural-born thief himself, and proud than otherwise of the fact. Consequently, everything must be put out of reach that he can steal. He values his importance with-out conceit or vanity; throws himself down to sleep in the way of everybody by day or night, in delightful confidence that no one will touch or hurt him. In har-ness he is really proud of his work, and trots along with tail tightly curled, head up, and ears erect, with a happy, contented "smile." The poor "outside" dog—one feels sorry for him. He is often a pet or a game dog, and the drudgery of harness is galling to his pride. One meets him on the trail, tugging hard at a load of freight for his master, with tail and head down. He casts his eyes up into yours with a shamed expression which says, "Who ever thought that I would come to this!"

As an instance of the pride a dog takes in his work, one day a dog-team was coming down Bonanza trail. Just where the trail lifts from the creek into the woods is a raise of a few feet. There were two dogs in the team, and they were hauling a sled with a moderate load. When they came to the rise the pole-dog flunked. The driver "*mahsh-ed*," but to no effect. The lead-dog was willing enough, but every time he started the other stopped. The leader stood such nonsense as long as he could, then turned on the pole-dog, threw him down, and wiped the snow with him. When he got up the driver took the pole-dog out, and the leader pulled the load up the grade all alone. A good leader is all-important.

There are times when kindness won't work at all. If it is a dog that an Indian has raised and beaten without reason from the time it was a puppy tied to a string by the lodge fire, it is useless to expect that such a dog will always work when it should without a sound beating. He regards a gentle driver as easy, and shirks and sulks. At such a time it must be settled who is master, in a way that the dog can understand and remember; for, after all, he is a wolf in many ways, and in the wolf pack it is cruel brute force that masters.

Patience, above all things, is needed with dogs. They are most willing workers, but need encouragement. A dog - driver, one of the best on the Yukon, told me: "The half of them don't know how to treat their dogs. They don't whip them at the right time. When you have to, whip a dog so he will remember it. When I started to drive dogs, and one sulked, I used to go to the dog, give him a cut, and jump back to the gee-pole, and think I had done all right. Now I try to explain it to him till he understands, and then if he sulks I baste hell out of him."

FINEST DOG-TEAM IN THE KLONDIKE

The dog-driver who values his dogs never uses a club or stick ; yet he does use what seems more cruel, but really is not, the dog-chain, or he pounds his thick-hair sides with his fist. The regular dog-driver's whip, which a few carry, is a seal-leather, eight-strand, round plait as thick as one's thumb and five feet long, tapering to a point, with a wooden handle ten inches long. The leather is weighted for about twenty inches from the handle with a slender bag inside filled with shot.

The finest dog-team in the Klondike is a team of five powerful gray "huskies" from the Porcupine River. This winter they came into the possession of their present owner, Captain Barnett, of the Alaska Commercial Company, under peculiar circumstances. Three of the team of five were owned by Chief John Shuman, of the band of Indians at Rampart House, the Hudson's Bay post on the Porcupine. The Indians went on their usual fall hunt after caribou, but the caribou failed to run as they expected, and the village of about fifty souls, on the verge of starvation, started for Fort Yukon, a runner being sent ahead to inform the white men. Captain Barnett organized a party and met them on the river, eighty miles up. At that time the Indians had been for three days with nothing to eat but one rabbit and three or four "dormice" (ermines or weasels). A big "feed" was given, and Chief John Shuman, wishing to show his gratitude to the white men, arose during the feast and made a big speech, telling how well he had been treated, saying that he wanted to do something to show his gratitude. He had some fine dogs—white men had wanted to buy them before—but he had said that no white man should own his dogs. Now there was one white man whom he was willing should have those dogs, and he was Captain Barnett.

Captain Barnett gladly paid the Indian $1200 for three dogs, and he completed the team by the purchase of two more from another Indian, for which he paid $500, making $1700 for the whole team. Besides that, he took the Indians to Fort Yukon, where he feasted them again, and carried Chief John Shuman to Circle City to sell his furs, and only when he had done this did he then become the possessor of the dogs.

They are splendid fellows, taller than the Yukon dogs, and probably are what they are said to be—"huskies," the native dog of the Mackenzie River.

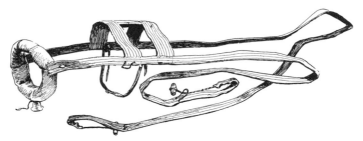

KLONDIKE INDIAN DOG HARNESS, MOOSE HIDE WITH DRILL TRACES

The manner of harnessing dogs differs somewhat throughout the Northwest. In the Hudson's Bay region south of Hudson's Bay the dog pulls from a collar by a single trace over the back, and there are as many separate traces as dogs. In the Upper Yukon the harness used by both Indians and white men is a collar, with side-traces and back-band, and, if more than one dog is used, they are hitched tandem, the traces of the dog ahead being fastened to the traces of the one behind, either close to the collar or at a point behind the back strap. One sort of collar is made of harness leather stuffed with hair and stiffened with quarter-inch iron

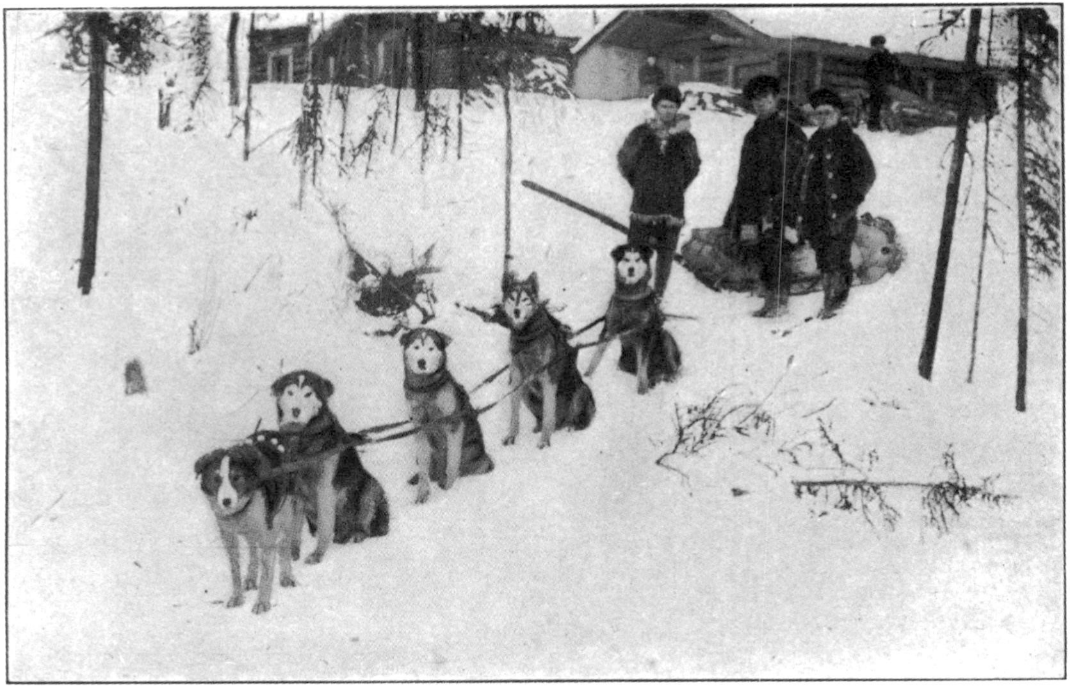

THE FINEST DOG-TEAM ON THE KLONDIKE

wire, serving as hames, but part of the collar itself; the back-strap and belly-strap are also leather, and the harness is fitted with metal snaps, the traces being of webbing.

The native Indian harness is made, the collar of tanned moose-hide, stuffed with moose-hair, and the back-band, traces, etc., of the same material or of a double thickness of stout canvas or twill; the traces taper to a point, with a wooden pin which passes through a slit or loop at the sled or in the harness of the dog behind, and is brought back and buttoned into a hole in the trace. This is readily unfastened in cold weather.

If a Yukon freight sleigh, with a gee-pole for steering, is used, the pole-dog is hitched to a short singletree connected with the sled by a single long rope, so that the dog is just ahead of the man at the pole. It is amusing to see the driver jumping from side to side of this rope, which threatens to trip him up at every turn.

Another kind of harness is, strangely enough, rarely seen on the upper river; it is the Eskimo harness. The Eskimo harness is rather hard to describe intelligibly in words. It is made of a strip of fresh bear-hide about two feet long and, say, a foot wide. The Eskimo cuts three slits lengthwise in this. The middle slit is about a foot long; the two other slits, one on each side of this, are larger. In this condition it has no resemblance to a harness, but the middle slit is pulled over the dog's head, and the fore-legs are lifted and thrust through first one slit and then the other. The end on the dog's back is connected with a snap and swivel to a single long seal-hide trace, the dogs being hitched either tandem at intervals of about five feet, or else in pairs side by side at the same distance apart, with a single leader. The raw bear-skin, by pulling, stretches into shape. Another harness is made of the right form at once out of rope or cloth. The disadvantage of the Eskimo method is that in wooded country one dog may go one side of a tree while

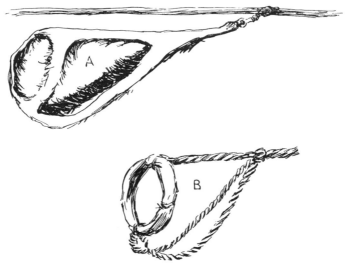

ESKIMO DOG HARNESS
A. Bear-skin. B. Rope

another goes the other. But it has this decided advantage, that, when two teams meet and there arises a difference, as generally happens, the swivels enable the respective owners, after they have untangled their teams, to straighten the dogs out at once without untwisting. Or when, as also happens, the sled gets a start on the dogs and everything lands in a heap at the foot of the hill, the swivel then is a great advantage.

What is now called the "Yukon" sleigh was an invention of the Cassiar miners, and is the sleigh in general use for freighting. The distinctive sleigh of the Yukon is the "basket" sleigh, originally built on the lower river. It is a light, elastic frame of hickory, oak, or white birch, lashed with rawhide, runners half a foot high, the vertical side timbers of the runners extending above the bed one foot at the front and two feet at the rear, finished off with a rail on top, the interstices being filled with

BASKET SLEIGH

a netting of cord or rawhide. Two handles, after the manner of plough-handles, are placed at the rear, and by these the driver steers and prevents upsetting. The inland Eskimo sled is of white birch, which is not strong, but on the coast it is made of driftwood, much heavier, and shod with bone. In length the basket sleigh is eight to twelve feet, and in width twenty to twenty-two inches. The flat Indian toboggan, made of white birch, bent up in front, is used by the natives in hunting, but is not serviceable for the trail.

For the following details of an equipment, such as has hitherto been necessary for the trip from Dawson to Dyea, I am indebted to Mr. A. D. Nash, one of the best dog-drivers on the Yukon.

On his last trip out he figured on provisions for thirty days. The party consisted of four men, with six dogs to a basket sleigh and six to a freight sleigh, both with 22-inch track. He sent beforehand to Fort Selkirk by steamer 350 pounds of food, consisting of 100 lbs. of dried salmon, 100 lbs. of bacon, and 100 lbs. of rice for the dogs, and 50 lbs. of provisions, including one cooked ham, for the men.

When he left Dawson he carried, for the men : 45 lbs. of bacon ; 1½ 50-lb. sacks of flour, 15 lbs. of which were made up into doughnuts, which were frozen and put into a sack ; 20 lbs. of rice ; 15 lbs. of beans ; 10 lbs. of rolled oats ; 20 lbs. of dried fruit ; 10 lbs. of corn-meal ; 30 lbs. of butter ; tea, coffee, and beef extract (the last is all right, but a man can't live on it) ; 6 cans of cocoa ; 1 doz. cans of milk ; a few cans of beef and mutton ; 1 ham, ready cooked. And for the dogs the following . 175 lbs. of rice ; 235 lbs. of bacon ; 150 lbs. of salmon. The rest of the equipment consisted of 4 robes, 1 lynx, 1 bear, 2 caribou ; canvas bed-cover, 6 × 7 ft., to lay on the ground ; 10 × 10 drill-tent, with 2-ft. wall ; sheet-iron stove, without oven, 9 × 12 × 24 in., with 3 joints of pipe stowed inside loose, a damper in the first joint, and a chain at rear for lifting the stove each morning without burning the mittens. A tank was made of copper to fit around stove-pipe, to hold 1 gallon, for melting snow and ice, with a half-cover top ; a cooking outfit of 2 frying-pans and 2 small kettles, and a spoon, tin plate, and tin cup for each man. Two axes ; a repair kit, with rawhide for replacing the lashings of the basket sleigh ; snow-shoes, two pairs ; one long "trail-breaker," five or six feet long by fifteen inches wide ; and "trail shoes," two and a half feet long by nine inches wide. A couple of dog-chains go with the outfit for rough-locks under the sleighs when going down steep grades.

For cooking the dog-food a special tank was made of 4x tin, into which the stove telescoped, with ¾-inch iron handles riveted to each end, and hinged so as to drop out of the way. This tank was put on an open fire, while the stove was used to warm the tent. The open fire cooks in less time than the stove.

The daily allowance of each dog was one cup of rice and one pound of bacon, and one-half pound of fish at night. Dogs are fed only once a day, but sometimes, when the men stop at noon to boil a kettle of tea and eat a doughnut, each are given a doughnut; but the rule is to give them all they can eat once a day.

To load the sleigh, the bed-cover is placed over the sleigh, and the goods laid on, and the cover folded over close and lashed tight, so that if the sleigh rolls over nothing can spill out.

The tent is rigged with a ridge-pole of rope, so as to be swung between two trees, with a rope inside to hang clothes to dry.

DOG
MOCCASINS

The native dog needs no care, further than if his feet get sore he may come into the tent and dry them. Dog moccasins (little pockets with leather soles and cloth tops) are sometimes used.

It is better, all travellers say, to avoid a cabin at night, as one cannot so completely dry off as in one's own tent.

One who pictures the frozen smooth river as a pond cannot understand the difficulties of the trail. The first team up from Circle City this winter was thirty-five days making the journey, and chopped its way forty times across the river.

Twenty-five to thirty days was considered good time

out to Dyea in early winter, and eighteen in returning in spring. The quickest time between Dawson and the coast is claimed by Bob Ensley in sixteen days.*

One of the longest dog journeys on record was made by young Charles Hamilton, of the North American Transportation and Trading Company, who, in order to communicate before the next spring with the officers of his company at Chicago, left St. Michael on November 26th, 1892, with 1000 pounds of outfit on three sleds drawn by twenty-one dogs. He reached the coast on March 19th the next year, having travelled a distance

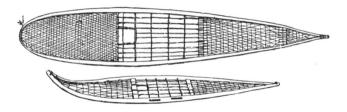

KLONDIKE HUNTING SNOW-SHOE AND TRAIL SNOW-SHOE

of over 1800 river-miles, a distance made hundreds of miles greater by the devious windings of the trail. He walked much of the distance on snow-shoes, guided by Indians, meeting with much hardship but no serious mishap. This winter "Jack" Carr, a United States mail-carrier, made the same trip, but lost several of his dogs from exhaustion.

The life of a dog-freighter is one of hardest work; but the clear, ruddy complexion, elastic step, with the swagger and snap that show mastery of his team, are proof

* As these words are written news arrives that in March, 1899, one team of dogs has made the trip in ten days, and that the mounted police have sent mail out in less time by relays.

enough that hardship, instead of something to be shirked, is necessary to the most vigorous health, to a vigorous body and a clear brain. Waldron told of his last trip on the river last winter.

"Last winter, when grub was high, I went down with a dog-team to Circle. The wind blew so hard at one time that it blew the trail-sled, piled with stuff, clean over, and blew the dogs out in a string. You sweat like everything when you are travelling, and the Mackinaws freeze like a board. My coat froze, and I turned it to the fire and burned a hole in the back. I sews that up, but that made it so I couldn't button it in front; so I lets in a piece of gunny-sack in front. I had gunny-sacks around my legs and a mukluk on one foot and a moccasin on the other. I froze both feet, the tips of my fingers, and my nose, face, and ears. I was a pretty-looking sight when I got into Circle. The boys didn't know me. It is impossible to cover up the face so it will not freeze when it blows on the river. I didn't want any more of that, and I came up with a load and gave up freighting between here and Circle."

One of these dogs is a Malamut, jet black, with a bob-tail, and fur so thick that one can hardly separate the hairs to see to the skin. His fur is like that of a very thick black-bear-skin. He weighs eighty pounds, and he looks so much like a black bear that if a man saw him on the trail at a distance he would shoot him. He is as kind as a kitten, and loves to be petted, but is too heavy to get into Waldron's lap, as he tries to do.

GOLD mining is of two kinds. One known as "bed-rock," or "quartz," mining, is performed by crushing the original vein-rock in which the gold has been deposited by nature, and separating the metal. Gold occurs not alone in quartz, but in mica-schist, feldspar, and other "metamorphic" rock, so that the term "bed-rock" mining is in one sense more proper than "quartz" mining; but as quartz is, in the United States, the commonest rock in which gold is found in considerable quantity, "quartz" mining is the term in universal use here.

The other kind of mining is known as "placer," or stream-bed, mining. In placer or stream-bed deposits nature, operating with water and air, has already done the work of the crusher, and to a certain extent that of the separator also. The particles of metal which grew in the veins have, by the wearing down of the mountain masses, found their way into the valleys of creeks and rivers, and rest on, in, or near bed-rock—bed-rock as understood by the placer-miner being not necessarily the hard rock-formation, but any substance, even clay, sufficiently dense to hold the gold, which, by reason of its great weight, seeks the lowest level. In placer mining expensive machinery is not usually required, but only such as a man can easily carry with him or make with his own hands; hence placer mining is frequently spoken of as "poor-man's" mining. As placer gold is commonly within the reach of every man with strong hands, the discovery of rich placer deposits has always aroused more excitement than the discovery of vastly richer gold-bearing veins.

Often the bed of the stream in which the gold first fell has continued to wear deeper, and wherever that has happened the bulk of the gold has found a new level ; but a considerable portion may remain hundreds of feet above the newer stream-bed, in situations that in no way suggest a river channel until the surface of the ground is removed and water-worn gravel found beneath. Such deposits are termed "bench," or "hill-side" diggings, and are to be looked for by experienced miners alongside rich gold-bearing streams.

Gold in its metallic forms is variously known as "flour" gold, "leaf" or "float" gold, "wire" gold, "fine" gold, "coarse" gold, and "nuggets." Flour gold may be so fine as to be scarcely visible to the unaided eye; leaf gold is in thin flattened pieces up to half an inch or more square, and wire gold is gold in short wire-like pieces. Coarse gold is a general term that includes everything above fine or flour gold, or, say, from the size of coarse corn-meal to that of grains of wheat or larger. "Nugget" is likewise a flexible term. Where fine gold predominates, a smaller piece might be called a nugget than where coarse gold is the rule. Nuggets run in weight from, say, a pennyweight to as much as an ordinary man can lift with his hands.

Gold when found in nature in the metallic state is termed "native," and is never found perfectly pure, but alloyed with other metals, such as silver, antimony, tin, copper, etc., the proportion varying greatly in different

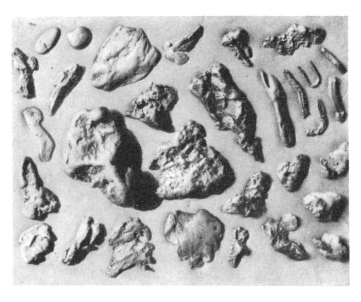

KLONDIKE NUGGETS—TWO-THIRDS NATURAL SIZE

localities, and determining the relative "fineness" of the gold.

To separate the gold from the dirt and gravel in placer mining the same general principle is employed as by nature—namely, water in motion. The simplest tool for this purpose, and that which every placer-miner provides himself, is the "pan," a dish of sheet-iron two or three inches deep, with flaring sides, about a foot in diameter at the bottom, and seventeen or eighteen inches at the top ; a pick, and a shovel with a round point and long handle, complete the essential tools of the placer-miner.

" PANNING "

"Panning" is performed by filling the pan with the gravel believed to contain gold and taking it to a stream or vessel of water; then, holding the pan in both hands, it is dipped into the water and shaken so as to disturb the contents and allow the gold to fall to the bottom. The larger rocks being removed by hand, the dirty water and light stones are allowed to run over the rim of the pan. The pan is again filled with water and shaken, and this operation is kept up until there remains in the bottom of the pan only the heavier sand and particles of other metal, such as magnetic iron, or "black sand," which is generally found in abundance with gold. When the contents of the pan have been reduced to the bulk of, say, a tablespoonful, a little clean water is taken into the pan, and the pan given a tilt which causes the water to swish back and forth, or else, by a peculiar rotary motion, around and around the pan. The lighter particles are carried ahead by the water, and, if there is gold in the dirt, little yellow grains will be observed to drag behind, plainly visible on the dark iron of the pan. When one has once seen *gold*, nothing else can be mistaken for it.* When the gold is "fine" there is danger of its floating off in the water ; so, when such is known to be the case, the miner puts a few drops of quicksilver into the pan. Gold and quicksilver have a strong affinity, and the instant they are brought together the two unite, forming an amalgam, which is easily secured. The pan containing the amalgam may be heated over a fire, which dissipates the quicksilver, leaving a mass of fine gold. But when it is desired to save the quicksilver, the amalgam is poured into a little sack of fine cloth and the quicksilver squeezed out, and when no more can be removed the lump is heated to dispel the remaining quicksilver. If the gold is "coarse," the pan is simply dried and the gold weighed on the scales, which every miner carries, and put into a little buckskin bag. A single grain of gold is called a "color." A prospector will say that he found so many "colors," but it has no direct reference to the value. What con-

* "Fools' gold," so often mistaken by the inexperienced, is sulphuret of iron, or iron pyrites.

stitutes "pay" dirt varies, of course, with the amount of wages a man is willing or able to work for. A "prospect" is simply the gold a miner finds in one panful,

" ROCKING "

and the term is usually employed to mean an amount sufficient to pay for the work.

The "pan" is the miner's basis of estimate. Two "shovelfuls" make one pan, 103 "pans" make one cubic yard of earth. In this way he will try to estimate the probable amount of gold which the gravel deposit contains.

When the prospector has, by panning, located a deposit of gold, he usually constructs a machine for more rapidly washing the gravel. The simplest contrivance, next to the pan, is what is called the "rocker," said to be a Chinese invention. The rocker is simply a box on rockers, like a cradle, with a perforated metal top, or "hopper," and a sloping blanket, or "apron," inside. It is set near the water and the dirt shovelled into the perforated hopper. Water is dipped up in a long-handled dipper and poured in with the dirt, the rocker being energetically rocked at the same time by means of an

MAKING A "CLEAN-UP" FROM A ROCKER

upright handle. The larger stones are removed by hand, the gold falls through perforations and lodges upon the apron, which at intervals is cleaned, the contents being placed in a bucket with quicksilver until all the fine particles of gold were taken up. The amalgam formed is squeezed in a cloth filter, and the remaining lump heated over a fire until practically all trace of the quicksilver disappears. If the gold is coarse, however, the contents of the apron are simply scraped into a pan, and then carefully panned out. The rocker may vary somewhat in details of construction, but the principle remains the same in all. The dipper is often made out of a round two-quart can, fitted with a stick about two feet long set at an acute angle. The rocker is especially useful where there is a scarcity of water, as it can be placed over a tank or reservoir, and the same water used again and again.

When there is what the miners call a sufficient "head" or fall and volume of water, the miner resorts to the "sluice-box" as the next most expeditious method. The sluice-box is a box about twelve feet long, with open ends; the bottom being a board fourteen inches wide at one end, twelve inches at the other, and the sides eight inches high. It is made narrower at one end so that the lower end of one box will just fit into the upper end of another, where several are placed together to form a continuous waterway.

On the floor of the box is placed a frame called a "riffle," made either of round or square poles two inches or less in diameter, placed lengthwise, or else short ones crosswise; the riffles are made so that they can be lifted out of the box. The length of a string of boxes depends on the fineness of the gold, for, obviously, the smaller gold will be carried farther by the water than the coarse before it settles in the interstices of the riffles; and as there must be sufficient rapidity of current to carry the light stones, it is also evident that the water must start at a sufficient elevation for the water leaving the boxes to run on down stream. So a dam is built at the upper end of the ground to be worked, with two sluice-gates, one opening into the sluice-boxes, and another into a ditch or flume, by which the water of the creek not needed for the boxes is diverted around the claim. Whenever the grade of the creek is so slight that the requisite head of water cannot be had in the length of a single claim, several miners often unite and build one dam.

At the lower end of a string of sluice-boxes is one two feet wide at the upper end, narrowing to a foot at the lower, and of the same length as a box, or shorter. This is called the "dump-box," and is also fitted with riffles. Some miners add two or three more boxes with riffles, known as "tail-boxes." The dirt and stones that have been worked over once in the rocker, or sluice-boxes, are called "tailings."

For ordinary coarse gold the grade is as follows : The upper, or "lead," boxes are set on a half-inch grade, the next four to six on a 6-inch grade, the last one on an 8-inch grade, and the "dump-box" on a 5-inch grade.

After the water is turned into the boxes the gold-bearing dirt is shovelled in—the big stones being forked out—until the crevices of the riffles are choked. Then the water is turned off, the riffles taken up, and a little water turned in and the gold carefully separated. This operation is called "cleaning up," and will be more particularly described later. A "box length" is an area of ground measured by the length of the box, twelve feet, one way and six feet each side the box, being as far as a man can reach with the long-handled shovel, the area being about one hundred and fifty-six square feet. The term is used in speaking of the amount of gold cleaned up from that extent of ground. The expression so many ounces or dollars of gold "to the shovel" means the amount in ounces or dollars that *one man* shovels into the boxes *in one day*, or a specified number of hours. The "pay streak" is that part of the stratum of gold-bearing gravel that is rich enough to pay to work. The "cut" is the opening in the steam-bed in which the sluice-box is set up.

There are other methods and contrivances for saving gold, such as hydraulicking ; but the foregoing general description of the simple tools known to all miners is all that is needed to prepare the reader for an account of gold discovery in the Yukon, and how certain methods of mining were discovered that make the Klondike different from all other gold-fields yet discovered.

As early as the year 1857, only nine years after the discovery of gold in California, a northward movement along the western coast resulted in the discovery in that year of placer gold on Fraser River, in British Columbia, and a stampede from California. In 1871 the rich "Caribou" District was discovered, and another excitement ensued, which resulted, in 1874, in the discovery of rich gold-fields in the Cassiar Mountains, both of which districts lie immediately south of the headwaters of the Lewes River. The Cassiar placers were in time exhausted, and the hardy miners pushed on, not directly over the mountains, but following bars of the Stikeen River, which was a large gold-producing stream, to its mouth, and thence northerly along the Alaskan coast. In 1880, Silver Bow Basin was discovered, back of the present town of Juneau, which was first called Harrisburg, in honor of Dick Harris, one of the two original discoverers, but was subsequently changed to Juneau, after Joe Juneau, the other partner. Reports had reached the outside from time to time that traces of gold had been discovered by employés of trading companies in the Yukon. But the pass over the mountains into the Yukon was guarded by the Chilkat and Chilkoot Indians, who opposed the entrance of all white men into the country for any purpose. The year of the Silver Bow strike a party of white men crossed over—the first whom the Indians allowed to go through. This party brought back good reports of the bars on the Lewes River, and from this time on other parties crossed the pass, built their boats on the other side, and descended the river farther and farther, working the bars—generally returning to the coast the same season. No mining was attempted in the winter, nor was it possible. All the work was done in the short summer between the breaking-up of the ice in the river and the freezing in early fall; but the almost continual daylight of that latitude and season somewhat increased their hours of work.

The "bar," as the term is used by the miner, does not necessarily mean a shallow portion of the river; rather it is an alluvial deposit of sand and gravel, often ten or twenty feet or more above the low-water level of the river. These high banks carried gold in fine particles, but so widely distributed that the miners did not even try to work them; but in the process of their washing down at freshet time the gravel was deposited inside the bends of the river, and the gold concentrated into layers, or strata, usually richest near the heads of the bars. The rocker was employed altogether to separate the gold, which was denominated "fine." The gold-bearing sands were near the surface, and some of these bars proved very rich. Cassiar Bar, below the mouth of the Hootalinqua, in 1886 yielded to five men on the head claims $6000 for thirty days' work.

FIRST MINERS IN THE YUKON

Another and important factor now entered into the development of the Yukon mines. The Alaska Commercial Company, soon after the purchase of Alaska by our government from Russia in 1867, was given a lease of the sealing rights of the Pribyloff Islands, which carried with it a practical monopoly of the fur-trade of Alaska, then solely a fur-producing country. From the company's main distributing-points, Kadiak and Unalaska, it supplied the sub-station of St. Michael, and from there, at first by one small steamer, the *Yukon*, goods were sent to different points on the Yukon where its agents were engaged in the Indian trade. Chief of these agents at this time were LeRoy N. McQuesten, better known as "Jack" McQuesten, Arthur Harper, and Al Mayo, who, with some others not so well known, came into the Yukon about the year 1871, from the Northwest Territory, by way of the Mackenzie and Porcupine rivers. The Indian population was larger then than now, and the furs from the Yukon were of a high grade, the sable being second only to the celebrated Russian sable from Kamtchatka. The traders occupied posts from time to time at different points on the Middle Yukon. McQuesten built Fort Reliance, six miles below the mouth of the Klondike River, in 1873, and occupied that post until 1882. Not a few of the first miners wintered at this post.

In 1885 rich bars were discovered on the Stewart River, and, with the rush of miners there the next summer, Messrs. Harper, McQuesten & Mayo established a post at the mouth of that river. During the winter which followed there was a shortage of provisions, and the little camp of seventy or eighty men was on the verge of starvation. The cause of the shortage at Stewart River was the report, brought to Stewart River just before the river closed, that *coarse gold* had been discovered on "Shitanda" Creek (a corruption of the Indian name "Zit-zen-duk"), now called Forty-Mile, from its having been estimated to be that distance from old Fort Reliance. It was late in the fall when the report came that Mickey O'Brien, Jim Adams, and two others, by the name of Lambert and Franklin, had found coarse gold. A stampede for the new diggings followed, for the miner does not bother with fine gold when he can get coarse gold. Those miners who thought they had not enough supplies for the winter bought all the trader would sell them and started for Forty-Mile. It was the late comers from up river who suffered in consequence.

A letter with the news of the find started out from Stewart River in January, carried by a man named Williams, with an Indian boy and three dogs. On the summit of Chilkoot they were overtaken by a storm, and were buried for three days in the snow. When the storm abated Williams could not walk, and was carried on the back of the Indian boy four miles to Sheep Camp, whence he was sledded into Dyea by some Indians, and died in the store of Captain John J. Healey. The dogs were never seen again. The miners congregated from all parts to know what had brought the man out, for the winter journey was considered almost certain death. The Indian boy, picking up a handful of beans, said, " Gold all same like this." The excitement was intense, and that spring over two hundred miners poured in over the pass to Forty-Mile.

The winter was a season of enforced idleness. The spring freshet at one end and freezing at the other shortened the working season to about sixty-five days, during which time an average of eight or ten dollars a day had to be made for the next year's grub-stake. Every man was a prospector and a hard worker, skilled at boating,

FORTY-MILE

accustomed to hardship, rough, yet generous to his fellows. One custom in particular that shows this feeling was that when the 1st of August came, any who had failed to locate a paying claim were given permission to go upon the claims of such as had struck it and to take out enough for the next season's outfit. This peaceable condition in general characterized the Yukon.

Forty-Mile, unlike other streams that had been prospected, proved to be what the miners call a "bed-rock" creek—that is, bed-rock came to or quite near the surface. Then Franklin Gulch, tributary of Forty-Mile, was discovered; in the bed of the small brook the gold was found under several feet of gravel. Other tributaries of Forty-Mile were afterwards discovered, all with good pay.

In the spring of 1886 the traders removed to Forty-Mile, and the rich diggings of that region were developed, with the post for a base of operations; in 1893 on Sixty-Mile, and in 1894 on Birch Creek, placers even richer than those on Forty-Mile were discovered.

With the discovery of coarse gold, sluice-boxes were introduced, though the rocker continued in common use. Thus far the frozen condition of the ground was the greatest obstacle to mining. The sun's rays, wherever they reached, were sufficient to thaw a foot or so each day, and each day the miners would remove the thawed dirt. In this manner bed-rock on Forty-Mile, which was rather shallow, could be reached in one season. Thawing the ground with fire had been thought of, but the idea was put to no practical use. Its possibilities were discovered in a curious way. At Franklin Gulch, in 1887, Fred Hutchinson (now of 7 Eldorado) was following a pay streak which extended under water, and he was obliged to leave off work. That winter, however, after the ice had formed, it occurred to him to chop the surface of the ice over the spot he wanted to work, but taking care not to break through. As the ice froze downwards he kept on chopping, until he reached the bed of the stream, thus having built a sort of coffer-dam

STARTING A HOLE

of ice, which kept the water out of the hole. Hutchinson built a fire on the ground, and took out a little pay dirt. His neighbors observed his freakish undertaking and laughed at him. But the following year two of them made fires on the ground, and, the diggings being shallow, took out considerable dirt. These first efforts were necessarily crude, but they demonstrated that ground might be worked which the sun's rays could not reach. In any event, it was a great leap forward, as twelve months' work was now possible instead of only two as before. Some, however, did not take kindly to this, and they said, "It's as bad now inside as outside—work winter and summer." After having reached bed-rock, the next step was to tunnel or drift along it. This was first done by O. C. Miller on Forty-Mile, but Miller only drifted to prospect a claim which he intended to work the following summer. From that time on winter work became more general, and the deeper diggings were reserved for that season. As deeper ground could be worked out by drifting than by the old way, the term "winter diggings" has come to mean ground too deep to work by open summer work.

The art of drifting, however, was not generally understood until two or three years before the Klondike discovery, and so much more is being learned that it may truthfully be said that it has taken the second year at Klondike to develop the Yukon "placer expert."

In the creeks of Klondike, as far as they have been prospected, the gold is known to be found in two situations. First on and in bed-rock in the beds of the creeks, covered by from twelve to fifty feet of gravel and muck; secondly, on the sides of the creeks, either at a uniform elevation of about two hundred feet over the present stream, being the remains of a former stream-bed, or else at lower elevations, where the gold-bearing dirt has slid down. These hill-side claims were unknown in the Yukon at the time of the Klondike discovery.

At least two men are required to work a creek claim in winter. Thirty cords of wood are required for the winter's burnings of two men. The wood, which grows in the valleys and on the hill-sides, is either procured in the summer or fall before drifting begins, or as needed from day to day. Drifting begins in late September, as soon as the surface water of the creeks is in a measure dried up by the frost. Contrary to a prevailing notion, the colder the weather, the better for winter work. When the miner is ready to place his first fire, he judges as well as he can where the pay streak is, but in this he has absolutely no surface indications to guide him. The

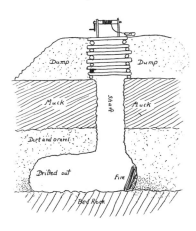

present stream winds from side to side of the valley, and the old stream underneath, in which the gold is found, apparently did the same; but the windings of the one afford no clew to the windings of the other. A hole must be put down simply at random, as a gunner fires a first shot to determine the range. When the shaft has reached bed-rock, the

SECTION OF A SHAFT, WINTER DRIFTING

direction in which the old creek lies is usually told by the " dip," or slant, of the bed-rock, so the miner drifts in that direction fifteen or twenty feet, which is as far as it is profitable to drag the dirt. Great difficulty is experienced in securing draught for the fire in the first drift. If the pay streak is not reached in the first drift, a second hole is put down thirty or more feet from the first and the drifting continued until the pay streak is found.

Then the pay gravel is drifted out, a hole twenty by thirty feet being often excavated, the roof being in such cases supported by timbers. The surface indications are further deceitful in that a slide of the mountain may have filled in the side of the creek, covering entirely the bed of the old stream.   Even on a rich creek the gold is not evenly distributed.   Rough, broken bed-rock holds the gold better than smooth, over which the gold appears to have been carried without lodging.   The common manner of " proving " a claim consists of sinking to bed-rock, and drifting on bed-rock across the creek; but if the creek should be " spotted," it may be necessary to " cross-cut " more than once.   When the pay streak has been found it is followed by a series of holes and drifts up and down. In order to know when he is on the pay streak the miner each day (perhaps several times a day) takes one or more pans of dirt from the hole and pans it out in a wooden tank of water in the cabin, carefully weighing the gold thus found.   If he has five cents to the pan it may pay to work, but only in summer.   Ten cents to the pan is considered pay for winter work ; twenty-five cents is very rich.   But this means *average* dirt.   Miners often

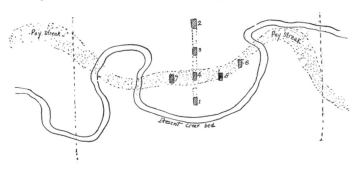

IDEAL PLAN OF CREEK CLAIM, SHOWING RELATION OF PAY STREAK
TO CREEK BED

deceive themselves by not averaging the dirt, and find on cleaning up that they have not the quantity of gold in their dump that they expected.

Formerly the first fire was placed on the muck, but

on account of there being so much water in the muck it was very slow work, and it has been found better to pick the muck. The hole is about four by six or seven feet, and is made true and square. When the hole has reached a depth at which the dirt cannot be shovelled

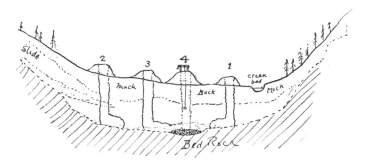

IDEAL SECTION SHOWING HOW A CLAIM IS "CROSS-CUT"

out, a windlass, made of a spruce log six inches thick and four and a half feet long, and resting on two posts about four feet high, is set over the hole, and the dirt is hoisted in a wooden bucket which holds about eight pans of dirt. One hundred buckets a day is a good day's work.* The fire is put in at night and in the morning the smoke has sufficiently cleared to allow a man to go into the hole. The smoke is very trying to the eyes, and not infrequently gases in the hole have overcome and killed the miner. As the height of the dump increases the windlass is raised on crib-work, so as to be on a level with the top of the dump. When the pay gravel has been found, it is carefully placed by it-

* At ten cents per pan, 100 buckets (800 pans)=$80 per day, or $40 per man, which must pay for all "dead" work—cabin-building, wood-cutting, freighting supplies, sluicing, etc.

self. Drifting continues until May, when usually the surface water runs in and puts out the fires. It often happens that work is hindered from that cause all winter, while there may be spots, at the side of the present stream, where burning can be continued all summer.

In April and May preparations are begun to sluice the dumps, by building a dam exactly as for summer sluicing. The water is led in a three-foot flume 'along the

A DUMP, WITH A WINDLASS RAISED ON CRIB-WORK

side of the claim, and at intervals tapped by cross lines of sluice-boxes, one leading past each dump; and when the sun has thawed the dumps the dirt is shovelled in, a process which will be described in detail later.

To sink a hole requires twenty to thirty days, and it may be necessary to put down a half-dozen holes or more before the pay is found. Thus a whole season's work may be put in without locating the pay, even when the claim is rich, or they may be so fortunate as to strike pay in the first hole.

Instead of risking all on a new claim in an undeveloped creek, many of the new-comers preferred to either work for wages on the developed creeks, or to take what is called a " lay "—a lease for one year of a section fifty feet wide across the creek—the conditions being to sink to bed-rock, drift on bed-rock to the pay and to the edges of the section, for a percentage varying from fifty to seventy-five per cent. of the proceeds. This is unsatisfactory to the "laymen," for the reason that the claim may be "spotted," and no "pay" in so small a section, and because the whole season's work may not locate the pay even when it is there. The custom is growing in disfavor with owners also, as a season's unsuccessful work diminishes the value of the claim, which would otherwise have at least a speculative value.

A "layman," when he finds the pay streak, may turn to and hire men payable on " bed-rock," that is, at the clean-up. Some lays are granted guaranteeing wages of $15 per day, in case the product should not be as large as was expected—that is, the wages are a first lien on the output.

For a concise statement of the methods that have been employed during the first year of Klondike, as well as the cost of developing a claim, both winter and summer diggings, I cannot do better than to quote a statement made by Alexander McDonald, to accompany a petition sent by the miners to the Governor-General of Canada, in December, 1897.*

* *Appeal of Yukon Miners to the Dominion of Canada, and incidentally some Account of the Mines and Mining of Alaska and the Provisional District of the Yukon,* published as a hand-book of 125 pages for distribution among members of Parliament by M. Landreville, A. E. Wills, and Edward J. Livernash, committee.

A MINER'S STATEMENT

" I, Alexander McDonald, do solemnly declare: That I am a resident of the Klondike Mining Division of the Yukon District, Northwest Territories, Dominion of Canada.

" That I am a holder of several placer-mining claims in said district, both in the Klondike and Indian divisions thereof.

" That I am a miner by occupation. Since 1880 I have been engaged in the business of mining, having mined within that period in Colorado, on Douglas Island, in the Forty-Mile Division of the Yukon District; and, since September, 1896, in the Klondike and Indian divisions of the Yukon district. My experience has been mainly confined to dealing with the precious metals, gold especially.

" That in said Yukon District I have had experience at mining for gold in summer and winter, have worked in and had charge of placer-mines, and am familiar with methods pursued in said district, the cost of mining therein, and the yield in general of the mineral belt thereof.

" That what is known in said district as 'summer work' begins in June and ends about the middle of September. Not much is accomplished in June, and the September work is uncertain.

" The ' summer work ' consists in opening pits or cuts (opencast mining) and sluicing the gravel.

*   *   *   *   *   *   *

" That all of the deposits between moss and the lowest-known pay point is frozen throughout the year, and this necessitates exposing surfaces for thawing by the sun's heat in summer working, and leads to corresponding slowness and difficulty in the working of pits. The muck thaws three inches a day, on an average ; the gravel, about ten inches.

" That my experience in mining in said district, and my observation of the mining by others in said district, convinces me that an effective bed-rock drain on Bonanza Creek would have to be at least 2000 feet long; on Eldorado Creek, 1000 feet.

" That there are not any steam - pumps in the district aforesaid, nor any electrical appliances whatever for use in drainage of summer pits. The rule is for the claims to be drained by hand-pumps of the most primitive order.

"There is not enough water available on more than a few claims to run water-power pumps.

"That the grade of the known creeks of said district is so slight that in damming water to a height requisite for ordinary sluicing water is backed 200 feet.

"That during the past season of 'summer work' $1.50 an hour was the universal price of ordinary unskilled labor in this district. The better laborers commanded $2 an hour. The working day averaged ten hours of labor.

" BURNING "

"That the cost of lumber undressed averaged 40 cents a board foot on the claims.

"That, as an average, 100 sluice-boxes are used on every claim worked as summer diggings, with dimensions as follows : Length, 12 feet; at top, 10 by 11 inches; at bottom, 10 by 13 inches; the 10 in each instance representing depth.

"That 72 sets of block riffles per claim are used during the summer season, as claims are worked at present in said district, and these cost an average of $5 a set.

" That the cost of sluice-boxes, riffles not included, averages $25 a box.

" That the cost of setting a line of sluice-boxes, and keeping said lines set during the summer, averages $2000.

" That the cost of building a rough dam sufficient for the ordinary working of the average 500-foot claim in said district is about $1000.

" That the cost of constructing a waste ditch on Claim No. 30 Eldorado (one of the claims of which I am a holder) was about $1200. I think it an average ditch.

" That the cost of handling the dirt, 'summer working,' from the ground-sluicing to the clean-up, averages (labor bills) $5 a cubic yard on the entire quantity moved.

" That the cost of pumping for drainage of summer pits 400 feet long by 30 feet wide averages $72 per twenty-four hours.

" That wheelbarrows cost $25 apiece; shovels, $3.50 apiece; mattocks, $5 apiece; blacksmiths' portable forges, about $200 apiece; average-weight grindstones, about $35 apiece; hammers, 60 cents a pound; saws, $5.50 apiece; nails, 40 cents a pound; rope, 50 cents a pound; gold-scales of average capacity, $50 a pair; quicksilver, $1.25 a pound; black powder, $1.25 a pound; fuse, $2\frac{1}{2}$ cents a foot.

" That what is known in said district as 'winter work' begins in September and ends late in July. In September the work is preparatory to sinking and drifting. After May 1st it is wholly sluicing.

" That said 'winter work' is what is known as drift-mining.

" That because of the frozen character of the dirt aforesaid, it is the practice to thaw the dirt to be handled, first by means of wood fires to release it from the breasts for hoisting it to the surface, and again by means of the spring sun's heat to free the gold in sluicing.

" That a fire banked 25 feet in length by $2\frac{1}{2}$ feet in height, one-half a cord of wood being used, thaws about 5 cubic yards of gravel as it lies in the deposit.

"That the wood used for such fuel costs at an average $25 a cord, delivered at the mouth of the shaft.

"That the cost of sinking untimbered shafts 4×6 feet, surface dimensions, is about $10 a foot.

"That the cost of handling dirt from shaft-sinking to clean-up, 'winter work,' averages (labor bills) $12 a cubic yard.

"That in drift-mining in said district it is impossible, with present methods, properly to clean up the bed-rock, and, in that the richest pay is on bed-rock or in bed-rock, great losses ensue.

"That the cost of a cabin 12×14 feet, ground dimensions, is about $600. Such cabin ordinarily houses three miners.

"That in summer it costs 25 to 30 cents a pound for transportation of supplies from Dawson to the mouth of Eldorado Creek; fifteen miles to the thirty-sixth claim above the mouth of Eldorado Creek, and on said creek, 35 cents; to the thirty-fifth claim above Discovery on Bonanza Creek, 35 cents; to Hunker Creek, 50 cents.

"That in winter it costs 10 cents a pound for transportation of supplies from Dawson to the mouth of Eldorado Creek, and other distances proportionately."

The above sufficiently shows that, while Klondike mines are "poor men's" mines, in the sense of being placer-deposits, still, when not only the expense of reaching the country, but the cost of living while there, and the cost of working the mines is considered, the Klondike is not *a poor man's country.*

CHAPTER XIII

IT was the morning of Thanksgiving Day, the 25th of November. The night before we had cooked enough dough-nuts to last two men a week, and threw them into an old tele-scope valise, along with a junk of bacon and tea and sugar, for one pack, and tied up a pair of twelve-pound blankets into another pack, ready for a start at day-break on our first trip to the mines. Our camp was on what was known as claim No. 97A, which meant that, if no mistake had been made in numbering or in measur-ing, there were ninety-seven 500-foot claims between ours and Discovery claim, which was seven claims be-low the "Grand Forks" of Bonanza and Eldorado creeks, which is the heart of the diggings—a mode of estimate in this instance misleading, owing to numerous short claims and one gap of five whole claims between 36 and 42, offset somewhat, however, by several long claims, off which fractions over and above said 500 feet had been taken and distinguished by the addition of the letter "A" to the claim number. The actual distance to the Forks was estimated at from eleven to thirteen miles, according as one followed the sled-trail in the windings of the creek, or the foot-trail, which cut off the long loops.

CABINS AND DUMPS

It was hardly daylight when we shouldered our respective packs and turned up the trail. The air was the kind which hardens quicksilver; so we started off at a lively trot, according to Yukon custom, and then settled down to a four or five mile gait. The run put a glow into our cheeks and a warmth into our bodies, but we had to keep rubbing chin, cheeks, and nose to prevent them turning white and hard—the first two

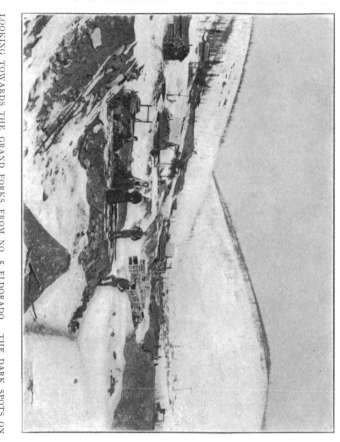

LOOKING TOWARDS THE GRAND FORKS FROM NO. 5 ELDORADO. THE DARK SPOTS ON THE HILL ON THE LEFT INDICATE LANCASTER'S FAMOUS "BENCH" DISCOVERY

indications in this keen, dry air that they are frozen. For the first four or five miles but little work of any kind had been done—only an occasional newly built cabin, or a crude windlass over a black hole in the ground which still emitted smoke from the night's fire. One early riser, out chopping wood for breakfast fire, looked at us curiously, then remarked, "Stampedin'?"—the inference being that two men with packs coming at that gait and that hour from the direction of town had received a "tip" of a strike somewhere. When we reached the "Sixties" below, we came suddenly upon a row of cabins, and heaps of dirt with windlasses on top. The day's work had just begun, and sleepy men in Mackinaws and old cloth "parkies," canvas mittens, with faces muffled and feet wrapped in sacking (the working miner cares little about looks, though doubtless many wore them for the sake of economy), had begun to turn creaking windlasses, hoisting dirt out of the holes. Others were busy sawing wood with long, single cross-cut saws, the slender blackened poles of spruce, cottonwood, and birch being laid on a long "horse," having pegs each side to keep the pole from rolling off. The first early travellers were coming down the trail. I shall not forget this first sight. A heavy bank of smoke from the night's fires hung over the valley, and the air was laden with the smell of burned wood. More cabins and smoking dumps ; then strings of cabins, first on one side, then on the other, the trail growing like the street of a village in which there were only men. Other men on the hill-sides were dragging down small poles for the fires, streaking the white snow with black.

We hurried on, clambering over dumps, now shuffling along the smooth, polished sled-trail, hardly comprehending the strange, weird sight. Three hours from camp we stood at the forks of Bonanza and Eldorado. The sight was one never to be forgotten. The sun, like a deep-red ball in a red glow, hung in the notch of Eldorado; the smoke settling down like a fog (for the evening fires were starting); men on the high dumps like spectres in the half-smoke, half-mist; faint outlines of scores of cabins; the creaking of windlasses—altogether a scene more suggestive of the infernal regions than any spot on earth. It was hard to believe that this was the spot towards which all the world was looking. Little more than a year ago this wilderness, now peopled by some thousands of white men, resounded only to the wolf's howl and the raven's hollow *klonk*. Well might one gaze in wonder, whether an old California miner or one who had never before seen men dig gold, for the world had seen nothing like this.

At the side of Bonanza Creek, where one could look into Eldorado, was a settlement of twenty or more cabins, some occupied by miners, others used for hotels and various purposes, but no stores or places of amusement, everything being hauled or carried up from town, and the miners going to Dawson for recreation. One hotel, known as the "Grand Forks," of which a Miss Belinda Mulrooney was proprietress, was evidently well supplied with food and refreshments, and meals could be had there, served on a clean table-cloth with china dishes, for $3.50 each, or $12 a day for meals and bed. Pelletier ran upon a one-time dog-driver from the north shore of Lake Superior, one Madden, who was here keeping a hotel. Just now the proprietor of the "Hotel Madden," like most of the other new-comers, was out of both provisions and whiskey, and was debating whether he should not have to go "outside" for more.

We were made welcome to the best in the house—

VIEW OF ELDORADO LOOKING UP FROM MOUTH OF FRENCH GULCH

namely, the use of a chair, a table, a stove for cooking, and a place on the floor to spread a blanket. The hotel was a two-storied log building, about 25 × 30 feet, a single room below, with a ladder to reach up-stairs. A large heating-stove stood in the middle of the floor, a cooking-stove and a long bare table at the other end. In one corner was what is even more essential than a dining-room to a Yukon hotel—the bar, a narrow counter of spruce boards, back of which on a shelf stood several long black bottles, one of which, it was announced gloomily, still contained a little rum, the house's entire stock of liquid refreshment. The walls were further decorated with some colored lithographs and cigarette photographs.

As a little daylight remained, we left our blanket and ran over to Eldorado, wending our way among the dumps—a matter of considerable difficulty to the stranger who tries to take a "cut-off." We made direct for a cabin, one of several on the right hand, on Claim No. 5, one of the first cabins built on the creek, and first occupied by Clarence Berry. Berry was, as we knew, in San Francisco with the $130,000 which he took out with him and showed, in the window of his hotel, to wonder-struck thousands. But Frank, his brother, was there, superintending the claim, doing his own house-work entirely alone, and feeling rather lonesome in consequence ; so it happened that before we had talked half that we wanted to say it was past time for starting, and we were bidden to remain for supper. Our host, with commendable dexterity, but no small amount of grumbling at the troubles of bachelor life, set before us, on a bare spruce table, a most grateful meal of stewed corn and tomatoes and beef-steak, the two first-mentioned articles being served, as was also the milk for our coffee, in the original tins. This "millionaire's" cabin—if one may speak of the half-owner of Nos. 4, 5, and 6 Eldorado and other claims as a millionaire—was about 12 × 16 feet, with a small window at each side, and the rear partitioned off for a sleeping-apartment by a screen of calico. The furniture consisted of the aforesaid table, one or two home-made chairs or stools, and two very rickety bedsteads, all of unplaned lumber. A sheet-iron stove stood by the door, and beside it the square "panning" tank of dirty water. Frying-pans and other cooking utensils hung on nails behind the stove. Near one window was a shelf, on which stood a small glass kerosene lamp, a small gold-scale, and a copper "blower." The ceiling was covered with calico; this and a bit of curtain at the windows marked it as a woman's cabin, something nicer than a rough miner would provide for himself; in fact, there is a bit of romance here, of a winter's trip, a new bride, and nuggets by the pocketful.

We talked into the small hours, of "winter diggings," "box lengths," and "pay streaks." Berry went over to Anton's cabin (Anton, who owns one-half the so-called "Berry claims") and brought a nugget that had lately been found. It was a beautiful lump of gold, flattish and much worn, of a bright "brassy" color, indicating a large alloy of silver. Putting it on the gold-scales, it weighed a scant fifteen and a half ounces, and had been taken from a "bench" just outside of the creek claim.

Twenty-five men were at work on claims Nos. 4, 5, and 6, and a fraction 5A. One man did nothing but take one panful of dirt out of each hole two or three times a day, so as to keep on the pay streak. There was a blacksmith-shop for sharpening picks, which wear out rapidly in the frozen ground. "Is Klondike a poor man's country?" was, of course, one of our questions. The reply was more emphatic than elegant. Our next question was, " Is the ground rich?" "There is one dump I know on Eldorado where a man can take a rocker and rock out $10,000 in a day, or he can pan $1000 in four pans. Those who have high-grade dirt will not sell for less than from $50,000 to $150,000. The 'pay' is hard to follow, it pinches out, and we have to follow it like a gopher-hole. If a man could only uncover the ground ! I came here and looked at this claim. Gold here? Why, I see a lot of nice trees sticking out of the ground ! Twenty-five-dollar nuggets are *common*. We have a thousand dollars' worth, averaging $10, that came out of our first cut. Some men won't stay at work at any wages when they see the ground. One man came to me and said he wanted to quit. 'Aren't you satisfied ?' 'Yes, I'm satisfied with you, but I won't work for any man in a country where there is dirt like this,' and he went up the hill-side and began sinking a hole."

Next morning we continued on up the creek for a distance of four miles to the junction of Chief Gulch. All the way up was the same; almost every claim was being worked. Some of the dumps are thirty feet high, and evidently on the "pay," for the windlasses are already set up on light crib-work, so as to shove the dirt well to the side of the creek. Paying such wages, and with a tax besides of 20 per cent. over them, there was no question that the claims were wonderfully rich. We stopped at several cabins. One of the miners expressed the feeling of probably a good many of the new "millionaires." "If we get any worse we'll all be crazy. I haven't anybody to laugh with. I suppose my people at home feel pretty good — never had anything till now." Everywhere we stopped we were received with a miner's cordiality, and given the best the camp afforded. On No.

30 we tumbled into a hornets' nest unawares. The fore-man was a belligerent, bullet-headed Irishman. Hardly had we responded to his "come in," when, learning that we were newspaper men, he turned in and gave us his opinion of the newspapers for sending the people into this country. He evidently took it for granted we wanted specific information to publish, and thereby bring more people into the country, deceiving them as to the true condition.

"No," said he, "I've got no informashun, I've got no informashun. You newspapers come here and want to know how much we're gittin'; and if I tell you I'm gittin' tin dollars to the pan out of wan hole, you'll go and say that we're gittin' that much all over the claim, when there is a hole over there where we're only gittin' a dol-lar to the pan."

We let him talk on, and found out about what we wanted to know—that the claim was very rich. He ended up by being quite civil, asking us to sit down; but it looked at first from his belligerent attitude as if he were going to put us out forcibly, which we after-wards heard he had done to a too-inquisitive corre-spondent.

Those working for wages, or on "lays," are more com-municative than the owners. One need not be long here to know that it was hardly less than impertinence to ask a mine-owner what his "prospects" were, unless he hap-pened to be a friend, or volunteered the information, and then the information might be confidential. For, with an iniquitous tax, a tax without precedent, with-out justification, only imposed in crass ignorance of the conditions of working and expense of mining, a tax that has been likened, even by Canadians themselves, to high-way robbery, it was small wonder that they would not

PREPARING FOR BIG DUMPS ON ELDORADO

divulge the richness of their claims. But they are all ready to talk about their neighbors.

The miners, most of whom were old-timers, lived comfortably in their cabins, which were overheated rather than cold.

In the evening, after work is done, they visit around or remain indoors reading papers and books. One finds all sorts of books, from a cheap novel to Gibbon's *Roman Empire* and Shakespeare, in the cabins of Bonanza and Eldorado.

There are many Swedes in Klondike—a fact attributed largely to the Treadwell Mine at Juneau having brought them there to work, and there they got the grub-stake which brought them into the Yukon. They are a hard-headed lot of men, accustomed to cold and hard, " bone " labor, patient, and satisfied with small returns in the absence of better. They are sometimes spoken of sneeringly, but that is a mistake. They have their share of the good things here, and, with the Norwegians, are often well-educated.

The old-timer is punctilious in the matter of washing dishes and clothes as far as that is practicable. Every cabin has its wash-tub and wash-board, and once a week the woollens are changed and scrubbed. He gives more care to the quality of his food and to its preparation than the new-comer, for he has learned by experience that it pays to do so.

Although the trading companies agree between themselves on prices—the highest that the miner can pay—still the competition is so keen that the quality of food is the very best. The old-timer never speculates in food. One who is better supplied lets his neighbor have flour at the price it cost him in the store.

The old-timer is often bitter against the new-comers.

He wonders what will become of the country and of them. What a change! Four years ago, if you told a man in Seattle you were going into the Yukon, he would set you down as a crazy fool.

The trouble seems to be that the old-timer has come to regard the country as his own, and naturally resents innovations, particularly those just now associated with "government," which they may well do, as "government" had small use for the country until they, the old-timers, by their own hands proved it to be rich. The greater number of the older miners are Americans, or have imbibed American ideas.

In Circle City no man was called an "old-timer" unless he had come in with the first rush of sixteen years ago. The old Cassiar men are here, but not many are owners of claims. When Klondike was struck, they said to their younger friends, "Don't be foolish; that country has been overrun by old California and Cassiar miners for ten years, and don't you go there a *chechahko** and expect to get rich." The country had to look just right, the willows had to lean a certain way, to suit these old, bearded men. In the "lower country" to what we should call "old fogies" the irreverent name of "sourdough stiffs" was given.

I heard an old-timer confess that "the longer a man stays in this country the less he knows. If he stays here long enough he gets so he don't know nawthin."

He has his own strict ideas of morality. Theft was as great a crime as murder, and when either happened, which was rarely, a miners' meeting was called, the accused was given a chance to be heard, and then by a vote the decision was rendered swiftly and surely. If

* Chinook jargon, meaning "new-comer."

guilty, he had to leave the country at once. *How* he left was a matter of no concern. *He had to leave!* Gambling was regarded as a legitimate amusement, but it did not mean that they all gambled. They considered that any one who chose to spend his money that way was as free to do so as in any other. But if he could, but would not, pay his debts, the recalcitrant was requested by a miners' meeting to settle—and he did. The professional gambler is respected as any other man who behaves himself, only he is considered in the light of a non-producer, and not in the same class or entitled to the same consideration as a prospector or a miner. A man who thoroughly knows the spirit of his fellow-miners says: "Here the man

WASH-DAY

who patronizes a saloon and the man who goes to church are on the same footing." A startling statement, but none the less true.

There is a dearth of blood-curdling tales that are expected to be the stock of every mining-camp. The Yukon has been too law-abiding for many stories of violence. The rigors of the country and the broadening effect of the life have made men behave themselves. The police have not, as is claimed, brought about this condition. It existed before there were any police here. The cold weather, the poor grub and little of it, incidents of a hard trip with dogs, the time there was no butter in Circle City—these constitute about the whole stock of conversation.

One night at No. 7 Eldorado, Fred Hutchinson's and Louis Empkins's claim, after work, a neighbor dropped in

A BOTTLE WINDOW

for a visit. He was a thin, solemn Irishman, past middle age, with a red face, red, drooping mustache, and a red marten-skin cap. He was introduced to us as "Red" Sullivan. Sullivan began to relate how they had found a nugget that day on the claim where he was working.

"Mike Young sees something bright like a pea in the bucket, and he brushed it off, and it kept gittin' bigger and bigger, and he pulled it out. You know Mike—nuthin' ever gits Mike excited, a regiment of soldiers wouldn't git Mike excited. He picked it up and come to the hole and hollered down, 'I've found a nugget!' 'How much?' I says. 'It may be forty, and it may be fifty.' 'Gosh darn,' says I, 'it'll go a *hunder* and fifty.' It went two hundred and twelve. It was like a frog. I called it 'The Frog.' I told him to take it to De-mars (a Frenchman who owns No. 8), and he'd give him double the price. Say, he'll kick him out of the house."

"Red" didn't know what would become of the new-comers. "They go out with toothpick shoes, fore-and-aft caps, half a pound of grub, and a bandanna handker-chief." Not much like an old-timer.

A man's real name is not of much consequence in this country. Not half a dozen men in camp know that "old man Harper's" front name is Arthur. Like as not some peculiarity of manner or appearance has instantaneously fixed a nickname upon a man, and the name has clung. "Swiftwater Bill" was plain William Gates. "Nigger Jim" in civilization was James Dougherty. And there is "Happy Jack," "Circle City Mickey," "Long Shorty," "Kink" Miller, "French Curly," "Skiff" Mitchell, "Siwash George," "Hootchinoo Albert," "Tom the Horse," "Dog-Salmon Bob," etc.

"Nick" Goff was one of those old-timers. Sixteen years ago he came into the Yukon, and has never once been "outside." For forty years altogether he has lived in the mines, and it is alleged that in all his life he never saw a railroad train. Last year he was asked why he didn't take a trip out to San Francisco for his health and see the sights, among the other things the fine hotels, where everything that a man could desire was done for his comfort. Nick listened attentively, and when the speaker was done he said: "You say they don't let a man cook his own meals and make his own bed?" "Why, no." "Then I ain't goin' to no place where I can't cook my own meals and make my own bed," and he didn't go.

Their sense of honor in the matter of debts is most strict, but, as unbusiness-like people often are, they are "touchy" about the presentation of a bill. This was one of the innovations of the new "N. A. T." Company which they inwardly resented. McQuesten gave credit whenever it was asked, and there is not a single instance where the bill was not paid when it was possible to do so. It was a keen understanding of the old-timer, his good traits and his prejudices, that endeared McQuesten to them, so that they spoke of him before any other man as the "Father of the Yukon."

HAIR-CUTTING

The credit system, while it often enabled the miners to tide a poor season, in the long run was neither to the advantage of the miner nor the company. Half of Circle City was in debt to McQuesten, and the miners turned their cabins over to the company when they stampeded for Klondike. As in the case of that other great monopolist, the Hudson's Bay Company, a nominal indebtedness on the books did not imply an actual loss, only so much less profit. As long as a man was in debt he would not leave the country, and as long as he stayed there the company was sure in time of getting about all he made, so that it was to the interest of the company to keep a man in debt. The advent of the new company at Forty-Mile, in 1892, immediately reduced prices, and compelled the supplying of better goods. Both companies undertook to do away with the credit system, but neither company has strictly enforced the rule.

But with all his whims and prejudices, the old-timer might serve as a model for courage and manliness and honor to some who pretend more. At the mines he is industrious and hard-working. It is only when he occasionally goes to town with a sack that he relaxes into often reckless dissipation. But when one has lived the dreary life, he has little blame in his heart for him who returns with empty " poke " and no apparent increase of wisdom.

The old-timers have been called "nondescripts." The new-comers are more distinguishable—photographers, newspaper men, physicians, mining engineers, farmers, lumbermen, and clerks. On one claim not far below Discovery, on Bonanza, a Salvation Army captain worked down in the hole, an ex-missionary turned the windlass and dumped the bucket, an archdeacon of the Church of England worked the rocker in the cabin, while the cook was a young man who had dealt faro.

I asked an old miner, foreman on a Bonanza claim, how Klondike compared with other places he had been in? He had been in California in 1852, and had mined in different parts of the world for fifty years. Said he: "In the Caribou country I saw 113 ounces [about $1921] of gold taken up in one pan of dirt, and I saw 102 pounds cleaned up in an eight-hour shift by five men.* But

---

* Equivalent to about $545—one man shovelling one hour. Assuming a rate of not over three hundred shovels an hour, the dirt would go about $1.80 to the shovel=$3.60 to the pan—phenomenally rich.

it was very limited, not over a mile of the rich dirt."
"Was it richer in Caribou than California?" " I have
seen spots in California—Scott's Bar, on Scott's River,
Siskiyou County—as rich as any in Caribou. Australia
does not compare, for the claims there are only ten feet
square. Thousands would be taken out of some holes,
but it was in spots ; some would get nothing."

We spent a week on Eldorado and Bonanza, returning
to our own cabin with a new experience and a higher ap-
preciation of the character of the class of men who ex-
plored and developed the Yukon.

DUMPING THE BUCKET

D AME FORTUNE was never in more capricious mood than when the golden treasures of the Klondike were ripe for discovery. The true story of that time, although so recent, is still obscured by the mists of uncertainty and contradiction, and there are still small points which the long and patient investigation I gave to the matter has not been able to clear up—such as exact dates—and it is doubtful that these ever will be. The first news of the discovery that reached the outside — even the official reports of Mr. Ogilvie — generally gave the credit of the discovery entirely to one Carmack, or "McCormick," as the miners call him. The story is fascinating from beginning to end, and in making this contribution to the history of that time I have been animated not less by a desire to gather together the scattered ends of report and hearsay than that tardy credit may be given to another man whom fortune, never more unkind, has thus far deprived of material compensation for a generous act and years of patient work.

The Klondike River had been known for many years, being only six miles from Fort Reliance, McQuesten's first post. According to Lieutenant Frederick Schwat-ka, who passed its mouth in 1883, it was known to the traders as " Deer River." Both Harper and McQuesten hunted moose in the present Bonanza Creek on the site of Discovery. Sixteen years ago a party of prospectors, among whom was General Carr, now of the State of

PROSPECTORS IN CAMP IN SUMMER

Washington, camped on the present Eldorado Creek. Other parties passed down the Klondike from the head-waters of Stewart River about the year 1886, but the river from its general appearance was not considered a gold-bearing stream, so year after year it was passed by for the more favored diggings of Forty-Mile and Birch Creek.

In the year 1890, one Joe Ladue, a French Canadian

originally from Plattsburg, New York, an agent of the Alaska Commercial Company, decided to establish an independent trading and outfitting post. Recognizing that his only chance was to grow up with a new region, and having faith that other creeks would be discovered as rich as the Forty-Mile diggings, he built the post, including a saw-mill in partnership with Mr. Harper, at the mouth of Sixty-Mile River, and began recommending all new-comers to prospect the bars or surface diggings of the latter stream, but more especially of Indian Creek or River, a stream entering the Yukon on the right or east side about twenty-five miles below his post, and thirty-three above the now abandoned Fort Reliance. For telling so-called "lies," especially about Indian Creek, Ladue was almost driven from Forty-Mile by the irate miners.

In the summer of 1894, among the crowd drawn in by the glowing reports from the Forty-Mile district was one Robert Henderson, hailing from the mines of Aspen, Colorado, of Scotch parentage, but a Canadian by birth, his father being lighthouse-keeper at Big Island, Pictou County, Nova Scotia. He was a rugged, earnest man, some thirty-seven years of age, six feet tall, with clear blue eyes. From boyhood he had been of an adventurous disposition, with a passion for gold-hunting that showed itself even at his Big Island home in solitary excursions about his bleak fisherman's isle, in which "Robbie," as he was called, was always looking for gold. Henderson had but ten cents in his pocket when he reached Ladue's post. Hearing what Ladue was saying about good diggings on Indian River, he said to Ladue: "I'm a determined man. I won't starve. Let me prospect for you. If it's good for me, it's good for you." Ladue gave him a grub-stake, and Henderson went upon Indian River and found it exactly as Ladue had said. He could make "wages," working the surface bars. On that account, he did not desert it for the just then more popular fields of Forty-Mile and Birch creeks, but determined to try again. With the experience of a miner, he knew that farther

ROBERT HENDERSON

on towards the heads of the tributaries of Indian River he would probably find coarse gold, though perhaps not on the surface, as it was on the river. Accordingly, the next summer found Henderson again on Indian River. He pushed on, and found "leaf" gold on what is now known as "Australia Creek," one of the main forks of

278

Indian River, seventy-five or eighty miles from the Yukon, one piece being, he says, as large as his thumbnail. Had he gone up the other fork sufficiently far he would have discovered the rich diggings of Dominion and Sulphur creeks. He returned to Sixty-Mile, and when winter came he put his goods on a sled, returned to Indian River, and went up Quartz Creek, a tributary of Indian River on the north, forty miles from the Yukon. Having had no dogs to help him, it was a very hard trip. It took thirty days for him to reach Quartz Creek. He worked all winter on Quartz Creek, and took out about $500, another $100 and more being taken out later by other parties from the same hole. In the spring he went back up in the direction of Australia Creek, getting only fair prospects, nothing that warranted the "opening up" of a claim. During this time Henderson was alone, having no partner, and depending mainly on the game that fell to his rifle. Returning from the head of the river he went up Quartz Creek again. This time he cast eyes longingly towards the ridge of hill at the head of Quartz Creek separating the waters of Indian River from those of the then almost unknown Klondike River. Crossing over the short, sharp divide (it is so sharp that if a cupful of water were poured upon the crest, one half would run one way, the other half the other way), he dropped down into a deep-cleft valley of a small stream running northward. He prospected, and found eight cents to the pan! That meant "wages"; such a prospect was then considered *good*. Enthusiastic over the find, Henderson went back over the divide. There were about twenty men on Indian River, working mostly on the bars at the mouth of Quartz Creek, some of them doing fairly well. Henderson persuaded three of the men — Ed Munson, Frank Swanson, and Albert Dalton—to go back with him.

The four men took over whip-saws, sawed lumber, built sluice - boxes, and "opened up" a claim in regular fashion about a quarter of a mile below the forks — a spot plainly visible from the divide—and began shovelling in the gold-bearing dirt.

He named the stream "Gold Bottom." It lay parallel with the present Bonanza Creek and entered the Klondike River about nine miles from its mouth. The amount

MOUTH OF KLONDIKE RIVER AT TIME OF THE STRIKE—CHIEF ISAAC'S SALMON-RACKS

that they shovelled in on Gold Bottom Creek was $750, *and that was the first gold taken out of Klondike.* It was equally divided between the four men. Now if a person had stood on the crest of the ridge and looked to the westward, he would have seen the valley of another large creek. That creek had never been prospected, but was known as "Rabbit Creek"; it was so close to Gold Bottom Creek that if one knows just the right spot on the divide, the cup of water would run not only into

Indian River and Gold Bottom Creek, but also into the source of this "Rabbit Creek." For in this manner the heads of a number of streams lie together, as the spokes of a wheel around the hub.

Early in August the party ran out of provisions, and, leaving the others at work, Henderson went down Indian River and back to Sixty-Mile. There were about a dozen men at the post and at Harper & Ladue's saw-mill, also a party who were on their way to Stewart River. Henderson told them what he had found. He persuaded the Stewart River party to turn back, telling them they would have to look for it, whereas he had *found it*. Ladue at once sent two horses overland with supplies, and all the others went with them excepting Ladue. Henderson repaired his boat, and with some supplies started down river, leaving Ladue to follow him. On account of low water he was unable to return up Indian River; besides, it was nearer by the mouth of the Klondike River.

GEORGE W. CARMACK

It was the fishing season. The salmon in the Yukon are very plentiful in August. Chief Isaac's Indians were taking the salmon in weirs and drying them on racks in the sun.

Across from the Indian village and a few hundred yards below the mouth of the river were the tents of a little party consisting of a white man and some Indians—a squaw, two Indian men, and a boy. The white man's name was George Washington Carmack; the squaw was his wife; the Indian men were respectively

281

Skookum Jim and Cultus (worthless) or "Takish" Charlie, while the boy was named K'neth—all Takish* Indians. Charlie was a big chief of the Takish. Jim would have been chief, being the son of the former chief,

SKOOKUM JIM

but among the Takish the descent is through the chief's sister. Jim and Charlie, therefore, though called brothers, were really cousins, and were called brothers-in-law of Carmack. This Carmack was originally a sailor on a man-of-war, but had taken up his abode with the Chilkoots at Dyea and married a Takish wife. Carmack liked the life with the Indians, and it used to be said that one couldn't please him more than to say, "Why, George, you're getting every day more like a Siwash!" "Siwash George" was the name by which he became generally known. Carmack had made excursions over the pass years before, and both he and the Indians, who were his inseparable companions, knew somewhat of mining, though they could hardly be called miners.

Carmack was outfitted by John J. Healy, who was then at Dyea to trade with the Takish and other interior Indians. Carmack built a post, still called "McCormick's Post," situated on the bank of the Yukon, about twenty miles above Five-Finger Rapids. Any one who took the trouble to stop there might have seen fastened against one of the rude log buildings a paper with some

* Same as Tagish—pronounced *Tah-keesk.*

writing upon it: "Gone to Forty-Mile for grub." Under the floor they might have found a bear-skin robe and some other things, left there when he started down river on the journey that was to make the name of Klondike known to the whole world. This notice was put up in the summer of 1895.

The white man and Indians secured an outfit at Fort Selkirk from Mr. Harper. The following spring Carmack dropped down to Forty - Mile, but presently returned as far as the mouth of the Klondike for the fishing, where he was joined by his Indians.* They set their nets just below the mouth of the Klondike, and were drying and curing their catch, Indian fashion, when Henderson came along, on his way to Gold Bottom.

As Henderson's boat touched shore he saw Carmack. "There," he thought, "is a poor devil who hasn't struck it." He went down to where Carmack was, told him of his prospects on Gold Bottom, and said to him that he had better come up and stake. At first Carmack did not want to go, but Henderson urged. At length Carmack consented to go, but wanted to take the Klondike Indians up also, as well as his own. Henderson demurred at that, and, being frank, may have said something not complimentary about "Siwashes" in general. It has been reported that Henderson said he "didn't intend to stake the whole Siwash tribe," and he added, "I want to give the preference to my old Sixty-Mile friends." What effect this may have had on subsequent events I do not know; I can only surmise that it did have some.

Next morning Henderson went on to his claim on

---

* Another white man, named Fritz Kloke, was also there fishing, and was drying fish under a rough shed of poles covered with canvas, which may be called the first white man's building on the site of what is now Dawson.

Gold Bottom. Carmack with two Indians followed soon, but, instead of taking the circuitous route by the mouth of Gold Bottom, went up "Rabbit Creek." Carmack arrived soon after Henderson, and showed some "colors" of gold that he had found on "Rabbit Creek." "Colors" and "pay" are by no means to be confounded. Traces, or "colors," of gold are to be found almost everywhere. The Indians and Carmack staked each a claim on Gold Bottom. When they were ready to go, Henderson asked Carmack if he intended to prospect on the way back, to which he replied that he did. Then Henderson asked him, if he found anything, to send back one of his Indians, saying that he had gold, and that he would pay him for the trouble; which, Henderson asserts, Carmack said he would do.

Leaving Henderson and his partners at work, Carmack returned homeward as he came. A few miles' walk along the bald crest of the divide brought him into the forks of "Rabbit Creek," some distance from its head. Five miles beyond, in the thick spruce - timbered valley, a tributary about as large as "Rabbit Creek" puts in on the left-hand side.

About half a mile below this large tributary the party stopped to rest. They had been panning here and there. Carmack, it is said, went to sleep; Skookum Jim, taking the pan, went to the "rim" of the valley at the foot of a birch-tree and filled it with dirt. Washing it in the creek, he found a large showing of gold. Right "under the grass - roots," Jim said, he found from ten cents to one dollar to the pan. In a little while, it is said, they filled a shot-gun cartridge with coarse gold. A strange circumstance was that this gold was not from bed-rock, which was many feet below the surface, nor even the present creek-bed, but, unsuspected by them, had slid

DISCOVERY CLAIM, BONANZA CREEK, SUMMER OF 1897

down from the "bench," or hill-side, a kind of diggings which were unknown at that time. Carmack staked off Discovery (a double claim) for himself, and five hundred feet above and below for his two Indian companions, Skookum Jim taking No. 1 above Discovery, and Cultus Charlie No. 1 below. The date of this is variously given as the 16th and 17th of August, the former date being generally regarded as the probable one.

After staking, they hastened to Forty-Mile, forgetting their promise to Henderson, who by every moral right was entitled to a claim near the rich ground they un-doubtedly had discovered. They recorded their claims before Inspector Constantine, the recorder or acting gold commissioner, and named the creek "Bonanza."

Carmack's own story of "$2.50 to the pan" was not be-lieved, though it was not doubted that he had found gold. A stampede followed. Drunken men were thrown into boats. One man was tied and made to go along. But there was no excitement beyond what attends a stam-pede for locations on any creek on which gold has been found. There are always persons about a mining camp ready to start on a stampede simply as a chance, wheth-er good prospects have been found or not. Whole creeks have been staked out in the belief that gold would sub-sequently be found. So the excitement of this earlier stage was of small significance. It was that of the pro-fessional "stampeder," so to speak—rounders about the saloons, some new arrivals, but few old miners, the latter being still in the diggings up the creek.

The first persons to arrive at the scene of the new dis-covery began staking down-stream. That also was a "stampeder's" custom. The chances were considered better there than above. It is all nonsense, the talk now of persons who would have one believe they "got in on choice locations" by reason of superior foresight. It was blind luck. The staking went on down-stream for six miles, and then began above, and continued for seven or eight miles up-stream before the side gulches, or "pups," as they are called, were thought of seriously.

Ladue, who had started for the mouth of the Klondike behind Henderson, was among the first to hear of Carmack's strike. Ladue staked a town-site at the mouth of the Klondike and started for Forty-Mile, but, meeting a man who wanted some lumber, he sent on his application by another party, returning to the mill at Sixty-Mile, and soon after returned to the mouth of the Klondike with nails, spikes, and lumber, built a rough warehouse, just opposite the present Alaska Commercial Company's warehouse, 22 × 40 feet, and a cabin—the first in Dawson —the name given the new town by the surveyor, Mr. Ogilvie, in honor of his chief, Dr. George M. Dawson, director of the Canadian Geological Survey. The Alaska Commercial Company's steamer *Arctic* having by this time reached Forty-Mile, bound for Fort Selkirk, pushed on through the ice that was running in the river to the new town, arriving in September with a few miners and a very limited amount of supplies. After discharging, she hurried back to Forty-Mile, but was frozen in before she could be placed in a safe place, and the next spring, in trying to get her free of the ice before she was crushed, a stick of dynamite, intended for the ice, destroyed her.

Among the first to hear of the strike were four men from up river—Dan McGilvray, Dave McKay, Dave Edwards, and Harry Waugh—and they located Nos. 3, 14, 15, and 16 below Discovery. These men did the *first sluicing* that was done on the creek, and they made the first clean-up, with five boxes set. The figures are lacking for their first shovelling, but on the second they cleaned up thirteen and a half ounces of gold ($329.50), being five hours' work of one man shovelling. The gold varied from the size of pinheads to nuggets, one of $12 being found. Now the Klondike magnifier began his work, with this curious result, that the " lies " of to-day were surpassed by the truth of to-morrow, until it came to be accepted that, " You can't tell no lies about Klondike." McGilvray and the rest had perhaps $1500—surely a large sum for the time they had worked. Ladue weighed the gold, and as he came out of the store he said to some assembled miners, " How's that for two and a half days' shovelling-in—$4008 ?" The liability to exaggeration about a mining camp is so great that it is impossible for any one to escape who writes or speaks in the midst of affairs concerning any specific find. A man with a town-site must also be allowed a great deal of latitude in such matters. But soon the joke was on the other side. Men actually on the spot would not believe anything they heard. Two of the men working on Indian River came down and heard of the strike. Said one to his partner, " Shall we go up and stake ?" Replied the other, " Why, I wouldn't go across the river on that old Siwash's word " (meaning Carmack). They went on down to Forty-Mile. Another party, one of whom was Swan Peterson, who bought in on No. 33 Eldorado, came along at the same time, and argued for three hours at the mouth of the Klondike whether they should go up, and finally went on to Circle City.

There were few old-timers in the procession. *They* knew all about Klondike. It was nothing but a "moose-pasture." It was not like other places where they had seen gold. They climbed the hills and walked along the divide until they could look down into the valley of

T   289

Bonanza. Here many of them stopped and threw up their hands in disgust. Others went the round of the creek, cursing and swearing at those who told them to come there. One old-timer got up as far as No. 20 above, where the last stakes were. He surveyed the prospect, and as he turned away remarked, "I'll leave it to the Swedes." (The Swedes were supposed to be willing to work the poorest ground.) Another, or it may have been the same, is said to have written on the stakes of No. 21, not the usual "I claim," etc., but, "*This moose-pasture is reserved for the Swedes and Chechahkoes.*" Louis Rhodes staked it right afterwards. After he had written his name he said to his companions, being ashamed of staking in such a place, that he would cut his name off for two bits (25 cents). The next summer he took out forty-four thousand and odd dollars.

But all that and much more was hidden in the future. A Klondike claim was not considered worth anything. One-half interest in one of the richest Eldorado claims was sold for a sack of flour. A few thousand dollars could have bought up the creek from end to end.

Some who had provisions remained to prospect, others returned to Forty-Mile, just as the miners were coming in from the diggings, to learn for the first time of a strike on Klondike. Among these was a Swede by the name of Charlie Anderson. By the time Anderson reached the new diggings there was nothing left. After a fruitless attempt to reach a distant creek from which gold had been reported, he returned discouraged to Dawson. There a gambler approached him and said, "Charlie, don't you want to buy a claim?" "I don't care if I do. How much do you want?" "I'll let you have No. 29 on Eldorado for $800." "I'll take it," replied Anderson, who had taken out a considerable sum that summer from a

THE SCENE OF CARMACK'S DISCOVERY—DISCOVERY CLAIM AS IT APPEARED IN AUGUST, 1898

claim on Miller Creek, at the head of Sixty-Mile River, and he weighed out the dust. The enterprising salesman went about boasting how he had played Charlie for a "sucker," only he wanted some one to kick him for not having asked him $1200. He believed he could have got it just as easily as he did the $800. The man who sold the claim is still a poor man. When Eldorado began to "prove up," even Anderson could not realize the enormous value of his claim, from which there will come out $400,000, if the remaining two-fifths are as rich as the three-fifths that have been worked thus far. Eldorado was not liked as well as Adams Creek, just below it. A late-comer went up Adams, found a man staking for himself and family (by this time the real excitement had begun). Said the late-comer : " I've come a good way. What you are doing is illegal, and I want a claim and mean to have one." The man who was staking told him he would like to have his friends near him, and offered him the stakes of No. 15 Eldorado, if that would do as well. It was accepted. Nothing more than "wages" has yet been found on Adams.

How was the news of the Klondike discovery received on the lower river? Forty-Mile, the seat of the recorder, was of course the first to hear all the reports and rumors. This can best be told in the words of one who was in Forty-Mile town at the time. "Nobody believed any of the first reports about gold on the Klondike. You see, there never was any money in the lower country. A man would come in after a hard summer's work with a 'poke' [sack] that a man would be ashamed of here in Dawson. They owed the stores for their last year's outfit, and they'd pay for that and get credit on next year's outfit. The stores had rather have it that way than not. They were sure a man would not leave the country without paying, or with a small stake, so they'd be sure sooner or later of getting all he made. They were a pretty good class of men in the lower country, and most of them could get credit. A man would come into a saloon, and all he'd have would be one drink or one dance. You'd never see them asking up three or four at once to drink. Why, there weren't but three men in Forty-Mile that could afford to get drunk. They did nothing all winter but sit around where it was warm, playing pedro, solitaire, and casino. Word came to Forty-Mile that Louis Rhodes had two men working for him, and was getting good pay. 'That's a lie,' said one man. 'Louis Rhodes! when was *he* able to hire two men?' Next word came down that Ben Wall was getting two-bit dirt. 'Hell!' says Nigger Jim; 'I've known Ben Wall these ten years, and he's the all-firedest liar in the Yukon.' When they heard that Berry was getting $1 to the pan, they laughed. Klondike was a bunco — nothing but a bunco." These words were spoken in what the miners called "josh," but they were true, nevertheless.

Circle City, 170 miles farther away than Forty-Mile, did not get the news so soon. The first report that reached Circle was of a discovery on Klondike—an ounce to the "shovel," shovelling off the surface. This, in miners' parlance, meant that one man had shovelled into the sluice-boxes gold to the value of one ounce ($17) per day. The next news was when Sam Bartlett came down with a raft of logs which he had failed to land at Forty-Mile. Bartlett said it was a "bilk"; that Joe Ladue was only trying to get men up to his town-site—he had stopped there, but would not stake. The next news came to Oscar Ashby, a saloon-keeper, from a friend, about the middle of November. The river was then

A TYPICAL CLAIM IN ELDORADO—SUMMER OF 1897

closed, and the letter came down over the ice.* There were about seventy-five men in Oscar's saloon when the letter was read. It was somewhat to this effect, telling Ashby to buy all the property he could on Klondike, it did not make any difference what the prices were: "This is one of the richest strikes in the world. It is a world-beater. I can't tell how much gold we are getting to the pan. I never saw or heard of the like of such a thing in my life. I myself saw $150 panned out of one pan of dirt, and I think they are getting as high as $1000." The crowd in the saloon had a big laugh, and thought so little of it that they never spoke of it again. "It disgusted them that men were so crazy as to write that way," to quote the words of one who was present. Soon after another letter came. This time it was to Harry Spencer and Frank Densmore, from a party with whom they were well acquainted. Densmore at once fitted out a dog-team and went up. After he got up he wrote back to Spencer, relating all the particulars. He repeated the words of the others —namely, that he really could not tell what they *were* finding: it was immensely rich; he had never seen anything like it. Now Spencer and Densmore had large interests in Circle City, so the men knew it could be no lie; they were compelled to believe it. The wildest stampede resulted. Every dog that could be bought, begged, or stolen was pressed into service, and those who could not get dogs started hauling their own sleds, men and even women, until in two weeks there were not twenty people left in Circle, and of those some were cripples and could not travel. In a short while there were not even

* Tom O'Brien and the general manager of the Alaska Commercial Company made the 250 trail-miles or more in a few hours over five days, travelling light, with basket sleigh and dogs — a record trip.

that number left, a report giving the actual number as two men and one woman. Those who had claims deserted them, and those who had outfits took what they could haul and left the rest in a cache, where they are to this day. One man, William Farrel, of No. 60 above on Bonanza, left a thousand dollars' worth of provisions, five full claims on one creek, and fully a dozen other interests, all considered good prospects; and, says he, "I haven't paid any attention to them since." By the time the Circle City crowd arrived Bonanza was staked to No. 60 below and into the 60's above, and also the side creeks, Eldorado and Adams. So that the late-comers had to go into the side-gulches, or else buy in, which latter many of them did, so that on such as Eldorado it soon came about that few of the original stakers were left, having sold out at ridiculous prices.

There were from three to four hundred miners at work about Circle City, and nearly all had money, the United States mint returns giving the amount of gold cleaned up that season in Birch Creek as $900,000!

The first mail that went outside by dog-team carried letters to friends and relatives, advising them that a big strike had been made. It reached them in January and February, and they started. Crossing the pass in spring, they came down on the high-water in June, and, though unable to get in on the main creeks, many of them located other creeks that are showing up rich. That the report of a strike of this magnitude should have been common property outside six months before the excitement is clear proof that the world's acute attack of insanity was caused by the adroit manipulation of the story of the miners' arrival by sensational newspapers, as the result of rivalry and to boom the Alaska outfitting business.

But where were Henderson and his partners while Bonanza and Eldorado were being staked?

Bonanza was staked into the 80's above and Eldorado to No. 33—or over three miles—when a party of miners, including George Wilson and James McNamee, went over the divide to Gold Bottom, where Henderson was still working.

Henderson asked them where they were from. They replied, " Bonanza Creek."

Henderson says that he did not want to display his ignorance. He had never heard of " Bonanza " Creek. At length he ventured to ask where " Bonanza " Creek was. They pointed over the hill.

" ' Rabbit Creek !' What have you got there ?"

" We have the biggest thing in the world."

" Who found it ?"

" McCormick."

It is said Henderson threw down his shovel and went and sat on the bank, so sick at heart that it was some time before he could speak.

There was nothing left for Henderson. Many another man would have been utterly discouraged. It is true, however, that there was very rich ground for a mile farther up on Eldorado, but the extent of the richness of the new creeks was not then suspected. Nor did Henderson's ill-fortune end here. He had been over the ridge, upon a large fork of Gold Bottom, and made discoveries, one of which amounted to 35 cents to the pan. He staked a claim there, according to the law then in force—one full claim, and another to which he was entitled by virtue of discovery. After cleaning up on Gold Bottom and dividing the money between his partners, he staked a discoverer's double claim and started for Forty-Mile, as winter was coming on. On the way he met

Andrew Hunker, a German by birth, who had staked and recorded No. 31 below on Bonanza Creek, and Charles Johnson, an Ohio man, who had staked No. 43 below on the same creek. They told Henderson that they had made a discovery of $3 to the pan on the other fork of Henderson's "Gold Bottom." They had staked between them Discovery and No. 1 above and No. 1 below, on September

STRIPPING THE MUCK OFF "SUMMER DIGGINGS"

6th. This was two miles below Henderson's discovery. They told Henderson they thought he could not hold Discovery as against them, and as their new find was apparently better than his own, he staked No. 3 above. This fork was first called Hunker's Fork of Gold Bottom, and was so shown on maps of that time. But as the subsequent staking began at Hunker's discovery, the whole creek to its mouth at the Klondike was recorded as Hunker Creek, Gold Bottom becoming a fork of Hunker

Creek. At Bear Creek, between Hunker and the Yukon, where Solomon Marpak, a Russian Finn, had just made a discovery, Henderson stopped and staked a claim. When he reached Forty-Mile, Henderson learned that instead of being allowed a claim on each separate creek, a new mining regulation just received from Ottawa provided that no person could hold more than one claim in a mining "district," the Klondike River and all its tributaries being considered a "district." Sixty days from the time of staking was allowed in which to record, and Henderson applied, he maintains, within the time, and there is no reason for doubting his general statement. Although his record is imperfect, much latitude must be allowed men who are isolated for months and necessarily have hazy ideas of dates. In general there is no doubt but that at the time Henderson drove his stakes he was entitled to either four or five claims, according as he chose his locations, on Hunker Creek, and the law which thus deprived him came into force between the time he staked and the day he reached Forty-Mile. And, I would ask, how could Henderson—and I would include all of his class, the hardy prospectors who were the real developers of the Yukon, who have given to Canada all that is at present shown to be of value there—how could he have made the original discoveries, that paved the way for the development of the great riches of Klondike, if he had remained, say, at Forty - Mile town, where he could have kept posted on changes in the mining law made from time to time at Ottawa ?

Hunker's discovery being better than his own, Henderson recorded No. 3 alone. He was laid up that winter, unable to work, from an injury he met with on Indian River. In the spring, far from being disheartened, and with energy and faith characteristic of the man, he took his tools, boat, and some provisions and went up the Klondike forty miles, to a large tributary then called "Too Much Gold," but known now as "Flat" Creek, prospecting. He soon returned and proceeded to a large creek, two miles below the mouth of Stewart River, and, eleven miles above the mouth of the creek, made a discovery of 10 cents to the pan, the creek being subsequently named "Henderson" Creek. From there he ascended the Stewart River a long distance, prospecting. Being favorably impressed by the outlook, he staked a town-site at the mouth of McQuesten Creek, eighty miles from the mouth of Stewart, and on his return made an application for the same to Ottawa. For some cause he received no reply to the application. (The town-site has since been taken up and stores built there.) Returning to the new camp which had sprung up at the mouth of the Klondike, he took steamer, intending to leave the country, but was frozen in with the rest of the refugees at Circle City. He was under the doctor's care all winter. Obliged to realize some money, he sold No. 3 above Discovery on Hunker Creek for $3000—a mere fraction of its value. Henderson, miner that he is, would have worked this claim had he been able to do so, and he would still have found himself in possession of a comfortable fortune, and thereby received some compensation for his many discouragements.

Although he did not himself make the discovery on Bonanza, he was yet the direct cause and means of that discovery being made. He was not the victim of his own negligence or failure to grasp an opportunity. He created the opportunity, and was prevented from profiting by it. It is beside the point, but yet of interest, that I have it, on Henderson's own word, which I am not disposed to question, that it was his intention, when done with Gold

TYPICAL SUMMER DIGGINGS (29 ELDORADO)

Bottom, to go down Rabbit Creek prospecting. When the news of the wonderful richness of Bonanza burst upon the world, Henderson was forgotten. Mr. Ogilvie, then at Forty-Mile, kept his government posted concerning the developments of that fall. Mr. Ogilvie gave the best information at his command. Carmack had made the discovery on Bonanza Creek : Henderson's part was not then understood, and Henderson was no man to press himself forward. But later Mr. Ogilvie gave the man full credit in the following words .

"The Klondike was prospected for forty miles up in 1887, without anything being found, and again in 1893, with a similar lack of result; but the difference is seen when the right course is taken, and this was led up to by Robert Henderson. This man is a born prospector, and you could not persuade him to stay on even the richest claim on Bonanza. He started up in a small boat to spend this summer and winter on Stewart River prospecting. This is the stuff the true prospector is made of, and I am proud to say he is a Canadian."*

When I first met Henderson I was impressed by the earnestness of the man. I asked him if he was not discouraged by all that had happened.

"No," replied he, "there are as rich mines yet to be discovered as any that have been found."

I was not quite sure that he believed that, but it was characteristic of the man to say so.

In October, 1898, I saw Henderson for the last time. He had just reached Seattle from the Yukon. Unsuspicious and trusting, he had been robbed on the steamer of all the money he had—$1100. He had one thing left. It was the golden (carpenter's) rule and myrtle-leaves badge of the Yukon Order of Pioneers, of which he was

* Extract from Victoria *Colonist*, November 6, 1897.

a member. For some reason he insisted on pinning it himself upon my vest, saying, "You keep this. I will lose it too. I am not fit to live among civilized men." He returned to Aspen, where his wife and child were, to work again at the same mine where he worked six years ago, before he went into the Yukon. Surely, if the Minister of the Interior could from Ottawa grant hundreds of miles of claims, supposed to be of great value, to men who never saw and never will see the Yukon, surely it would be a graceful act for him yet to do something for this man, who scorns to be a beggar and to whom the offer of a pension would be an insult as long as he can tramp and dig and look. Canada owes not less to Henderson than California to Marshall, the discoverer of gold at Sutter's mill.

The miners who knew have always given Henderson credit. "Siwash George would be fishing yet at the mouth of the Klondike if it hadn't been for Bob Henderson."

A DAWSON BAGGAGE EXPRESS

CHAPTER XV

AFTER Bonanza began to show up richer
than anything before known in the
Yukon, many who did not believe
the ground was particularly valuable until the true nature of the strike was
made evident by the labor of others began
to realize what good judgment they had
shown in picking out such "choice locations." To those who by mere chance held
their claims until after the first work was
done it matters little that the first opinion of Klondike
was poor, but upon those who thought the amount of a
year's "grub-stake" fair pay for a few days' hard travelling the sight of fortunes taken from ground they themselves had staked can well be imagined. If the truth
were to be confessed, the reason there were not more
sales was that there were few buyers. As the claims
"proved up," the buyer, conservative and cautious, was
nearly always a lap behind the seller, and when prices
rose into thousands and tens of thousands it is no wonder there was no basis of calculation. It was as easy to
believe there was a million or four millions as one hundred thousand dollars in a single claim. When a rich
claim on upper Bonanza sold for $3500 at Forty-Mile, a

well-known old-timer left the room where the sale was being negotiated, saying he "wouldn't stay and see an honest man buncoed."

No. 31 Eldorado was sold by the original stakers for $100, $80 being cash. Within six months it sold for $31,000, and one year later the owner refused $150,000. One-half of No. 30 Eldorado, it is said, was sold for a sack of flour. The owners, big Alec McDonald and Billy Chappel, did not think enough of it to work it themselves, but rather late in the season put it out on a "lay," and took a "lay" themselves on another claim. The "laymen" struck it the first hole, and out of thirty burnings took out $40,000.

On account of the distance to the seat of the recorder, the miners agreed upon a temporary recorder from among their own number (after the United States custom). They paid this man $2 for each claim, agreeing to pay in due season the $15 required by Canadian law. When he began to measure the claims, by some trick a 40-foot rope was introduced instead of a 50-foot one, which shortened each claim by 50 feet or more, and left fractions between, which by this time were of value. These were seized upon and staked the same as full claims, but when the deception was found out there was a big row, and Mr. William Ogilvie was called from Forty-Mile to settle the trouble. Mr. Ogilvie, being a magistrate, took testimony; the men repented, confessed, and were forgiven; and then Mr. Ogilvie made a partial survey of Bonanza and Eldorado. But many of the claims on Bonanza were short.

One of these short claims, however, was not the fault of the official measurer. It was on lower Bonanza—I never knew the exact spot; it was where the creek twisted very much and the valley was broad. The staker was a mounted policeman. He should have measured 500 feet in the direction of the valley, but not being able to see the direction, perhaps on account of the thick woods, he followed the winding creek. When the surveyor threw lines across the valley corresponding to his upper and lower stakes, the poor policeman had six feet less than a claim !

"Micky" Wilkins staked a claim near Discovery. "Micky" was not one of those who were thrown into boats and brought along against their will from Forty-Mile in the first stampede, but he *was* one of a party who helped tie a drunken man and throw him into a boat. "Micky" sold out for a few hundred dollars. When the claim was surveyed the new owner found only a few inches. I felt sorry for all who sold at the very start until I met "Micky."

A fraction of a claim would hardly seem worth having; but John Jacob Astor Dusel, who staked No. 2 above on Bonanza, was a good miner, and he wanted to take in the mouth of Skookum Gulch. Dick Lowe put the tape to Dusel's claim and found it about 78 feet too long, and took for himself a narrow slice directly opposite the mouth of Skookum. He did not think much of it at the time. He wanted $900 for it. No one was so foolish as to pay so much for the narrow strip of ground. He tried to let it out on a " lay," but no one wanted to work it for an interest. He had to work it himself, poor man ! The first hole was put down by his present foreman, and he did not find a cent. Further account of what is probably the richest piece of ground in the whole Klondike must be left till later, when he was sending the gold down on pack-horses.

On Eldorado the claims were almost all over 500 feet. It was as if they were measured by guess while on the run, and then a lot more added to make sure. No. 37 was 420 feet too long. Several fractions are from 100 to 160 feet in length. Sometimes the second man did not measure his fraction correctly, and a third man found and staked another slice. Nothing on Eldorado was too small. There is one 10-foot fraction

SLUICING THE WINTER DUMPS

thought to be worth $10,000 to $20,000. A 13-foot fraction was found next to No. 14. It was so narrow that the owner had to take a "lay" of 37 feet on the adjoining claim in order to work it.

Nor was all the luck confined to the mines. A butcher named "Long Shorty," otherwise Thorp, drove cattle in over the Dalton trail, and was trying to reach Forty-Mile late in the fall with the meat on a raft in the ice. He was frozen in at the mouth of the Klondike,

310

only to discover there a big mining - camp. That beef was a godsend to the miners, as provisions were very scarce. Flour had to be freighted with dogs from Forty-Mile, and sold at from $40 to $60 a fifty-pound sack. Beef was $1 to $2 a pound. Mining - tools also were scarce, shovels bringing $17 to $18 each. But wages were proportionately high, $1.50 to $2 an hour being paid for common labor, and often not to be had at that price. Wages were high, not because of the expense of living, but because of the opportunities for individual effort.

The first hole to be put down by burning is credited to Skookum Jim. Pages could be filled with the finds that day by day were made on those claims that were worked that winter. A personage known to fame as "Swiftwater Bill" took a 100-foot "lay" on No. 13 Eldorado. Seven holes were put down before the pay was struck (though many think there was pay in one of the first holes, and that they filled it up). At any rate, the buyer asked the price—$45,000—and with six others he bought the claim, paid $10,000 down, put in a rocker, and paid for the claim in six weeks.

Any claims not recorded within sixty days were open for relocation. There were several such claims left vacant by men who considered them no good, and who recorded elsewhere. Such a claim was No. 40 above on Bonanza. It was generally known that the claim was open, and a mounted policeman was there, with watch in hand, to announce when exactly twelve o'clock midnight came. It was in January. There were several parties on foot, and two men had dog outfits. Promptly at midnight all hands staked and started. One Lereaux and a companion, Vaughan, ran to No. 48 above, where one team was waiting. Lowerie, the other dog - man, started on the run for Dawson, where an Indian with five or six dogs was in waiting. Lereaux had the same number. At Dawson they were not far apart. Both were splendid teams, but dogs are poor things to race with, as every one knows. A dog has no ambition to pass ahead, like a horse; he prefers to follow. Besides, when the trail is narrow, it is hard for one team to pass another. They probably could not have passed each other at all, but it happened that every time they came to a cabin the leading team insisted on turning out, whereupon the hind team would seize the opportunity to dash by. When they reached Forty-Mile, Lowerie and the Indian were ahead. The Indian runner did not know the recorder's office was across the creek, or else the dogs determined to turn into Forty-Mile town. Lowerie saw the mistake, jumped from his sleigh, and made for the recorder's office on the dead run, with Lereaux just even with him. Both men reached the office at the same moment and fell against the door. They were both so exhausted that for a while they could not say what they had come for. When they recovered sufficient breath to announce their business, Captain Constantine told them he would wait to see if there were others behind; and, no one else coming, he divided the claim between them.

A detachment of mounted police came up to Dawson in the late winter or spring, bringing the record-books with them. Certificates of registry of that time were in manuscript, there being no printed blanks until later.

Wild scenes followed the clean-up. Men with never a penny to spare in their lives were suddenly made rich. There was no real disorder, there were no shootings, no hold-ups, none of the things associated in the popular mind with a real live mining-camp. Something in the

Yukon air discourages all that. It could not be the presence of the police, for there were no police at Circle City, and only a baker's dozen at Dawson. Gold flowed, and when it would not flow it was sowed, literally sowed, broadcast in drunken debauch over the sawdust floors of the saloons as if there were no end to the supply. Gold was panned out of the sawdust—whole saloonfuls of men would be asked up to drink, at half a dollar a drink. Sometimes orders were given to call in the town, and then the bartender would go out into the street and call everybody in, and all would have to drink. Whenever one of the new "millionaires" was backward in treating, which was not often, the crowd—always a good-natured one—would pick him up by the legs and arms and swing him like a battering-ram against the side of the house until he cried out "Enough!" There had never been seen anything like it before, nor will anything quite to equal it ever be seen again.

The afore-mentioned "Swiftwater Bill," whose chief claim to attention seems to have been the way he "blew in" money and the ease with which—speaking in the vernacular of the mining-camp—his "leg could be pulled" by the fair sex, spent $40,000, and had to borrow $5000 to go outside with. His claim was good for it, though. He quarrelled with his "lady friend," and, observing her order eggs in a restaurant, he bought up every egg in town—no fewer than nine hundred in all—at a cost of $1 each. He wore his *mukluks* in the streets of San Francisco, threw money into the streets, and, in other ways ostentatiously displayed his new wealth, his vanity and craving for notoriety making him ridiculous even in Dawson.

How much gold came out of the ground that first summer can never be known. Two and a half millions is probably not far from the mark. The richness of the fifteen miles reported by Mr. Ogilvie was much exaggerated. The pans of dirt that he saw washed out gave him reason for believing, upon computation, that there might be, as he stated, actually $4,000,000 in each claim. But these were not averages. Far, far from it. Nor was the enormous cost of working the richest, yet costliest, diggings in the Yukon taken into consideration, as it should have been; this might have prevented the imposition of the iniquitous laws of a Canadian cabinet, confessedly ignorant of the rudiments of gold-placer mining, and who, like the rest of the world, lost their heads in contemplating the richness of the country.

J. J. Clements panned out of four pans $2000, the largest being reported at $775. Clarence Berry showed gold in bottles that he said represented, respectively, $560, $230, and $175 pans. There were many others like these. Of course, they were picked and scraped off bedrock, and did not represent average dirt; $5, even $1, "straight," as it is called, would be enormously rich.

If the pay-streak were 100 feet wide and 3 feet deep, there would be 150,000 cubic feet, equal to, say, 675,000 pans of dirt. Think what an average of $1 to the pan, or even 25 cents, would be!

"Jimmie the Tough," otherwise McMann, got a "lay" on No. 15 above on Bonanza, sold dump in spring for $35,000, spent $28,000 in one bar-bill alone, and went out with $6000 to San Francisco; returning, landed at Dyea with $1200, invested in whiskey at $25 a gallon, landed at Dawson with $588, got drunk and spent $500 in one week, and then went down to Fort Yukon after grub with the rest of the crowd.

One hundred and thirty thousand dollars came out of the Berry-Anton claim No. 6 and the fraction. On No. 11

Eldorado five box-lengths cleaned up $61,000. Some say that they took out $15,000 to $20,000 to a box-length, one man, two shifts, shovelling twenty hours. There were spots on Bonanza as rich as Eldorado, but not so even and regular. One thousand dollars to the foot is the top figure, on an average, for best of Eldorado, but the cost is one-third for taking it out. The first year showed nuggets of all sizes up to one of $585 (estimated at 1 oz. = $17) from No. 36 Eldorado.

Not all the fortunate ones started for civilization with their new wealth. Many remained to work their claims, and these—perhaps not less happy or exultant—were not heard of outside in the excitement that accompanied the breaking of the good news to the world. The bulk of the gold, amounting to about $1,500,000, went out to St. Michael's, where waited the good steamer *Portland*, of the North American Transportation and Trading Company, and the *Excelsior*, of the Alaska Commercial Company, crowded with friends and relatives of the returning miners. Others, in parties of three and five, took to their poling-boats, and it was some of these, and still others fleeing for their lives from the threatened famine, that we met on our way in.

HOW ELDORADO WAS STAKED AND NAMED

The following account of how Eldorado was staked and named was given me by William D. Johns, formerly a newspaper man, but now a Klondike miner. Mr. Johns was in the neighborhood of Forty-Mile when word of Carmack's discovery arrived, and was one of those who did not believe the report. He was, therefore, not in the first stampede.

"Bonanza was staked as far down as the 80's and as far up as the 70's, but I determined to go anyway and try some of the 'pups,' believing it is never too late in a camp as new as this.

"Fred Bruceth, the man with whom I planned to go, said it was no use. So when, on the morning of the day that we were to start from Forty-Mile, we found that our boat had been stolen, he threw up his hands and refused to go. But upon inquiry I found that it was still possible for us to go. I found some men who owned a boat, and they told us that if certain parties to whom they had promised the use of it did not return in fifteen minutes we could take the boat.

"The men did not turn up, and in half an hour we were towing the boat up the Yukon. Only two weeks before we had passed the mouth of the Klondike and camped on the site of the present Dawson. At that very time Siwash George was making his discovery on Bonanza—of course unknown to us. On the third day we reached the mouth of the Klondike, and camped in our old camping-place, and the next morning, after making a cache of our supplies, and taking a pack, crossed the mouth of the Klondike to the Indian village (where Klondike City now is), and then took a trail which leads over the hills and along the ridge parallel with Bonanza. After a hard tramp we reached Discovery in the afternoon. Siwash George and three Indians were working at the side of the bank, sluicing with two boxes in the crudest sort of way. I took a pan, and panned my first gold in Klondike, off the side of the bank, getting 50 cents. We went on to No. 3 above Discovery, and made camp under a brush shelter. That night two men, Anton (his full name is Anton Stander, an Austrian) and Frank Keller, whom we had seen before on the Yukon, came to our camp, and sat by our fire for an hour and a half talking. Anton told us their camp was farther up—

" WINTER DIGGINGS "

Shovelling gold-bearing gravel off the dumps into the sluice-boxes, Bonanza Creek

on upper Bonanza we inferred. They said they had found 10 cents to the pan on upper Bonanza, and they advised us to try there.

"Next morning we took our packs, and with two others, Knut Halstead and John Ericson, both Norwegians, prospected along till we got into the 30's. There we left everything but picks, shovels, and pans, and went up into the 70's, a distance of rather more than seven miles from Discovery. We prospected as we went, but found nothing. The boys agreed in declaring that if the ground had not been already staked they would not take the trouble to do so themselves. We returned to camp, and decided to prospect a large 'pup' that came in just above on No. 7. Our attention had been drawn to this 'pup' before we got to Discovery, on the day of our arrival, by meeting two men going down the creek.

"They were a party of four Miller Creek men. We asked them, 'How's the creek?'

"'No good,' 'Skim diggings,' 'Bar diggings,' 'Moose flat,' were the answers received.

"'Did you stake on the creek?' we asked.

"'No,' they replied.

"'Where are Demars and Louis Empkins?' we asked, referring to the two other members of their party.

"'Oh, they have gone up a "pup" to stake.'

"'Why didn't you stake?'

"'Oh, to hell with the "pups!"' was their answer as they went away down the creek.

"Pretty soon we met Demars and Empkins. 'Where have you been?' we asked.

"'On that "pup,"' they replied.

"'Any good?'

"'Don't know anything about it; as long as we were up, we thought we might as well stake somewhere,' and they hurried on after their companions. They were rich men, but they did not know it.

"Next morning, before we were ready to start, Keller came down to our camp dressed in corduroys and with a rifle on his shoulder, as if he were starting out on a hunt. He inquired how we had made out. We told him we had found nothing. He still favored Bonanza ; he thought it was all right. We asked him where his camp was ; we had not seen it the day before. 'Over on the other side,' he replied, indicating the way, and we thought no more of it then. 'Where are you going to-day ?' he asked us. 'To prospect that "pup,"' I replied ; 'do you know anything about it ?'

"'Oh, I found a five-cent piece* on rim rock, about a mile up.'

"He left us. We still thought he was off on a little hunt.

"We started towards the 'pup.' When we reached the mouth, Fred Bruceth stopped and pointed to the brook.

"'Some one is working ; the water is muddy,' said he.

"Like hunters who have scented game, we lapsed into silence, and, with eyes and ears alert, kept on. We had gone only a little way when suddenly we came upon four men. Three of them were standing around the fourth, who was holding a gold-pan. All were intently looking into the pan. The man with the pan was Anton, and the other three were J. J. Clements, Frank Phiscater, and old man Whipple. When they looked up and saw us, they acted like a cat caught in a cream-pitcher. Seeing that we had found them out, they loosened up and told us all they knew. They showed us then what they had in the pan. There was not less than 50 cents.

* Five cents to the pan—scant wages.

While we were talking, along came Keller. He had taken off his corduroys and was in his working-clothes, his attempt to steer us away having been a failure. The five men had staked off their claims.* Anton's was the highest up the creek. Above his were the two claims that Empkins and Demar had staked.

"Anton told Ericson that he might have his claim, as he was going to take Discovery claim. We all went up to stake. Pretty soon Anton came all a-sweating and begged and pleaded with Ericson for his claim back, as the old man Whipple had declared that no one should have Discovery but himself. Ericson cut his name off the stakes, and Anton restaked the claim—the present No. 6 Eldorado. Ericson went above Empkins and Demars (Nos. 7 and 8) and staked No. 10. Bruceth and I went on far enough to be out of the way of a clash and staked—he taking No. 11, and I No. 12.

"Regarding the discovery, it was the custom in the lower country—not only on the American side, but within Canadian territory—to allow a discovery (consequently a double claim) upon each gulch. But the edict had recently gone forth from Forty-Mile that there could be but one discovery on a creek, and none on a 'pup' of a main creek. The discovery had been allowed to Siwash George, so that there could be no discovery claim on this fork.

"Another custom was that if a person, after having

* Whipple was No. 1; Phiscater, No. 2; Clements, No. 4; Keller, No. 5; and Anton, No. 6. "Discovery" was the present No. 3. Empkins, in relating to me how he got in on Eldorado, said that he and his three companions had come up the "pup" and found Anton and the others, and they had a small prospect on the surface, but they were told it was not encouraging. On that account two of the party did not stake. Empkins sold a share in the claim to Fred Hutchinson, and last spring received $100,000 for the remaining interest.

staked in one place, wished to locate in another, he must, before he could hold the second, cut his name off the first. Anton and Keller had already staked on upper Bonanza, and so might have been sincere in recommending that part of the creek as good. While, according to old custom, they might have held a discovery on Eldorado, they could not legally do so now. Consequently, Halstead

VIEW FROM THE BOTTOM OF A "CUT," SUMMER DIGGINGS
(NO. 12 ELDORADO)

promptly jumped the so-called 'discovery' claim that Whipple was trying to reserve for himself, still leaving him, however, with one claim on the 'pup,' besides his Bonanza claim. He was stoutly trying to hold all three.

"A party of Finns soon came along, headed by a man named Cobb. They did not stake, but went on and turned up Bonanza. They were the only other persons on the creek that day. That night in camp we discussed nam-

ing the new creek. Old man Whipple wanted it called
'Whipple Creek.' But we were rather hot at the Whipple crowd for having used us so ill in trying to steer us

ONE MILLION FIVE HUNDRED THOUSAND DOLLARS IN GOLD-
DUST, IN NORTH AMERICAN TRANSPORTATION AND TRAD-
ING COMPANY'S WAREHOUSE

away from the creek; and, besides, old man Whipple had
once tried to jump Halstead and Ericson's claim on
American Creek. After several names were mentioned,

Knut Halstead suggested ' Eldorado,' and that was the name determined upon. I make this point, as certain later comers have claimed the honor of naming the creek.

" Next morning Fred Bruceth got up at five o'clock and went down after McKay, whom the miners had appointed as their recorder, letting out the news on the way. Among the first to arrive were Cobb and his crowd. Hearing of the prospect, and knowing that the Whipple crowd had staked Bonanza also, Cobb stated emphatically to Whipple that unless his crowd took their names off Bonanza he would jump their claims here. Just then Anton, Clements, and Keller came up to where we were talking, and Bruceth and I, who felt that though they had tried to job us, yet they really had made the discovery and were entitled to the ground, tried our best to persuade them to go up and cut off their names, or they would lose their Eldorado claims—they certainly could not hold both. Whipple kept insisting that they could. At this juncture Phiscater came along.

" He treated with disdain Cobb's threat to jump their claims, and said he would go and see the recorder. McKay arrived on the scene, and he told them that if they cut their names off Bonanza he would put their names down on the new creek. This Clements, Anton, and Keller did.

" The first of a gang of stampeders who had arrived at Dawson on the steamer now appeared. Among these were William Scouse and William Sloan, who took Nos. 14 and 15.*

" We all went over to the creek, and began to measure and record.

* Some one staked No. 13 in a fictitious name, to try to hold for a friend, and this was afterwards jumped by a man named Hollingshead.

"JUMPING" CLAIMS

" Cobb jumped Phiscater's claim, as he would not take his name off Bonanza. The name of the creek was formally declared to be ' Eldorado,' as agreed upon at the meeting the night before.

"Cobb lost his claim, for Captain Constantine, the acting gold commissioner, decided that at the time he jumped there was plenty of as good ground farther up the creek, and that it was hoggish, to say the least, to jump ground where a discovery of gold had been made. Had all the five claims been jumped, instead of only one, and this been done after the creek had been staked, there is a chance whether Anton, Keller, and company would not have lost their claims, to which they had not the slightest legal right until they had taken their names off Bonanza, and the reason that barred Cobb would not have applied to late-comers, when there was no more ground on the creek above.

" The spot where the gold was discovered was, like the discovery on Bonanza, at the edge of the creek, on the line of Nos. 2 and 3. It was taken from a cut in the bank, and was practically surface gold that had slid down from the old channel on the hill-side. It was nothing more nor less than ' bench' gold, the existence of which was not even suspected at that time. From a hole eighteen inches deep in the creek-bed, and under water, as high as \$2 was taken out. Bed-rock, where the real richness lay, was fifteen or sixteen feet below the surface, under muck and gravel.

" The next morning, at 6 A.M., we started back, and reached the Indian village at 1 P.M., crossed over to our cache, and had dinner. Then we started for Forty-Mile, which we reached at 10.30 that night, and next day we recorded again, and finally, at Constantine's office."

Mr. Johns little realizing the value of his claim, sold a half-interest to Knut Langlow for $500, one-half cash, and one-half to be paid "on bed-rock." It was considered he made a good sale. Some while after (information having privately reached parties in Forty-Mile) he sold the other half for $2500; a good sale—also a good *buy*.

WILLIAM D. JOHNS ON A "STAMPEDE"

Anton went to Forty - Mile after staking. He was short of grub, and wanted to work his claim. Ordinarily any man could get credit in the lower country, but when Anton applied to the Alaska Commercial Company the temporary agent would not let him have it unless it was guaranteed. Clarence Berry came forward, guaranteed Anton's bill, and received in return a half-interest in the claim. Berry further traded him a half-interest in an upper Bonanza claim, then supposed to be of no value. Berry was sometimes spoken of as a "tin-horn gambler," was not supposed to have much money, and he was never called upon to make the guarantee good. It was whispered about the camp that the agent was to profit by the transaction. However, he did not. Afterwards Anton and Berry bought controlling interests in Nos. 4 and 5 and a fraction between 5 and 6. Their group of claims became known through the public press as "the Berry claims."

"Old man" Whipple sold out for a song to Skiff Mitchell, Tom O'Brien, and two others known as the "Big Four." Phiscater sold a half-interest in No. 2 to a man named Price for $800, and then bought out his interest in the claim, together with half a dump they had taken out during the winter, for $15,000, paid $2000 down, and the balance out of the dump when it was sluiced, with a big margin besides.

OPENING UP A NEW CLAIM

Such was the beginning of gold-mining on the richest creek in the Klondike.

SIX thousand souls wintered in Dawson, of whom five-sixths did not know whether their stock of provisions would last till spring.

The meagre stock remaining in the stores was doled out a few pounds at a time, after an interview with the agent in person. The North American Trading and Transportation Company had about seventy duplicate orders, left by men who took outfits from the other store. These outfits, comprising each a sack or two of flour, were sold at the regular store prices ; indeed, although the miners whose outfits were short, and others who for any cause were refused provisions, vehemently asserted that the agent was speculating in the necessaries of life, no pound of goods was sold by that store for more than the original price. The fact of two such extremely differing prices existing at the same moment is incomprehensible until the conditions are understood.

On the 10th of January the speculative price of provisions still averaged $1 a pound; but in Dawson flour had fallen to $50 a sack for first-grade, and $35 a sack for second-grade. And as bearing out the contention of Captain Healy, that the miners in the gulches were, on the whole, well provided for, flour on the same date was selling in open market on Eldorado for $25 a sack; and butter, which had risen from the store-price of $1 a pound, was freighted to Dawson from Bonanza Creek, one whole case of forty-eight two-pound tins being purchased by the "Eldorado" restaurant for $480. In one miner's cache on Eldorado there was known to be eighty-one sacks of flour, and long before relief came from outside a general unloading began and flour dropped to the moderate price of $100 for six sacks.

Parties went out, intending to bring in over the ice large quantities of food, believing it would sell at $2 a pound before spring, but they did not realize that the market was limited, that a few persons might pay fabulous prices, but the great majority could not do so even if they starved. One man in Dawson tried to corner flour. At considerable expense he secured one hundred and eighty sacks from down river and other sources. He refused $75 a sack, expecting to realize $100, when flour fell in price, and he just saved himself by unloading.

Captain Healy, whose firm and certainly arbitrary attitude in the matter of food earned for him the reputation of being the most unpopular man in Dawson, none the less was an unusual and interesting personality. For forty years he was a trader on the northwestern frontier; a member of the Elk or Warrior band of the Blackfeet; scout in the campaign against Chief Joseph; sheriff at Fort Benton, on the Missouri River; next, trader at Dyea, and now in the Yukon; in person, rather small, with sallow complexion, gray hair, mustache, and goatee, and a cold, unflinching blue eye—the type of man in whose exploits the history of the West abounds, to whom personal fear is unknown, accustomed to deal single-handed with any emergency; but he has confessed that from the start the problem of overcoming the natural obstacles and of meeting the growing demands of the Yukon had been one of the hardest purely business "propositions" he had ever had to face.

With the fear of famine over us, and some allowing themselves but one meal a day, or indulging even in bacon only twice a week, there were few with the equanimity of our genial friend Captain Anderson, Arizona frontiersman, who wrote to the anxious ones at home that he didn't know whether there was going to be starvation or not, but, anyhow, he was eating the best first and saving the poorest till last. Some verses written at the time by my versatile neighbor, Russell Bates, draw no imaginary picture:

"THE LONE FLAPJACK

"One cold Alaska's winter day
　　I sat within my lonely shack;
Without, old Boreas held full sway,
　　While cold came in through every crack.
　　Upon the stove was scarce a snack—
　　My daily meal, a lone flapjack.

"Upon the floor my flour lay—
　　In all 'twas less than half a sack.
My beans and bacon on that day
　　Would hardly constitute a pack.
Could I live on till first of May
Upon one lone flapjack a day?

"While pondering thus, and looking back—
　　For I never in my life did lack

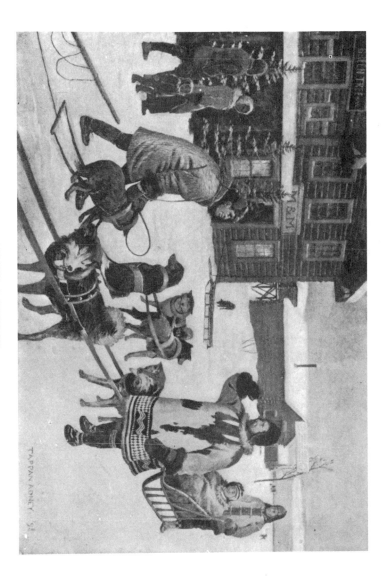

CHRISTMAS DINNER

Three sumptuous, hearty meals a day—
Judge Mastason, to my dismay,
Came in and said, ' My dear old Mac,
Can you give me a hot flapjack ?'

" My friend has gone, the days seem black,
I miss his hearty, genial way.
His friends at home will test his sack
Mid popping corks, as good friends may ;
But should the spring convey him back,
He's welcome to my lone flapjack!"

It was reported that a turkey reached Dawson at Christmas. That was a mistake. On April 10th, however, a turkey, ready cooked and dressed, was brought by a Dutchman over the ice from Skagway and was exhibited for several days to the wistful gaze of the public in the " Pioneer " saloon, where it was finally raffled off, netting the owner $174; but the owner said he would not go through the hardships of the trip in for the same price again.

The day before Christmas my cabin partner announced that he had invited some friends to dinner. Heavens ! I looked under the bunk where our stock of grub was safely stored. There was still plenty of bacon, but bacon three times a day loses its zest in course of time. There was plenty of flour, but neither of us could bake bread. We had been living on soup-vegetables and beans for several days, in consequence of forgetting to sweeten eighteen loaves of sour-dough bread with soda, which loaves not even passing dogs would eat. The outlook, therefore, was a dinner of soup, flapjacks, and beans—not even the usual " three B's," bread, beans, and bacon, of Alaska fare. Our last tin of condensed milk was gone, and there was none to be had for love or money. Our remaining butter—part of a firkin bought at Dyea—we now called either "butter" or "cheese"; it might pass for either. It looked as if it would have to be flapjack and beans for dinner. Pelletier, with a wise look on his face, said, "Leave it to me!" That night he came back with some bundles, which he threw down on the table, and proudly unwrapped a can of condensed cream, two cans of French pease, and—a can of *turkey!* A man of marvellous resources was he, but even yet I do not understand how he managed to get the turkey.

By means of the turkey (though the cranberry sauce was lacking), and under the direction of old Joe Liberty, an old Juneau pioneer who was living with us, we made out well. One of our guests was about to start for the coast, and to him it was a farewell dinner as well—a better one than many a poor fellow was having on the trail that day.

I heard a man say Dawson was the first place he was ever in where it was no disgrace to be "dead broke." Gold-dust was, of course, the medium of exchange. But the profits of mine-owners and the wages of workmen, amounting to millions, were frozen fast in the dumps of Eldorado and Bonanza, and there was but little money to spend. A man with a good claim could get a certain amount of credit, but the bulk of the business was transacted in cash. Money commanded 5 to 10 per cent. a month. The commercial companies and the saloons were the custodians of dust. A miner would hand his sack containing perhaps thousands of dollars to a saloon-keeper, who put it in an unlocked drawer, where it was as safe as in a bank outside.

In a new mining-camp the saloon is the centre of social life. At Dawson, shut out from the world, under conditions that tried the very souls of men, it was less wonder that men were drawn together into the only

public places where a friendly fire burned by day and
night, and where, in the dim light of a kerosene lamp,
they might see one another's faces. The Yukon saloon
was a peculiar institution (I feel that I am describing
something that passed away when the horde of new-
comers came later). Most of the proprietors were old-

A DAWSON SALOON

timers who had been miners, men of honor and character, respected in a community where a man was valued,
not according to his pretensions or position in "society,"
but in proportion to his manliness and intrinsic worth.
Class lines are not drawn sharply in a mining-camp, and
the freedom from the restraint of society and home
makes temptation greater than many can withstand.

Taken as a whole, the experience of a year in the Klondike is such as to search out the flaw in the weak but to strengthen the character of the strong.

Of the half-dozen or more places of amusement and recreation, the most pretentious was the "Opera-House," a large log building, with a bar and various gambling lay-outs in the front, and a theatre in the rear, with a stage, boxes at each side, and benches on the floor for the audience. It gave vaudeville performances, lasting several hours each evening, the performers being mostly a troupe who stampeded with the rest from Circle City. The price of admission, strange to say, was at the low price of "four bits," or half a dollar, admission being secured, according to the usual Yukon custom, by first purchasing for that sum a drink or a cigar at the bar. At the end of the performance the benches were taken up, and dancing began and continued all night. The receipts of the place were enormous, footing upwards of $22,000 a month. Early on Thanksgiving morning, after an uproarious masquerade ball, the dry building caught fire, and next morning saw only the blackened ruins of Dawson's first theatre. After the burning of the "Opera-House," the talent took to various occupations, most of the women securing work at the one remaining dance-hall, the "M. & M.," generally known as "Pete's Place," within whose hospitable walls on cold nights it cost the "busted" *chechahko* nothing to warm himself at the stove, to listen to the music, to look on at the scene of gayety, and wet his dry throat at the water-barrel. A water-barrel in a saloon, think of it! Yes, in the old-time Yukon saloon it stood in a corner, or at the end of the bar, and was kept filled with pure cold water at a cost of $10 a barrel, while a tin dipper hung on a nail for the use of all.

"PETE'S PLACE"

"Pete's" was a two-story log building, the upper story being the living-rooms of the proprietor. One entered from the street, in a whisk of steam that coated the door-jamb with snowy frost, into a low-ceiled room some thirty by forty feet in dimensions. The bar, a pine counter stained red, with a large mirror and bottles and glasses behind, was on the left hand. A lunch-counter stood on the right, while in the rear, and fenced off by a low wooden railing, but leaving a way clear to the bar, was the space reserved for dancing. Here, in the glow of three or four dim, smoky kerosene lamps, around a great sheet-iron "ram-down" stove, kept always red-hot, would always be found a motley crowd—miners, government officials, mounted policemen in uniform, gamblers, both amateur and professional, in "citified" clothes and boiled shirts, old-timers and new-comers, claim-brokers and men with claims to sell, busted men and millionaires—they elbowed each other, talking and laughing, or silently looking on, all in friendly good-nature.

Pete himself, one of the few saloon-keepers who had not been miners in the "lower country," served the drinks behind the bar in shirt-sleeves, with his round head and bull-dog expression, hair carefully oiled and parted, and dark, curled mustache, smiling, courteous, and ignorant—a typical "outside" bar-tender.

The orchestra consisted of a piano, violin, and flute, and occupied chairs on a raised platform in one corner of the dance-floor. The ladies were never backward in importuning partners for the dance; but any reluctance upon the part of would-be dancers was overcome by a young man in shirt-sleeves, who in a loud, penetrating voice would begin to exhort:

"Come on, boys—you can all waltz—let's have a nice,

long, juicy waltz ;" and then, when three or four couples had taken the floor, "Fire away!" he would call to the musicians, and then the fun began. When the dancers had circled around the room five or six times the music would stop with a jerk, and the couples, with a precision derived from long practice, would swing towards the bar, and push their way through the surging mass of interested lookers-on, or "rubber-necks," in fur-caps, Mackinaws, and *parkas*, and line up in front of the bar.

"What 'll you have, gents—a little whiskey ?"

Sacks were tossed out on the bar, Pete pushed in front of each "gent" a small "blower," and the "gent" poured in some gold-dust, which Pete took to a large gold-scale at the end of the bar, weighed out $1, and returned the balance to the sack. The lady received as her commission on the dance a round, white ivory chip, good for 25 cents.

Hardly had the dancers stopped before the caller-off, "Eddy," upon whose skill in keeping the dances going depended the profits of the house, began again in his loud voice, coaxing, imploring — "Come on, boys," or, "Grab a lady, boys, 'n' have a nice quadrille." And so it went on all night, one hundred and twenty-five dances being not unusual before daylight appeared through the frosted panes. Often the same men danced and caroused night after night, until their "pokes," or gold-sacks, grew lean, and then they disappeared up the gulch again.

Whenever a man started in to dance more than one dance he usually paid for several in advance, receiving what are called "allemande left" chips. There was a difference of opinion, which I believe has never been settled, as to when a *chechahko* is entitled to call himself an "old-timer." Some say after his first winter in the

Yukon ; others contend not until after he has bought his first "allemande left" chip.

Some of the women were employed at a salary of $125 a week and commissions on extras such as champagne, which cost those who cared to indulge in that luxury $40 a quart. The majority of women received only the 25 cents' commission, but sometimes, if industrious or good-looking, they made $25 or even more a night.

The whiskey varied greatly in quality, some being very bad, while the best, by the time it reached the consumer, was apt to be diluted to the last degree.

Whenever whiskey runs short the Yukoner falls back upon a villanous decoction made of sour dough, or dough and brown sugar, or sugar alone, and known as " hootch-inoo," or "hootch." The still is made of coal-oil cans, the worm of pieces of India-rubber boot-tops cemented together. This crude still is heated over an ordinary Yukon stove. The liquor obtained is clear white, and is flavored with blueberries or dried peaches, to suit the taste. It must be very bad, for its manufacture is forbidden by law ; they say it will drive a man crazy; but there were persons willing to take their oath that the regular whiskey sold over some of the bars was worse than "hootch." A home-brewed beer, or ale, was also served, a whiskey glassful costing 50 cents. Cigars were mostly a poor five-cent grade.

An example of the better class of Dawson saloon was the " Pioneer," or " Moosehorn," a favorite resort of old-timers. The proprietors, Messrs. Densmore, Spencer & McPhee, were types of the early Yukon pioneer. Frank Densmore, in fact, was among the first who crossed the pass, and he rocked for gold on the bars of the upper Yukon a dozen years before the Klondike was known. I recall the " Pioneer " as a large, comfortable

room, with the usual bar on one side, having a massive
mirror behind, and several large moose and caribou antlers
on the walls, a number of unpainted tables and benches
and chairs, the latter always filled with men talking over
their pipes, reading much-worn newspapers (six months
out of date), a few engaged in games of poker, and nine-
tenths "dead broke," but as welcome, apparently, as the
most reckless rounder who spilled his dust over the bar.
It struck the outsider with wonder, the seeming indif-
ference of the proprietors whether one patronized the
bar or not, for what other interpretation can one place
on a water-barrel at the end of the bar? Then, too,
the "busted" man of to-day might be the "millionaire"
of to-morrow; but the reason lay deeper than that.
There were men destined not to have fortunes. Very
late at night, when Dawson had turned in for a snatch
of sleep, one might see them lying on benches and tables, homeless, stranded men, half-sick and dependent
from day to day on the charity of strangers, and who,
but for this welcome bench or table, had no place to
lay their heads. Something of the generous spirit of
the old Yukon life made these men welcome.

Gambling is a miner's proper amusement, provided he
also pays his bills. Every saloon had its gambling lay-
outs. "Black-jack," poker, roulette, and craps were
played assiduously, some having a preference for one,
some for another, but the favorite game was faro. A
crowd might always be found around the faro-table, either
keeping track of "cases," or simply looking on at the
play. Twenty-five cents was the lowest chip, the white,
the reds and blues being respectively $1 and $5. The
"dealer," sitting behind the table and turning the cards
with mechanical regularity, and the "lookout," who saw
that "no bets were overlooked," were paid a salary of

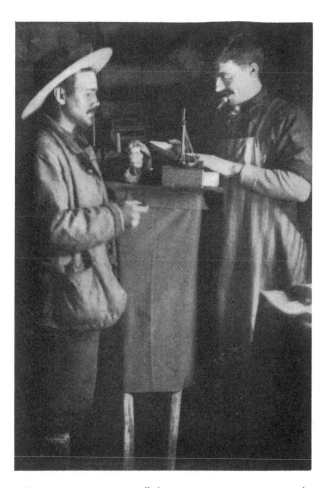

"HITTING THE BLOWER" (PAYING A BILL IN GOLD-DUST)

$15 to $20 a day, and each faro-table had to win from $50 to $80 every day to make a profit for the house, from which a moral may be deduced as to the wickedness of playing faro—on the wrong side of the table. At times the play was very large and correspondingly exciting. A young boy who had sold a rich claim "dropped" $18,000 in the course of thirty-six hours' play. Hundreds of dollars were made or lost on the turn of a card. One day a "dog-puncher," Joe Brand, walked in and threw down his sack on the "high card," saying, "That's good for a hundred." He won, and was given an order on the weigher for $100. Holding up the slip, he asked, "Is this good for the drinks?" "It is," was the reply, and he ordered up glasses to the number of two hundred, had them filled with whiskey, and then invited every one up to drink. A number in the saloon hung back, whom he vainly sought to make drink. He passed off the refusal with a laugh, saying that it must be pretty mean whiskey when no one would drink it. The balance was placed to his credit for another time.

I saw another man, a well-known character, at a "black-jack" table in a few minutes coolly lose an even $1000, and then just to show he didn't mind, he "ordered up" the whole house, treating every one in the saloon, at half a dollar a head, to whiskey and cigars.

Jake, a little Jew who ran a lunch-counter at "Pete's," was particularly fond of dancing and "craps," a game he doubtless learned when a messenger boy in Philadelphia. After a prosperous day's business Jake would "stake" a dollar, and if he won a sufficient sum he would spend the night dancing. He was too good a business man to spend the profits of business dancing, and so we always knew when we saw Jake on the floor that he had been lucky that day at craps.

Naturally a restaurant was a profitable undertaking to a person with a well-filled cache. The articles on the bill of fare were limited in number, uncertain in quantity, but unfailingly high in price. An eating-place, with the high-sounding name of "The Eldorado," stood in a space hardly more than ten feet wide, between two larger buildings, and consisted of a room front and back, the front room being supplied with three unpainted spruce tables and rough board stools, and a narrow counter between the door and window, on which stood the gold-scales. In the rear was the kitchen. The rough log walls of this "Delmonico's" of Dawson were plastered with signs, *à la* Bowery, reading: "Meal, $3.50"; "Porterhouse Steak, $8"; "Sirloin Steak, $5." The meal consisted of a bit of moose meat, or beef, beans, a small dish of stewed apples or peaches, one "helping" of bread and butter, and one cup of tea or coffee. In a tent on the water-front a man and his wife were said to have accumulated $30,000 as the winter's profits, selling coffee and pies, etc. In the "Dominion" saloon was a lunch-counter kept by a free-thinking Jew, who discussed philosophy with his customers as he served out plates of soup at $1 each. At Jake's there hung all winter the following bill of fare, drawn in large black letters on a sheet of Bristol-board:

BILL OF FARE

Sandwiches	$ .75	each.
Dough-nuts	.75	per order.
Pies	.75	" cut.
Turnovers	.75	" order.
Ginger cake	.75	" cut.
Coffee cake	1.00	" "
Caviare sandwiches	1.00	each.
Sardine "	1.00	"

AN EXPENSIVE *MENU*

Stewed fruits	. . . .	\$ .50 per dish.
Canned fruits	. . . .	1.00 " "
Sardines	. . . .	1.25 " order.
Cold meats	. . . .	1.50 " "
Raw Hamburg steak	. . . . . .	2.00 " "
Chocolate or cocoa	. . . .	.75 " cup.
Tea or coffee	. . . .	.50 " "

The card and the printing together cost $15, probably one of the most expensive *menu* cards in the world. Jake's visible stock seldom consisted, at any one time, of more than a bottle of Worcestershire sauce, a pie, a few tins of sardines, some tins of milk, a pan of beans, and a loaf of bread, which were temptingly displayed on three rude shelves against the back wall. In April, some oysters came in by dog-team. Jake paid $18 and $20 for several tins holding two dozen oysters—less than a pint. Thereafter an oyster-stew could be had for the modest sum of $15. Another person gave $25 each for two of the same tins. A shrewd Yankee, with a winning smile, started a bakery in the Ladue cabin in the middle of the street and made bread and pies, selling them for $1 each. Later he branched out into a restaurant, and took out a fortune.

Gold-dust is not an economical or convenient currency. Out of every $50 expended in making small purchases, there would be a regular loss of $4 to $6, due partly to the custom of the weigher taking the "turn" of the scale, partly to carelessness, and partly to actual theft. In changing dollars and cents into ounces and pennyweights, it is easy to purposely miscalculate or substitute larger weights. And then the small traders had only the pocket prospector's scales, which often were considerably out of balance. The proprietor of one restaurant told me that although he made it a rule not to take the "turn" of the scale, he invariably found himself several dollars ahead at the end of the day.

When the miner came to town on business, or on pleasure bent, unless he had a cabin, or friends to take him in, he was obliged to choose between staying up all night in the saloons or going to one of the half-dozen establishments by courtesy designated "hotels." Not even a person whose sensibilities had been blunted by a year in

"JAKE'S," WHERE AN OYSTER-STEW COST $15

the Yukon could abide in one even for one night in comfort or safety. The "hotel" was a two-story building. On the first floor was the bar, which served for the clerk's desk as well, the rear of the place being the family quarters of the proprietor. Upon payment of $2, always demanded in advance, the clerk, bar-tender, or proprietor—who was often one and the same person— would lead the way with a candle up a rickety stairs to an upper room, which commonly extended the whole length of the building, with only the rafters overhead. Sometimes this room was divided into small rooms or pens by partitions as high as one's head, with just space for a single cot ; or else the interior was filled with tiers of double-decked bunks of rude scantling, accommodating twenty or thirty sleepers. The bedding in each bunk consisted of rough blankets and a very small pillow. There was a nail in the wall to hang one's coat upon (for that was all a person was expected to take off, except his shoes or moccasins), and the landlord left a bit of candle to light the guest to bed. The only ventilation to this upper room was through generous cracks in the floor and a small window at each end, which in cold weather were kept scrupulously shut. When heated to a torrid pitch by a large stove on the lower floor, with every bunk full of unwashed men who have taken off their rubber boots or *mukluks*, the air of this veritable "bull-pen" before morning was such that no one could be induced to repeat the experience except when confronted with the positive alternative of lying out of doors without protection from the cold. Even worse than the thick, nauseating atmosphere were the vermin with which the blankets were alive, as there was no possible means in winter of getting rid of them short of destruction of the bedding. They are already the bane of the diggings, hardly one of the cabins on the older creeks being free from the unwelcome occupants. Clothes-washing was an expensive item, unless one did it himself. No article was less than 50 cents, and it was by no means a large wash that came to $10. Heavy blankets could not be washed at all. Persons regarded themselves as particularly cleanly if they changed underwear every two weeks.

The hard life led by the miner in winter often brings

on a disease known as "scurvy." It is not the same as ship scurvy, and the symptoms vary in different persons, the more common being a hardening of the tendons, especially those under the knee, a darkening of the skin, and an apparent lifelessness of the tissue, so that when a finger is pressed against the skin a dent remains for some time afterwards. It is rarely fatal, though it may incapacitate the victim for work for a whole season. It yields readily to a treatment of spruce-leaf tea, taken internally. Various specific causes are given, such as lack of fresh meat and vegetables, improperly cooked food, exposure and vitiated air, but physicians say that the real cause is yet unknown.

Physicians did uncommonly well. The charge for a visit in town was never less than $5, while a visit to the mines was sometimes as high as $500, the charge being regulated according to the "victim's" ability to pay; and the price of drugs was proportionately high. One young doctor was said to have earned $1200 to $1500 a month, while another who invested his earnings judiciously in mines was reputed to have made $200,000. The hospital, although a sectarian institution, was maintained by local subscriptions. Three ounces of gold-dust ($51) entitled a person to a ticket for treatment during one year, and a certain number of weeks in the hospital, with board and nursing free. To non-subscribers the charge was $5 a day, and $5 extra for the doctor's usually daily visit. From its establishment in the fall of 1897 up to April 1st, 1898, the number of deaths was twenty-four, of which seven or eight were from typhoid fever. The hospital was a godsend, and many a man came out from under the tender care of the venerable Father Judge and the little band of Sisters with a broader view of religious work and a better personal understanding of what it

meant to devote one's life to doing good for his fellow-
men.

Now and then we witnessed the sad sight of a funeral — some poor fellow borne to his last resting-place
far from his own people, but never without friends.   In
order to make a grave, it was necessary to burn the
frosty ground exactly as if for mining.   A sight witnessed perhaps no place else in the world was a hearse

A FUNERAL PROCESSION IN DAWSON

drawn by dogs.   The rude coffin of spruce was placed on
a Yukon sled, to which was hitched a team of four gray
Malamut dogs.   The minister and improvised hearse
went ahead, followed by a procession of friends, to a
spot on the hill-side overlooking the Yukon, where the
funeral service was read, and then the coffin lowered
into its resting-place, where the body will lie unchanged
until the earth itself changes.

The aurora borealis, or northern lights, of which we
expected to see so much, failed to show the brilliant con-

ventional arc of light represented in pictures of the Arctic regions. A clear yellow glow on the horizon, like that from the rising of the sun, lay in the north, and from this at times streams of light shot upward, often to the zenith, and took the form of waving bands or curtains of light, pink and green, swiftly, silently moving and shifting. Sometimes the light seemed very near, and then it seemed that we could hear a rustling, but whether it was the rustling of the light or the rushing of the river beneath the ice we could never tell, it was so subtle and illusive; and again it seemed as if its rays caught the pale-green light of the moon, which shone as bright as day in the cloudless sky.

The dry, crisp cold was no greater than one could stand, but from the first of December until the middle of January the cold and darkness combined to weigh upon body and mind. Even with plenty of work to do the short, dull days and interminable nights were gloomy and dispiriting. After the middle of January the days grew rapidly longer, for the coming and going of the seasons are much more rapid than nearer the equator. At Dawson the valley of the river lay north and south, and the sun was visible in the south for several hours at the edge of the distant hill-top; but in all the deep valleys which lay in the other direction the sun was not visible from November until February. Fifty-four degrees below zero, registered on a private spirit-thermometer at the barracks, was said to have been the lowest; but probably at higher elevations the temperature was considerably lower than that. Fortunately the extreme cold was accompanied with little or no wind, but the slightest movement of air cut like a knife. In the woods there was absolutely no air stirring.

The snow clung to the trees in curiously formed masses,

exceeding in size anything ever seen in the deep-snow regions of southern Canada. On the tops of the mountains the most beautiful effects were observed, each twig and tree being surrounded with white crystals of snow, giving to the landscape the appearance of having been chiselled from spotless marble. In February, under the increasing breezes, the snow began dropping; in March there were moderate gales. The sky in winter was nearly cloudless, and the snow seemed to come mostly from banks of mist that rose from air-holes in the river and drifted into the valleys. The snow-fall did not exceed two or three feet. It was as light as powder, and did not settle to any appreciable ex-

A "DRILL" PARKA

tent until the sunny days of early spring. Snow-shoeing was exceedingly tiresome, and off the trail quite impossible with anything but the largest Alaska shoes or with the Norwegian *skis*.

When travelling in cold weather it is necessary to cover well the hands and feet and to guard the face. The body cares for itself. A heavy blanket-coat over woollen underwear is amply warm, especially if provided with a hood, but an objection to wool is that perspiration strikes through and freezes, especially over the back and shoulders. When one enters a warm cabin this melts,

z 353

and unless thoroughly dried is apt to cause a severe chill. Deer-skin coats, although very "swell," are considered too heavy when travelling fast, the miner preferring the ordinary drill *parka*, with fox-tails around the hood, and a puckering-string to draw it around the face. The principal danger is of breaking through thin shell-ice. Even in the severest weather water from so-called "soda-springs" flows out of the hill-sides and over the ice in the creeks, often building up masses of ice known to the miners as "glaciers." So thin in some places is the ice that the Indians, when making a new trail on the river, always carry a stick with which to feel their way, testing the ice ahead of them.

Snow-glasses are a part of every Klondike outfit, as at the approach of spring the sun shining upon the snow produces an inflammation of the eyes known as "snow-blindness." The victims of snow-blindness are compelled to lie in-doors often for a week, suffering excruciating pain. The ordinary snow-glass is a goggle of smoke-colored glass, the sides being of fine wire netting. Another kind is made of blue-stained mica, with a rim of felt. Both are held on with a rubber band around the head. The Indians blacken their cheeks with lamp-black and grease, which modifies the intense glare. At Dawson not one person in ten wore glasses or took any other precautions, and I did not know of a case of snow-blindness. By a curious paradox it is said that strong eyes are more liable to snow-blindness than weak ones.

One naturally wonders how women endure the discomforts of life in the Yukon. But we who lived roughly were astonished to observe how the hand of woman could transform an interior, and what an air of comfort could be given, especially in the houses of the traders and other well-to-do persons who could afford proper furniture. The number of women in camp was a continual subject of comment; and there were a few children.

Dawson was, in the main, a city composed of grown people and dogs. Four years ago there were four white women in the Yukon. Two years later a theatrical troupe increased the number. This winter there were probably two hundred, most of whom were the wives of fortunate miners, and all of whom were as intent as the men upon earning, or helping to earn, a fortune.

Nearly all the first old-timers married Indian women, who have shared the good fortunes of their husbands in the Klondike strike,

INDIAN WOMAN IN FANCY PARKA

and are treated with the same respect that would be accorded a white woman. At Pioneer Hall, on New Year's eve, the " Yukon Order of Pioneers " gave a grand ball, at which, it is needless to say, " boiled " shirts were not *de rigueur*, but several were in evidence, in which their wearers, more accustomed to flannels, looked extremely uncomfortable. They brought their Indian wives, who in turn brought the children, and it made a quaint sight, the men, some in fur *parkas*, others in black broad-cloth, and all in moccasins; the women decked out in their best and newest "store" clothes, not much behind the fashion either; the babies in odd little *parkas*, playing on the floor under the feet of the dancers; and, as a final touch to the picture, here and there a lost dog looking for its owner. Tickets to this, the swell event of the season, were $12.50, which included an excellent supper.

The Yukon Order of Pioneers was organized by "Jack" McQuesten, at Circle City, for the purpose of furthering

BADGE OF YUKON
ORDER OF PIONEERS

the interests of its members, caring for them when sick, burying them when dead. No one is eligible who came into the Yukon since 1895. It numbers seventy or eighty active members, and one honorary member, Captain Constantine. The badge of the society is of gold—a carpenter's rule partly folded, the two arms being crossed with a spray of laurel, with the letters Y. O. O. P. inside.

No news of the outside world reached us until January 4th, when Andrew Flett, a Mackenzie River half-breed, arrived from Little Salmon with a team of four dogs and mail for the officials, bringing the news, received with mingled joy and disgust, that he had left at that place nine other teams loaded with public mail. He had left it behind, not daring to bring all the dogs to Dawson until he knew he could secure food. We learned for the first time from the messenger of the general anxiety about our safety, of the action of Congress for our relief, and the despatching of a reindeer relief expedition. There was also at Little Salmon half a ton of old mail, some of which had passed Lindeman before my departure, and was "held up" at Tagish awaiting the new governor, Major James M. Walsh, and other officers of the government, who, however, started so late that they were all frozen in near Little Salmon.

As early as Christmas, private dog-teams were offered to bring this mail into Dawson, but the authorities declined, expecting their own dogs to arrive soon. On February 26th every pound of mail that forty dogs could pull came in, and there was great rejoicing. Clippings of important news (we did not yet know of the loss of the *Maine*) were enclosed in letters, and these were passed around from hand to hand and eagerly read. After this teams from the coast arrived frequently. Every responsible private outfit that went out carried its batch of letters sealed in waterproof tin boxes. The government charge was only three cents a letter, the same as in other parts of Canada, but the first government mail did not leave until March. More than one precious parcel of letters may have been thrown by the way-side by these private carriers—indeed, one such parcel was found, and the fellow was caught, but he explained that he had been obliged to leave it and had intended to go back for it in the spring. A different sort of man was Patrick, or "Pat," Galvin, as he is familiarly known, formerly tin-smith at Circle City, but now a man who pays his bills in golden eagles manufactured from his own Klondike gold by Uncle Sam. Just before the break-up Galvin came in on the run, and, hastily finishing some business, started back, making Fort Selkirk, one hundred and seventy-five miles, in the remarkable time of three and a half days. There he left his dogs, and, with an Indian guide, continued on, carrying twenty-eight pounds of mail. The pack contained, besides letters with drafts aggregating $40,000, a parcel, encased in tin, of manuscript and sketches for HARPER'S WEEKLY, weighing nearly three pounds, which Galvin had undertaken to carry for me to the coast, a service for which he scorned a cent of pay. The Indian deserted him after he had told him of a short cut that would save much time. Galvin stopped two men on their way in and turned them back. They lost their way in the cut-off, and wandered for six days, most of the time without food. At one time they gave up all as lost, and left their names on birch-bark on the top of a mountain, but, pushing on with remarkable fortitude, they at length recovered the trail. During these six days the men Galvin had turned back would not share with him a pound of the load of mail. In due season a parcel reached Franklin Square, accompanied by a hastily scrawled note, which those who opened it perhaps little understood. Galvin had written, "I would not do it again for $25,000," and any one who knows Galvin knows he meant every word he said. As an example of faithfulness to trust, of pure bull-dog grit, this experience of Galvin's has few equals.

The dreary expanse of snow between Dawson and the coast saw trains of human beings and dogs going out, meeting other trains bound in, or living in cabins wherever they were stopped by the ice. The police, with stations at White Horse Rapids, Lake Labarge, Hootalinqua, Big Salmon, Freeman's Point, and Little Salmon, furnished relief, except for which many would have gone to their death by the side of the narrow white trail.

The more eager new-comers left the main part of their outfits in charge of one of their party, and pushed on to Dawson, where they exchanged provisions, pound for pound, with outgoing parties — an arrangement of the greatest advantage to both.

CHAPTER XVII

Spring in the Yukon—Last Dog-Teams from Outside—Horde of New-Comers at the Head of the River, Waiting for the Ice to Go Out—Failure of the Reindeer Relief Expedition—Preparing for the "Boom"—The "Clean-up" Begun — The Klondike Breaks Loose — Terrific Force of the Ice—The Yukon still Solid—Will Dawson be Washed Away?—"The Ice is Going Out"—"Chechahkos!"—Eggs a Dollar and a Half—The "June Rise"—Dawson Under Water

THE moment the spring sun gained a place in the sky the snow on the southern hillsides dwindled away like magic, turning the creek trails into streams of water which grew in volume with each succeeding day. The forests seemed to burst into life and the air was laden with the song and twitter of birds. By the middle of April the snow was gone from the flat at Dawson, and the sun, although not so high in the heavens, was shining for as many hours as in the middle United States on the longest day of the year. Moccasins and furs were laid away, and their places were taken by rubber hip-boots and broad-brimmed felt hats. At night, however, enough winter returned to freeze the trails for the dog-teams hurrying supplies and lumber to the mines before the final break-up.

The last teams in from the outside brought confirming news of the magnitude of the Klondike stampede. The crowd pouring over the passes was such as the world had never seen before. At Skagway the woods were cleared off, buildings were going up "faster than they could get the lumber," and the town contained seven thousand people, and was growing fast. A toll-road, known as "Brackett's Road," had been constructed over White Pass for wagons and horse-sleds, and freighting was reduced to 15 cents a pound from Skagway to Bennett. Where three thousand horses lay dead, a stream of men, dogs, and horses were moving easily. Dyea, which in December consisted of three white men's houses, was a mile and a half long and contained from five to six thousand souls. A stream of human beings dragged their hand-sleds up the now smooth trail, and over the summit all day long marched a thin black line of men with packs, locking step, so close together that they could touch. First a whim, or endless cable, was put, for drawing loaded sleds to the top, and later an "aërial tramway," a steel cable elevated on posts, with swinging buckets, was operating between Sheep Camp and Crater Lake, goods being carried from Dyea to Lindeman for 8 cents a pound. The Canadian government had made good its claim to the passes as the international boundary by establishing custom offices at both summits and there taking duties on American goods. The mounted police, in fear of famine, had been allowing no person without credentials to cross the summit without a thousand pounds of provisions. Along the lakes the new-comers were putting boats together, ready to start for Dawson with the opening of the river in May.

The effort of the United States government, when apparent confirmation of rumors of a serious shortage of food was received from Dawson, to send a relief expe-

dition by reindeer, came to a disastrous end, the deer having reached no farther than the coast end of the Dalton trail, over which it had been intended they should proceed to the relief of Dawson and Circle City. Although, happily, the help was not needed, it was a matter of keen regret to all who had followed closely the introduction of domesticated reindeer into Alaska that this the first practical opportunity to demonstrate their usefulness ended in disaster; for if reindeer had failed, there was no means under heaven by which help could have reached us. The domesticated reindeer will no doubt prove to be as well adapted for the Yukon valley as its near relative, the wild reindeer or caribou, of the same region, or the domesticated herds of eastern Siberia. For upward of eight years the government, through Dr. Sheldon Jackson, General Agent of Education for Alaska, had endeavored to effect the introduction into western Alaska of the domesticated deer, which they secured annually from the Siberian herdsmen, until, along with their natural increase, the herd numbered upward of fifteen hundred deer, stationed at the Teller Reindeer Station, Port Clarence, and at Golovin Bay, Behring Sea. The main purpose of the movers in this enterprise was to furnish food and clothing to the starving Eskimos, and, eventually, means of transportation in winter to and from our far northern stations, a service which deer should perform as well in Alaska as in Lapland.

When the news of our perilous situation reached the government, it happened that the revenue-cutter *Bear* had just departed from Port Townsend, Washington, with an expedition, under Lieutenant D. H. Jarvis, for the relief of eight whaling-vessels imprisoned in the ice at Point Barrow. Lieutenant Jarvis was instructed to take all the available government deer, and he ultimately reached Point Barrow, having successfully driven 382 deer a distance of over eight hundred miles. Consequently, there being no government deer available, Congress, on the 18th of December, passed "An act authorizing the Secretary of War, in his discretion, to purchase subsistence stores, supplies, and materials for the relief of people who are in the Yukon River country, to provide means for their transportation and distribution," and made an appropriation therefor. Dr. Jackson was

UNITED STATES GOVERNMENT REINDEER RELIEF EXPEDITION — DEER
HARNESSED TO SLEDS

despatched to Norway to purchase deer, and on the 28th of February reached New York with 539 deer, also sleds and harness complete, and 114 Lapps and Finns to drive the deer. The deer reached Seattle on March 7th, having lost but one of their number; but here, while waiting nine days for transportation, they were fed on grass, through the desire of the officer having them in charge to save the reindeer-moss that came with them, and several died. Finally, the herd reached

364

Haine's Mission, Pyramid Harbor, from which point they should have been at once driven to the moss-fields, a few miles distant ; but instructions regarding them sent to the officer in command of the United States soldiers at Dyea, though mailed at Skagway, did not reach him, four miles distant, until a week later, so that when the order came to move it was too late ; they were so weakened by unaccustomed food that they began to die rapidly, and by the time they reached abundant pasturage in the Chilkat pass, only fifty miles distant, but 183 deer remained alive, and the expedition was abandoned. The survivors were subsequently driven to Circle City.

At Dawson buildings of every description sprang up like mushrooms in a night, from the black, reeking bog. Many of them were of substantial logs and lumber, but the greater part, both large and small, were mere coverings, intended to last only through the summer.

First a frame of rough scantling went up, then a covering of white or blue drilling hastily stitched together into the form of a tent and thrown over, with openings for windows and doors ; fitted with seats and tables for restaurants, with shelves and counters for stores, and with the appropriate furniture for gambling-houses and saloons. Several buildings of dressed lumber, intended for use as stores, hotels, and theatres, were as handsome as one would care to see. The river-front was leased by the government officials to a favored individual for about $1 a foot per month, and re-leased by him to builders at $8 to $12 a foot per month ; and this was solidly packed with tent-covered frames, excepting a few hundred feet reserved for the landing of steamers and at the ends of two cross-streets. Building lots were held at extravagant prices. As high as $20,000 was paid for a desirable corner lot for a saloon, while a two - story log building in the centre of town was worth with the lot anywhere from $30,000 to $40,000. The government surveyed what public land had not been previously granted to town-site claimants into 40 × 60-foot lots for cabins, and assessed locators from $200 to $500 each, prices which they justified as being only half the "market value." Three saw-mills, running night and day, were unable to supply the demand for lumber, which was worth at the mill $150 to $200 per thousand feet. Men stood with teams waiting, taking the boards as they fell from the saw. Nails were so scarce that a keg of 100 pounds brought $500; a single pound cost $6, and $3.50 per pound was paid for burned nails from the ruins of the "Opera-house." So that a building of the size of some of those that went up cost $500 to probably $10,000 for the shell alone. One of the trading companies had a large stock of cotton drilling, worth perhaps 8 cents a yard, which it disposed of at 75 cents a yard.

A wood-working establishment, which worked all winter turning out well-made furniture and cabinet-work, supplied most of the fittings of saloons and stores.

The final thaw came on so suddenly that I succeeded in getting only one sled-load of stuff from the cabin to town. On May 1st muddy water in Bonanza Creek showed that sluicing had begun. On the 3d it came over the low bank, flooding the woods and rising three inches on the floor of the cabin. It is not exactly enjoyable having to wade about the house in rubber boots, fighting mosquitoes, trying to cook a flapjack or make a cup of tea over the stove, and climbing in and out of a high bunk with boots on. At the end of just two days I struck for town. The Klondike was still frozen fast to the bottom, but the river was running bank-full, to all appearances open. Two bridges over the Klondike had just been finished: one on seven stout piers at the mill, and the other at the mouth of the Klondike, a suspension foot-bridge in two spans (one for each channel), built of boards and scantling suspended from an inch-wire cable over large spruce spars. A crowd, mostly miners on their way up the gulch, and others just loafers (for mankind in general is as prone to loaf as hard at $15 a day as at $1), was gathered at the Dawson end of the latter. The ground-ice, loosening from the bottom, now began to heave, and was jamming dangerously on the shoals. The ice was already level with the floor of the bridge when some dynamite loosened the jam and the ice moved out. Just then a cry was raised, " The upper bridge is gone !" and, looking, we saw some sticks of sawed timber float by.

What had taken place shows the power of ice. Only two piers remained, and icebergs as large as small cabins were setting about in the river-bed and among the stumps and cabins on the flat. Several men, who were wringing out clothes and drying portions of outfits in the sun, said they saw the ice jam above the piers and begin to pile up, with the water behind it. Suddenly it broke over the brink and started across the flat, making for the cabins. The same moment a gigantic floe in the middle of the jam—and that was all that saved seventy-five to one hundred cabins and twice that many lives—started, picked the bridge up as if it had been a bunch of matches, and the rest followed crashing, bearing five spans before it ; and, thus relieved, the water fell as quickly as it rose, leaving the flat strewn with ice, logs, and lumber. The ice crowded again below into a slough at the mouth of Bonanza Creek, and the cabins of the settlement were flooded to the eaves for several days, their occupants, some of

whom were sick, escaping to the roofs, where they remained until boats came to their rescue.

On the 6th of May the Yukon began to rise rapidly,
lifting the ice, which, however, remained fast in front of
the town. Hundreds of anxious men kept to the streets
that night, believing, as the old-timers said, that if it
jammed as the Klondike had it would sweep the town
away. The water stood within two feet of the top of

YUKON ICE-FLOES

the bank. Captain Constantine, who knew what the
river might do, walked along the water-front and regarded the situation with evident anxiety. The sight
was one to inspire respect. When a big floe, forty feet
across, struck the front of the barrier, it half rose out
of the water, then dived under, or turned on edge,
crunched into the front with a dull roar, and remained
there. Now and then an empty boat was seen to strike,
careen, and go under. At four o'clock on the morning
of the 8th the cry was raised, "The ice is going out!"

and everybody rushed out in time to see the bridge of ice crack, groan, then slowly push together and stop; then slowly, slowly the whole mass began to move, and in a few minutes there was nothing but a swift river, with cakes of ice as big as cabins strewn along the banks.

The old-timers said we should see a *chechahko* "on the tail of the last cake of ice," implying thereby that the old-timers knew enough to give ice-jams a wide berth. Not long after the ice went out, the cry " *Chechahko!*" was heard. All eyes were turned towards Klondike City, and we could see a boat just coming into sight, with several men in it. As it drew nearer it proved to be a large Yukon boat containing five men and some sled-dogs and sleds. As it drifted down a crowd numbering several hundred followed it about a mile, when it pulled in-shore. When the crowd learned that they were only from Stewart River, they were disgusted. We had hardly got back when two men in a bright-green new "Peterborough" slipped in, and as they stepped ashore they were greeted with hearty handshakes and other signs of recognition, and then we knew they were not *chechahkos*, and that an old-timer had broken the rule. A crowd immediately surrounded them, asking questions. They had left Bennett six days before, rowed day and night, taking turns alternately rowing and sleeping, and sledded over Labarge. Several thousand people were around the shores of that lake, with boats built, waiting for the ice to go out.

Presently came another Peterborough, then another —there were three or four canoes in now; in one was a *chechahko*. One of the canoes brought a case of fresh eggs, which were snatched up, at $18 a dozen, by the miners, famished for something fresh and new. A few more boats got in, bringing word that the lake had opened up a narrow crack, through which they had worked at great risk ; it had closed after them. We noted the eagerness of the first to get in, and compared it with our own. How they were straining every nerve and muscle to be a day, an hour, ahead of the crowd!

The moment the ice went out five foolish persons, of whom I myself was one, paid $100 for a worn-out poling-boat (new ones being worth $250 to $300 each) and started for White River, where a late-comer over the ice reported having found a vein of very rich quartz. There had been hope that the "mother lode," from which the Bonanza and Eldorado placers came, would eventually be found. During the winter Captain Healy set men to work tunnelling in several places in the neighborhood of Dawson, but without encouraging result, none of the ore found proving sufficiently high-grade to work. The samples alleged to come from White River showed ore of immense richness, although suspiciously like ore from Cripple Creek, Colorado. Consequently the town was agog.

Five parties set out in boats and canoes. Ours was the first boat to reach Stewart River, making the sixty-eight miles in seven days of the hardest struggle. Two besides ours reached the ledge, but only by leaving their boats and proceeding overland, being unable to face the terrific force of the river against the tall, often perpendicular cliffs that line the Yukon for miles. After ten days of truly fearful exertion, often at the same time poling, rowing, towing, and chopping trees, great numbers of which had been undermined and fallen into the water, we reached our destination, and discovered the hoax. Starting back, we met the advance-guard of the new-comers, and learned that Labarge was clear. A few hours later, borne on the bosom of the flood, or "June rise," caused by the melting snows and glaciers in the mountains, we found Klondike City under water, the mouth of the Klondike like a mill - pond, the suspension-bridge gone, and numbers of people, many of whom we recognized as new-comers, going about in boats where we had lately walked in fancied security.

RAFT OF HOUSE LOGS ON THE KLONDIKE RIVER

CHAPTER XVIII

PROBABLY two hundred boats of various kinds, from Lake Superior birch-canoes to scows with horses on them, were tied up at Klondike City and the Dawson bank of the Klondike, and the hill-side was white with tents of new-comers and others who had been driven out of the cabins on the low ground. The central part of Dawson was under from one to five feet of water. The barracks were cut off, and people were going for their mail in boats and canoes, while the gold commissioner and his staff were driven to a tent on higher ground. Enterprising boatmen were carrying passengers along the main street, charging 50 cents a head.

It was now at midnight as bright as day. The sun rose behind Moosehide Mountain, swung around half-way to the zenith, and disappeared behind the mountain again after twenty hours continuous shining. From the hill-tops the sun was clearly visible during the twenty-four hours. In the tents it was uncomfortably hot, and the glare was trying to the eyes and nerves. Not only could one easily see to read inside a tent at midnight, but it was light enough out-doors for a "snap-shot" with a good photographic lens. During mid-day the temperature rose to 70° in the shade. The very sparrows and snow-birds in the brush on the hill-side lay still by day and sang and hunted at night. No one ever felt like going to bed. It was a considerable bother, without

A *CHECHAHKO'S* SCOW

watch or compass, to tell the time of day. A man would ask another, "What time is it?" "Ten o'clock," the answer might be. "Morning or evening?"

A few persons lived on the tops of their cabins, with a tent and stove, and a boat tied at the corner of the roof to get ashore with. From my own tent, on a steep bluff overlooking the whole scene, I would see a man at, say, 11 P.M., push off from shore, pole over to a cabin, clamber out onto the roof, take off his shoes, walk over to a pile of blankets, unroll them, then take off his coat, place it for a pillow, and turn in for a night's sleep—all in broad daylight.

The river subsided rapidly, and the new-comers continued to pour in. Each one said that the crowd was behind him. The authorities turned over to them temporarily a portion of the military reservation. Their tents whitened the hill-sides, and whole acres were covered so thickly that from a little distance they appeared as masses of white. At Klondike City, along the Klondike for a mile, and down the bank of the Yukon to the far end of town, among bowlders and rocks, wherever there was a space of ground large and dry enough, there were tents. A morass in the middle of the town-site was the only ground not occupied. A part of the overflow crossed the Yukon. From the point of hill above my tent I counted twenty-eight hundred tents, including those on scows, in each of which three to five or more persons were then living.

The boats, from the graceful Peterborough canoe to freight-scows forty feet long, carrying twenty tons, were tied up side by side along one and three-quarter miles of water-front, a solid phalanx from one to six feet deep!

Who is there that can describe the crowd, curious, listless, dazed, dragging its way with slow, lagging step along the main street? Can this be the "rush" that newspapers are accustomed to describe as the movement of gold-seekers? Have the hard, weary months of work on the trails exhausted their vitality? or is it the heavy shoes that make them drag their feet so wearily along the street?

It is a motley throng—every degree of person gathered from every corner of the earth, from every State

of the Union, and from every city — weather - beaten, sunburned, with snow - glasses over their hats, just as they came from the passes. Australians with upturned sleeves and a swagger; young Englishmen in golf-stockings and tweeds; would-be miners in Mackinaws and rubber boots, or heavy, high-laced shoes; Japanese, negroes — and women, too, everywhere. It is a vast herd; they crowd the boats and fill the streets, looking at Dawson. Some are disappointed. "This is not as big as Skagway," they say. The old-timer (we are all old-timers now) is lost. The mere recognition of a face seen last winter is now excuse for a friendly nod and a "How-de-do?" The crowd is good-natured, elbowing and slowly tramping back and forth.

It was a sight just to walk along the water-front and see the people, how they lived. Some slept in tents on their scows, one stumbled over others on the ground under robes or blankets.

Outfits of all descriptions were placarded "for sale," and these were surrounded by representatives of eating-places buying provisions, or old - timers buying underwear and tobacco. Tinned goods, butter, milk, fresh potatoes were eagerly asked for.

The first to get in with provisions made small fortunes, for by good - luck they brought the very things that would sell best. The first case of thirty dozen eggs brought $300. Soon the market was better supplied, and eggs fell to $150 a case, and in two weeks came down to $3 a dozen; milk, $1 a can; tinned mutton, $2.50 a pound; oranges, apples, and lemons, $1 each; potatoes brought 50 cents a pound; a watermelon, $25. Regular market-stands were opened for the sale of vegetables of all kinds, and the water - front looked like a row of booths at a fair.

Every conceivable thing was displayed for sale—clothing, furs, moccasins, hats and shoes, groceries, meat, jewelry. There were hardware and thoroughly equipped drug and dry-goods stores. Here is one of the signs :

DRUGS DRUGS

Rubber boots, Shoes, Etc.
Bacon, flour, rolled oats, rice, sugar, potatoes,
onions, tea and coffee, fruits,
corn meal, german sausage,
Dogs Dogs

In the brief space of a few days there seemed to be nothing that could not be purchased in Dawson, from fresh grapes to an opera-glass, from a safety - pin to an ice-cream freezer.

A sack of flour actually sold on the water-front for $3, less than cost, the owners being disgusted and selling out to leave the country. There was no fixed price. A few men in town could afford to pay the high prices asked at first for everything ; but we of the rank and file, of varying degrees of "bustedness," went without until prices came down.

When meals dropped to $2.50, what a treat it was !—no longer obliged to stand up before a rough board, nor to live on " home-made " flapjacks, beans, and bacon, until, as one man expressed it, he was "ashamed to look a hog in the face." Instead, we sat down at tables covered with clean linen. What a feast, the fresh vegetables and the curried mutton ! They have tried to tell us that when a man left this country he didn't feel he had a square meal without bacon and beans. The man was only joking. We could understand now how Pat Reagan felt when describing an outfit which a

Dutchman lost in Five-Fingers the year Pat came in.
"It was a foine outfit," said Pat. "He had two whole
cases of condensed milk."

Two popular young ladies were set up in the ice-cream
business by a certain young man about town. A large
stock of condensed cream and $100 worth of ice were
provided (ice was as expensive as anything else, on account of having to be handled by men at $1 an hour).

THE WATER-FRONT

A few days later the young man called around to ask
how business was getting on. "Oh," they replied,
"we're doing just splendid ; we have sold $45 worth of
ice-cream, but we'll have to have a little more ice."

The best restaurant at this time was the "Arcade," a
rough frame of scantling twenty feet wide and fifty feet
deep covered with blue drilling, with a door and two
windows in front. At the right, as one entered, was the
usual little counter with the gold-scales, behind which
sat the proprietress, with a few shelves behind her on

which were the tins and stuff that constituted the stock in trade for that day. The back was curtained off for the kitchen, and along each wall in the front were little board tables seating four, with stools. The waiters here were attired in regulation short black coats, and carried towels on their arms in professional style. The bill of fare was somewhat variable. The waiter would approach, throw his gaze at the ceiling, and call off: "Hamburger, beefsteak — no, no, we're out of beefsteak, but we've got some nice sausages. Will you have some sausage and a little Hamburger on the side?" The waiter was so *à la mode* that one instinctively felt for a tip until one remembered that it was Dawson, and that a man making $7 a day and board would probably scorn anything less than a nugget.

As soon as the new-comers had taken a look at Dawson they began to spread out over the country prospecting, stampeding new creeks, looking at the mines, or hunting for "jobs." In this last particular they met with disappointment. Thousands of men came in expecting to find work at wages. There was plenty to do for the man of resource, who could make his own job. The camp was, as it will be for some time to come, largely a *prospectors'* camp.

Many, after a few days or a few weeks, condemned the country off-hand, whereas *we* knew that six months or a year was required to fully comprehend the "genius" of Klondike.

As an instance of what many were expecting, an old man—I should judge him to have been sixty years old—came in to where I was working on a large map in the Mining Exchange, and judging from that that I might have some acquaintance with the country, he began to ask me if I knew of any "bars" in the neighborhood where he could work out enough gold to get out of the country. He wanted to go over to Indian River, of which he had apparently read something; but he did not know that he was not physically strong enough to carry more provisions than would take him there and back, much less stop and work. He had not a cent of money, and only twenty pounds of grub, but, as he said

OUTFITS FOR SALE

he had a shovel, I advised him, as he was one of the first of the new-comers, to proceed at once to Eldorado and get a job shovelling-in at $1.50 an hour. Then, when he had a little money, he might think of prospecting. That man, or any man fixed as he was, might stake the richest claim in Klondike and not be able to get the gold out, or even to know it was there. How many there were who certainly went away cursing the country, cursing those who persisted against evidence in calling it a "poor man's country"!

Among the throng there was none who interested me more than a tall figure I used to see from day to day. He wore a pair of deer-skin pants fringed on the outer seam, a loose blue-flannel shirt, belted in, and a wide-brimmed gray hat, from beneath which locks as soft as a girl's straggled to his shoulders. There was a look almost poetic in the gentle blue eyes of this picturesque individual. His whole air, indeed, suggested, as he doubtless intended it should, a romantic type of "cowboy." I was sitting in the tent of a Seattle mining broker; the day was hot and sweltering. This man, strolling along the street as we had seen him for the past few days, approached the open door, and, leaning in the welcome shade against the door-post, began talking to Mr. Hannon. The conversation proceeded for a while, touching matters of general interest. At length, and there was a tone of sadness in his voice, he looked squarely in Mr. Hannon's eyes as he said, " You don't remember me?" "No, I can't say that I do," replied Mr. Hannon. "Why, don't you know me? I'm the barber, across from your place in Seattle." And two friends, who had parted eight months before in Seattle, wrung hands in silence while a tear trickled down the cheek of each.

But, seriously, if it were not for persons like this, who for the past year have cultivated a "frontier" air, there would be little in Dawson to suggest the frontier town. Such as these simply amuse the old plainsman, who wore his hair long twenty or thirty years ago, because it was considered only fair to offer the Indian an acceptable scalp.

Bewildering as was the crowd pouring in from above, hardly less so were the preparations for supplying the Yukon by way of St. Michael. Figures alone can give an idea of the magnitude of the business, for the display was of a different sort. Where last year two ocean vessels met at St. Michael the five steamers that supplied Dawson, more than twenty ocean steamers were headed for St. Michael, and forty-seven river steamers, some of twice the tonnage of the largest previously on the river, and equalling in equipment and passenger accommodations the best Ohio and Mississippi river packets, were either on the stocks at Seattle or in sections on the deck of steamers for putting together at Dutch Harbor and St. Michael, or were already at St. Michael and within the Yukon, awaiting the breaking-up of the river. Never before was such activity seen on the West Coast. At one ship-yard (Moran's) in Seattle there were, at one time, fourteen river steamers ordered by new companies. Every ocean-going steam-vessel not already in the Skagway service, even from the "bone yards" of Seattle and San Francisco, was bought or chartered by companies of every degree of reliability. Six large steamers came around the Horn, five being Red Star and American transatlantic liners. Nor are vessels that sailed from New York during the winter with passengers direct for St. Michael included in this count, but only the vessels of companies organized for a permanent business in the Yukon. The two old companies advertised that they had more than doubled their previous equipment of river and ocean vessels. Besides, there were at St. Michael numbers of prospecting parties, each with a small steamer or motor-launch bound mostly for the headwaters of the Koyukuk River, thirty of which reached their destination. And if it had been any but a "Klondike" year, the stampede to Kotzebue Sound, *via* St. Michael, chartering every available steam and sailing vessel on the Pacific coast and landing 2000 miners at the scene of an alleged discovery of gold, would have commanded universal attention.

The Canadian Minister of the Interior, the Honorable Clifford Sifton, granted to a firm of contractors, Messrs. Mackenzie & Mann, provisional right to construct a railroad from the Stikeen River to Teslin Lake, in return for immense grants of gold-bearing land in the Klondike. Surveys were made and material delivered at the terminus of the proposed road, and tickets were sold in the principal cities of Europe and the United States for through passage to Dawson! In all, some thousands of unfortunate dupes ascended the Stikeen River, to find no railroad in existence, and 150 miles of horse trail on which there was insufficient forage for horses. On this, the most practicable of the "all-Canadian" routes into the Yukon, a fleet of steamers were to ply on the Stikeen River, and a small steamer, the *Anglian*, was already built on Lake Teslin to ply between the lake and Dawson. Before the agreement with Mackenzie & Mann was ratified by Parliament, however, a committee of miners, sent out from Dawson in the fall of 1897 to protest against the royalty tax, discovered and pointed out to Parliament the true inwardness of the proposed franchise, the profits on which had already been figured out as $34,000,000, and, as a result of the flood of light they let in upon Parliament concerning the Yukon, the bill was killed.*

* 3,750,000 acres of mineral land in Klondike were to be granted to the contractors, whereas the whole area about Dawson that had been prospected contained only 864,000 acres. They were to be allowed to run their lines along 960 miles of creeks, whereas Bonanza and Eldorado are only thirty-one miles long; the land was to be held in fee simple, instead of by annual lease; and royalties on gold were to be only one per cent., instead of ten per cent., which were required of all others. In return for which they were to build a narrow-gauge railroad, from a terminus only twenty-six

RAILWAY OVER WHITE PASS

On the 15th of June the first mile of a narrow-gauge railroad over White Pass was laid in Skagway. The general name of "White Pass and Yukon Route" included three distinct charters. The Pacific and Arctic Railway and Navigation Company operate to the summit; the British Columbia Yukon Railway Company is to operate from there across British Columbia; while the British-Yukon Mining, Trading, and Transportation Company will build to Dawson. By November 15, 1899, the twenty miles to the summit was opened for traffic; the fare for a passenger was $5, or 25 cents a mile, making it probably the most expensive railroad travel in the world.

At Bennett a fleet of small steamers, the largest ninety feet in length, was built or put together for navigating the river and lakes to Dawson.

A few months had turned Skagway into a city with broad, graded streets and sidewalks, lighted by 1200 sixteen-candle-power incandescent lights and fifty street arc-lights, and with one of the finest water supplies in the world, brought in pipes from a high mountain lake. It had a daily newspaper, and claimed to be the largest city in Alaska. It was governed by a civil council without tax-levying power, and preserved order with *one* United States marshal.

Probably no fewer than 60,000 persons reached Seattle and neighboring cities prepared to bear down upon Dawson.* The war with Spain intervened, and in three weeks

miles nearer Dawson than Skagway—150 miles of tracks, useless for seven months of the year—with right to charge exorbitant tolls, and with a monopoly of railway ingress to the Yukon for five years. It was a grab of nearly everything worth having in the Yukon district.

* A writer in the *Review of Reviews* estimates that at this date not fewer than 100,000 persons had started from different parts of the world for Klondike.

the Klondike boom was flat. But probably 40,000 reached the headwaters of the Yukon. The police at Tagish reported that up to the 18th of June, 7200 boats, averaging about five persons each, had passed. The number who reached Dawson is impossible to determine. Four to five thousand stopped at Stewart to prospect that river, and thousands, after remaining a few days or weeks in Dawson, left for the camps in American territory or for home. A police census of the population encamped on the Dawson flat in midsummer made the number 17,000 to 18,000. Four to five thousand people were in the mines, or in a radius of fifty miles, prospecting.

Besides those who took the direct route to Dawson, probably 2000 started in by way of Edmonton. Of those who tried the Peace-Pelly-rivers route from there (the Hudson's Bay Company route of forty years ago), not one, so far as is known, reached the Yukon, and the unfortunate victims of their own folly and the greed of Edmonton merchants met with sufferings untold, the way being marked with abandoned outfits, dead horses, and dead and dying men. Those who took the longer, Mackenzie-Porcupine-rivers route, fared not much better; a miserable few reached the Porcupine, while a number that one could count on the fingers of a hand reached Dawson at the end of summer, but only by leaving their outfits beyond McDougall's Pass. The unfortunate ones who remained with their outfits were able to proceed either forward or backward at best but a few miles a day. It is perhaps no exaggeration to say that this pitiable endeavor to reach Klondike by an all-Canadian route will cost the lives, directly and indirectly, from exposure and disease, of 500 persons. This is the price that the Canadian government pays for an all-Canadian route, and for the development of the supposed resources of the Mackenzie River valley. With a full knowledge of the situation, obtained through its own surveyors, it should have sounded a note of warning, instead of giving it public approval, as it did by official maps and reports.

Nearly two thousand miners ascended the Copper River, led by reports of gold and copper on the headwaters of this dangerous and difficult river. Practically nothing was accomplished, and many lost their lives crossing the treacherous Valdez Glacier. By this river, however, will run, sometime in the near future, an all-American railway to the gold-fields of the Yukon, striking that river probably at Eagle City.

The Yukon had been open a month lacking a few hours and there was no steamer yet from below. Speculation as to which would arrive first favored the *Bella* and the *Weare*, which had but to go from Circle City to Fort Yukon to load. At four o'clock on the morning of the 8th of June the cry " Steamboat !" was raised for the fiftieth time and passed along the street, and as usual all hands rushed to the water-front and looked. A tiny speck and smoke could be faintly seen two miles below; odds favored its being the *Bella*, from its having but one smoke-stack, whereas the *Weare* has two. The arrival of the first steamer in the spring at the starved-out camps has been always hailed with the same delight as would a column coming to the relief of a beleaguered garrison. It was an event in which not only every miner was expected to turn out and take part by waving his hat and cheering, but as the deep whistle of the incoming boat was blown every Malamut dog lifted its voice in a doleful wail. This wail began, we were told, at the first blast of the whistle, and the singular thing is that the leader struck the exact pitch, high or low, of the steamboat. Then in waves the moan arose, breaking out in renewed and louder howls, each succeeding wave louder than the former, until a volume of dissonance had risen over the whole camp, from a thousand dogs' throats, that drowned the very whistle, and was prolonged for several minutes afterwards. We had heard upon previous occasions this dismal concert, generally at the time one wanted to sleep, and made doubly irritating by the deep barkings of hundreds of big " outside" dogs, who, unlike their "inside" relatives, did not, when once aroused, know when to quit.

Now, however, the cravings and yearnings of the stomach having been appeased by the abundance brought in from up river, there was but little excitement except among the saloon-keepers, who were, all but one, out of whiskey ; while the dogs, being used to the daily blasts of several saw-mills, hardly so much as pricked up their ears. When the steamer drew into the wharf she proved to be the *May West*, a stranded boat that wintered near the Tanana River. She reported the *Weare* and the *Bella* high and dry on the bank at Circle City, where the ice had shoved them. Another stranded boat, the *Seattle No. 1*, came in soon after, followed by the Alaska Commercial Company's boat *Victoria ;* and on the 30th the *Merwin*, with the ill-fated *Eliza Anderson* party, arrived at their destination after just one year of misfortune and hardships. Finally the *Bella* and the *Weare* arrived, but not a word from St. Michael until the arrival of the *Healy* on the 8th of July. After that it occupied the staff of two newspapers to keep track of the doings on the water-front. The two old companies were clearly unmatched as to equipment, but there were at least six or seven new ones firmly established on the river, with warehouses at Dawson and other points, and a large fleet of excellent steamboats. One of the strongest of the new companies, the Empire Line (a connection of the American and Red Star transatlantic lines), was crippled by the withdrawal of their ocean vessels as government transports to the Philippines ; while a number of river steamers, estimated by one authority at twenty, belonging to this and other companies, were lost or delayed on the ocean voyage from Seattle and from Dutch Harbor, so that their passengers, who had paid for transportation to Dawson, were put to much delay and trouble at St. Michael. Their managers for the most part were able to purchase steamers outright after the first trip up, or else their own arrived in time to start them for Dawson before navigation closed.

Notwithstanding these delays, by September 1st (according to the figures given at the customs office at Dawson) fifty-six steamboats delivered cargoes of freight and passengers. The amount of provisions landed was 7540 tons, of which about half was brought up by the two old companies, the tonnage of the Alaska Commercial Company being the largest on the river. The North American Transportation and Trading Company, in addition to their own boats, chartered a number of steamers, or bought them outright, including their cargoes. By the date above mentioned nearly twenty steamers were on their way from St. Michael, most of which reached Dawson.

On the 14th of June a tiny whistle was heard in the river above town, and a diminutive steamer came puffing down to the wharf. She was 35 feet long and 8 feet wide, the *Bellingham* by name, and came under her own steam all the way from Bennett, successfully running both the Canyon and White Horse rapids. She attracted much attention as being the first steamer to arrive from up river. It was generally supposed that she was the first steamer that ever made the trip. But in the spring of 1895 a small propeller named the *Witch-Hazel*, 27 feet long, was hoisted over Chilkoot by Frank Atkins and E. L. Bushnell, of Portland, Oregon, shot the rapids, and reached Fort Cudahy, where the hull now lies.

Within the next few days eight more steamers reached Dawson from the lakes. Two others, the *Kalamazoo* and the *Joseph Clossett*, were wrecked, one on Thirty-Mile River, the other in the Canyon. The Upper Yukon had never been previously ascended by a steamer above Fort Selkirk, and the experiment of transportation out that way was watched with interest. On the 23d of June the *Victoria* departed for Rink Rapids, where 350 horses were waiting to carry passengers out over the Dalton trail. The fare to Pyramid Harbor was $250, which entitled each passenger to board, one saddle-horse, and two pairs of blankets as baggage. The steamer also carried Canadian mail and light express. The experiment was not repeated, as by the time the *Victoria* returned to Dawson it had been demonstrated that a steamer with the aid of a windlass could ascend Five-Finger Rapids, and, by connecting with small steamers above the Canyon, establish an easier and quicker route. The *Flora* and the *Nora* (each 80 × 16 feet), of the Bennett Lake and Klondike Navigation Company, made connection at White Horse with their steamer *Ora*. The fare from Dawson to Bennett was $175, and from Bennett to Dawson $75, with board, but passengers were required to furnish their own bedding. The time was five to six days up to White Horse ; to Bennett, seven. The *Willie Irving* (90 feet), the *Goddard* (40 feet) and the *Anglian* (Canadian Development Company) carried passengers to White Horse.

STEAMBOAT FARES

The journey out to Seattle was made in thirteen days, while, by a series of fortuitous connections, the trip from New York to Dawson was made by one Bartlett, a packer, in thirteen and a half days, the schedule being as follows: New York to Seattle, five days; Seattle to Skagway, three and a half days; Skagway to Bennett, one day; Bennett to Dawson, four days. About 1500

DEPARTURE OF STEAMER FOR ST. MICHAEL

persons went out this way. As soon as the up-river route was proven a success, several steamers from St. Michael were placed in the service. The fare remained about the same until September 14th, when the *Clara* made a rate of $95 to Bennett, meals $1 each and berths free.

The *May West*, the first steamer to start for below, left on June 18th, with 68 passengers at $100 each, to St.

Michael only. To meet the expected rush for passage on first steamers out, the North American Transportation and Trading Company made a rate of $300 to Seattle (an increase of $125 over last year), and passengers were required to send with them, by express, at least $1000 in gold-dust. Their steamer *Hamilton* left on the 23d of June with 178 passengers, and the *Weare*, on the 24th, with about 40 passengers and $1,500,000 in gold-dust. The Alaska Commercial Company charged for their first trip $250 for first-class, and $200 for second (according to accommodations on the ocean vessel); and on the 28th the *Bella* left with 150 passengers and $1,000,000 in gold. The *Seattle No. 1* cut to $150 to Seattle, and left on the 30th with 146 passengers. The North American Transportation and Trading Company made a $100 second-class rate on 100 passengers; but the cost of a ticket to Seattle remained during the season at about $200 on the best boats. Passage included meals and berth in state-room on both river and ocean steamer. The record time from St. Michael to Dawson was twelve and a half days, held by the North American Transportation and Trading Company's boat *John Cudahy*, her round trip consuming nineteen and a half days.

Upon the arrival of steamers from St. Michael, food and supplies of all kinds were more plentiful, but when lists were issued by the companies prices were somewhat advanced, flour being $8 per sack. Several new restaurants were opened, some of which would have been a credit to a city in civilization, both in the variety of food offered and in the manner of its service. The "Fairview Hotel," a three-story frame building, opened by Alec McDonald and Miss Mulrooney, was the handsomest building in town. It was intended, when darkness and cold made it necessary, several months later, to light it by electricity and heat it with hot air. Although the inevitable bar occupied the front, the Fairview could lay claim to being a respectable hotel, as there was a side entrance for ladies, who might not like to pass through the bar - room, and it possessed a bath-room. One of the best *chefs* was employed, and meals were served on linen - covered tables, with silver and china. The price of a meal—considered by some the best in Dawson—was $2. Board, with a 10 × 12-foot room, was $125 to $250 a month, according to location, and for transients $6.50 a day. Board without room was at first $25 a week, but was afterwards raised to $35 a week.

The "Regina Café," alongside the North American Transportation and Trading Company's warehouse gave, in my estimation, the best meal in town. It was in charge of one of the best San Francisco *chefs*. The linen was white and neat, there were arm-chairs of oak, and the service was of china and silver, such as one would find in a fairly well-to-do household at home. Here, besides every conceivable variety of food that is canned, one could order an oyster-pattie or a mayonnaise dressing ! The price of dinner was $2.50; breakfast, $1.50; or a ticket entitling one to twenty-one meals could be purchased for $30. Cigars and liquors here were only 25 cents, although elsewhere the price was 50 cents. At all the other restaurants the price of meals dropped first from $2.50 to $2, then to $1.50, which remained about the average price for a "square"meal, although a "Jap" sold a pretty good "staver-off" for $1 at a lunch-counter.

CHAPTER XIX

Hundreds of Miles of Claims—Wild Stampedes—Gold Under the Yukon—Gold on the Hill-Tops—Fickleness of Fortune—The "Clean-up" Begun—Bonanza Creek in Summer—A Clean-up on No. 13 Eldorado—High Pans of Gold—Richest Ground in Klondike—Newcomers' Good-Fortune—French and Gold Hills—Total Output—Bringing Down the Gold—Values of Klondike Gold—Banks—Unique Bank-Check—Improvements in Methods of Mining—"King of the Klondike"

IMPORTANT discoveries of gold followed those on Bonanza, Hunker, and Bear creeks. In June, 1897, two men reported gold on Dominion Creek, a large tributary of Indian River having its source opposite Hunker Creek. Both men claimed separate discovery, and the Gold Commissioner, being unable to decide who had the prior right to discovery, allowed two discoveries, which subsequently proved to be five miles apart, and are known respectively as "Upper" and "Lower" Discoveries. The prospects were excellent, but no work of consequence was done until winter. About Christmas reports of half-ounce nuggets being found resulted in a stampede, and everything on the main creek, which was larger than Bonanza, was staked, and staking continued on the numerous tributaries until, in July, 1898, there were two hundred and seventy-five 500-foot claims on the main creek, which, added to thirty or forty tributaries, reached the extraordinary length of 140 to 150 miles of staked claims. Between Discoveries the ground proved very rich, and single claims were purchased by Eldorado owners for as high as $40,000.

In June, 1897, four men, two of whom were named Whitmore and Hunter, made an important discovery about five or six miles from the head of another large creek lying between Dominion and Quartz Creek and heading directly opposite one fork of Gold Bottom. The creek, which was called Sulphur Creek, was staked by successive waves of stampeders. During the winter about a dozen holes were put down at intervals over nine miles of creek, but nearly every shaft disclosed rich pay and demonstrated the creek to be comparable in richness to Bonanza Creek. In July, 1898, over thirty miles of creek and tributaries were staked in 500-foot claims, and those in the best locations were selling for from $30,000 to $40,000.

Quartz Creek, although its situation and history should have drawn the attention of stampeders to it earlier, was overlooked until September and October, 1897, when a thousand men went over the head of Eldorado staking in succession everything in sight. In July, 1898, about thirty-five miles of creeks and tributaries were staked in 500-foot claims. "Eureka" Creek, with about thirteen miles of claims and good prospects; "Ninemile," "Ophir," "Big," "Wolf," and "Gold Run" were located in the Indian River district, the last-named creek, with twelve or fifteen miles of claims, "proving up" rich. On Bonanza everything in sight was staked, even to the tops of the gulches, until there were one hundred and eleven claims below and one hundred and nineteen above Discovery, and over forty "pups," or tributaries (including Eldorado), with a total length of about eighty-five miles of claims.

Hunker Creek was located for eighty-one claims below and fifty above Discovery, with eighteen or twenty "pups," including Gold Bottom, footing up about sixty miles of claims. Bear Creek, a very rich creek, but only five or six miles long, was all located. "All Gold," with about eighty-five 500-foot claims, and more on tributaries, was located, and developments gave claims a market value of $5000 for half-interests. "Too Much Gold," with eight miles of 500-foot claims, and "Leotta," with five miles of 200-foot claims, were also located. These are all tributaries of Klondike. Discoveries were reported on creeks entering the Yukon near Dawson, but it apparently did not matter to the stampeders whether there was gold in them or not. They spent much of their time about the saloons looking for "tips" from more energetic actual prospectors, and some by the end of winter, particularly those who purchased information of unrecorded claims from the Gold Commissioner's Office, possessed from forty to two hundred claims and interests each. By the 1st of July, 1898, between nine thousand and ten thousand placer-mining claims had been recorded.

Every one of this number was believed to have great value, and so inflamed did the imaginations of the owners become that claims on creeks in which not a pick had been stuck were valued at thousands of dollars. During the winter large numbers of these claims were offered for sale outside, in the belief that the popular mind was so inflamed that anything to which the name "Klondike" was attached would sell. From the old-timers' point of view the camp was spoiled. One of them expressed the prevailing feeling when he said,

"Prospecting's done away with. All the prospecting tools a man needs now is an axe and a lead-pencil."

Nothing could exceed the excitement of some of the stampedes that took place during the winter. An old man living in a cabin on the Yukon above Dawson reported at the recorder's office that he had found gold on "Rosebud" Creek about fifty miles above Dawson. The news got around to the rest of the camp, and all who could do so started. All one night, by match and candle light, they measured and staked. It turned out that no gold whatever had been found on the creek. On February 14th "Swede" Creek, six miles from town, was similarly stampeded. Two Swedes who had been prospecting there came down to record, and let out the news. It was two o'clock in the morning, and a bright moon was shining, and a stream of people, numbering over three hundred, marched up there and staked all that day and into the night. Five men were badly frozen, two having to suffer partial amputation of both feet. It was, indeed, the wonder of all who saw the *chechahkos* starting out in the dead of winter, often dressed only in house clothes, some wearing even shoes, that more were not frozen, but it seemed, as has been truly said, that "Providence was with the *chechahko*."

In April a sensational discovery was reported by two Swedes cutting wood on an island in the Yukon opposite Ensley Creek, eighteen miles from Dawson. During the winter they sank a shaft to a depth of thirty-eight feet and found gold on bed-rock. A mining inspector went up from Dawson and "proved" the discovery, obtaining, it is said, single pans as high as $8. The island was located in 250-foot claims and named "Monte Cristo." Other islands below were immediately staked and holes put down, but the rise of water in the river flooded their holes and stopped work. During the next summer the original discoverers of Monte Cristo panned out $300 on their dump, and sank another hole thirty-four feet and took out $200. At the same time several parties worked on a flat at the side of the river, sank eighteen holes, and then came down to record, whereupon there was another stampede, one hundred and eighty men going up in one day. Soon after the "Monte Cristo" discovery two holes were put down in the flat at Dawson. One night after dark the town-site was staked off, but the parties were not allowed to record.

The discovery of gold in these locations was startling, but not more so than the finding of gold on the "hill-tops." Shortly after Carmack's discovery on Bonanza Creek, H. A. Ferguson found gold higher up the hill, above Carmack's claim, but no one thought seriously of hill-side gold until July, 1897, almost a year later, when Albert Lancaster, a California miner, climbed up the west side of Eldorado, off No. 2, and began digging. He was laughed at by the miners, but he worked all winter, in plain sight of the busiest part of the mines. He recorded his claim, a plot 100 × 100 feet, on August 4, 1897 — the first "bench" or hill-side claim recorded in the Klondike. Soon after Lancaster's discovery, one William Diedrick, better known as "Caribou" Billy, made a similar discovery at the junction of Skookum Gulch and Bonanza Creek; and about the same time a man named Peterson made a discovery on the opposite side of the same gulch. Peterson dug a few feet into the hill-side and took out $6000. Immediately after these discoveries the ground in their neighborhood was staked, not by the old-timers in the Bonanza Creek, as one would think, but by new-comers and hangers-on from town. Holes were sunk near Lancaster, and a nugget was found weighing over a pound, and another worth $550 at the mouth of Skookum. Still the miners, for a reason hard to understand, could not realize that vast riches lay in plain sight along the hill-side, nor could they understand the theory of an old stream-bed, from which all the gold in the creek-bed perhaps originally came. Caribou Billy, however, seems to have

" BENCH " OR HILL-SIDE CLAIMS, FRENCH HILL, IN AUGUST, 1898

understood this, for he kept examining the sides of Eldorado, and on the 16th of March, with Joe Staley, a newcomer from Dayton, Ohio, began digging on the hill-side on the west side, off No. 16, at the mouth of French Gulch. Joe Staley, with his brother Ben, had left home before the Klondike excitement, attracted by reports from Miller Creek, and reached Dawson in June, 1897. His lot was about that of the average new-comer, until he fell in with the old Caribou miner. On the brow of the hill, two hundred feet above the valley of Eldorado, the two men began digging. Four feet down they found gold, and, without waiting to see how much, they pitched the gravel back and put in another fire so as to make believe they had not reached bed-rock, for not twenty feet from their hole was a path down which the miners of Eldorado daily dragged wood for their fires. Joe hunted up his brother, and on the 19th of March he staked Discovery, 100 feet square, and Ben the same area alongside. They sank another hole, striking bed-rock at nine feet. Caribou Billy went down into the hole, and, after looking around, called up, "We've got it!" A pan was passed down to him and he sent up three pans of dirt, which were put into a sack and taken to the creek to pan. There was $189.75 in the sack. Before they could get back to the hole another "party" had been down and found a nugget as large as his thumb. Joe threw water into the hole and froze it and then recorded the claim. A stampede followed. I was making my last round before the thaw of the creeks at the time. I saw men going up a path in the snow, which was nothing unusual, and some heaps of yellow earth, at which men were working with picks and shovels. The hill was completely staked off, and Dominion surveyors were trying to straighten out the lines of the stampeders. I looked over the ground, admired the view from the hill, and then went down and talked with Joe Putrow, foreman for Professor Lippy, on No. 16 Eldorado, who was putting in a dam for sluicing, and asked him what they had up there. Putrow didn't think there was anything there. Neither did others I talked with; none of the men in the creek had been up to stake.

That evening, at the Grand Forks Hotel, the survey-

ors, who did not know more than any one else, offered me a set of stakes that were not taken. On the way back in the morning I met an acquaintance who had been working all winter on Bonanza. He had his sled and prospecting tools; he had spent several days digging on the hill, and was on his way back. When I asked what there was up there, he replied, in his picturesque language, "I'm from Missouri, and you've got to show it to me. I couldn't find 'colors' in holes they were throwing half-ounce nuggets out of. I think it's mostly 'salted.'" A Missourian, I believe, takes nothing on hearsay. I turned back, and we both went over to Dominion Creek and then returned to town, to cogitate, a few weeks later, on the fickleness of fortune.

The "clean-up" had been under way several weeks before I could again visit the mines. Unfortunately much of the work of sluicing the winter's dumps was over, and considerable of the gold, with its happy owners, had come down the gulch. But the scarcity of water after the subsidence of the freshet, owing to the small rainfall, was holding back the work on Eldorado, where the largest dumps were; and, besides, all the summer work of "ground-sluicing" was yet to be done.

Along the beaten trail to the diggings the aspect of nature was that of another clime. The thermometer had been indicating 70° in the shade at mid-day, and there were no clouds to intercept and modify the rays of the sun. Pack-horses and mules loaded with sacks and boxes plodded along in single file towards the mines, or were returning empty to town. Stampeders, in squads of three and five, with coats off, and mining pans and shovels on their backs, picked their way from tussock to tussock, following the winding trail in and out among the trees in the valley of lower Bonanza, or they lay on the ground, resting in the shade of the birches by rivulets of cold, clear water that trickled out of the side-gulches. Now and then one overtook a miner, leading one or more dogs with little canvas side-pouches stuffed out with cans of provisions, going to his claim. Summer had changed beyond recognition the winter's trail. Dams of crib-work filled with stones, flumes, and sluice-boxes lay across our path; heaps of "tailings" glistened in the sunlight beside yawning holes with windlasses tumbled in; cabins were deserted —the whole creek, wherever work had been done, was ripped and gutted. Nothing but flood and fire is so ruthless as the miner.

Pretty soon we came to some miners at work. One man was filling a wheelbarrow at a dump and unloading the earth and stones into a string of sluice-boxes extending from a long flume at the side of the valley; another man in rubber boots, with a close-tined pitchfork, stood ankle-deep in a torrent of water that half filled the boxes, and forked out the larger stones. A little farther on three men were "stripping" muck off a claim, ready for "ground-sluicing." A string of sluice-boxes running through the middle of the claim brought water from a dam above, and as the water fell upon the frozen muck they "picked" it out in chunks as black as coal, which the water gradually dissolved and carried off. In several places "stripping" was finished and the sluice-boxes were in place for sluicing, and crews of eight and ten men, in their shirt-sleeves, all wearing rubber boots, were engaged, some in wheeling the top dirt off in barrows and dumping it at one side of the creek, while others shovelled dirt from bed-rock into the boxes.

One man stood inside the sluice with an implement

like a hoe with tines, or with a round disk of wood on the end, with which he raked the heavier stones towards the dump-box, where another man stood pitching them out with a fork, while still another, at the end of the dump-box, shovelled the small stones into a heap each side. Although most of the water passes through the boxes or flumes, a considerable portion leaks into the

REMOVING RIFFLES, PREPARATORY TO "CLEANING-UP"

bottom of the cut, so that nearly every claim had a "china wheel" rigged for pumping the water out. The "china wheel" is an endless belt, with buckets every foot or so, running over two wheels placed as far apart as the depth of the cut makes necessary, the upper wheel being worked by a sluice-head of water against a small overshot wheel. When there is not enough water the pump is turned by hand.

No one seemed ready to make a "clean-up," so I kept on to No. 13 Eldorado, where I knew one of the "bosses." Here a big flume, higher than the eaves of the cabins, was tapped at right angles by strings of sluice-boxes, one for each dump, which were not yet all sluiced. Four claims, Nos. 13, 14, 15, and 16, were using the same dam and flume. Half a dozen men were lying around idle, and I was told they had been nearly a week waiting for a turn at the water. The flume was as dry as a tinder-box. I had the good-fortune not to have been there long before the flume began to drip, and pretty soon a good volume of water was pouring through. I noticed three men standing beside one of the dumps; they were "Bill" Leggett, one of the owners of the claim, and two workmen. George Wilson, partner of Swiftwater Bill, said, "If you want to see a clean-up you'd better go over there." A tin tub, a whisk-broom, and two or three small copper scoops lay on the ground beside the boxes, the riffles of which were clogged with dirt. The first the men did was to lift out the riffles, and then they shovelled the dirt from the bottom of the boxes into the tub. In the appearance of this dirt there was nothing strikingly handsome; at a little distance it looked like dirt one could dig out of the ground anywhere. Mr. Leggett climbed up on the flume, raised a little gate at the head of the string of boxes, sufficient to allow half a sluice-head of water to run through. Then he took a position beside the boxes, which stood about two feet off the ground, with the whisk-broom in one hand. One of the men then shovelled the dirt out of the tub into the sluice-box, and Mr. Leggett began sweeping it upward against the current. The lighter stones and gravel were immediately carried off, with a lot of dirty water, into the dump-box. The sweeping was kept up until there remained in the bottom of the box a mass of black mag-netic sand. The man with the broom continued sweep-ing; little by little the black sand worked downward, and at the upper edge blotches of yellow began to appear. In probably five minutes there lay on the bottom a mass of yellow, from which nearly all the black sand was gone. The yellow was not bright and glittering, but dull—almost the color of the new-sawn wood of the boxes. The water was turned off and the gold carefully scooped

"CLEANING-UP" SUMMER DIGGINGS, NO. 36 ELDORADO

up into the pan, where it looked like fat wheat, with here and there a grain as large as a hazel-nut. There was only $800 in the pan, Mr. Leggett said—a small clean-up for Eldorado.

On No. 36, two miles above, summer work had begun. The claim had been "stripped" the summer before, and now a crew of half a dozen men had just finished their

first shovelling into three strings of boxes. As I stood
on the bank looking down into the "cut," I saw a man
go up to the dam and shut off the water. Then a tall,
middle-aged man, in a flannel shirt and rubber boots, who
appeared to be the "boss," and who proved to be Mr.
Styles, half-owner of the claim with Alec McDonald,
walked out upon the boxes and picked up some nuggets, which he dropped into the pockets of his overalls.
Another man then followed him out, and they lifted the
riffles out, tapping each frame against the side of the box
to shake off any gold that might cling to it, and passed
them to a third man, who laid them in the dump-box.
Then Mr. Styles took a tool made from an old shovel,
bent and trimmed off square at the end like a hoe, and
with this he hoed the dirt into a heap in the second
box up-stream. Half a sluice-head of water was turned
on, which carried away considerable mud. Three tall
"horses" were next placed alongside the boxes and a
plank laid over them, so that a man could walk along
and look into the boxes. The water was now turned
off entirely, and the lower end of the last box was lifted
up and allowed to rest upon a stick laid across the
dump-box, a heavy stone being placed on top to hold it
firm. A very small quantity of water was now let
through. Mr. Styles and an assistant took a gold-pan,
a whisk-broom each, some little scoops, and a wooden
paddle about a foot long, and walked out on the trestle.
Mr. Styles began pushing the dirt against the current
with the paddle. Considerable mud and light dirt was
worked off, and then each took a whisk-broom and began
sweeping the remaining sand with the upward movement before described, and when no more sand could
be worked out the gold was scooped up into the pan.
The same operation was gone through with at the two

other boxes, the gold from each being put into a separate pan and then taken to the owners' cabin. In the photograph below, showing Mr. Styles at the door of his cabin, there are *four* pans that *seem* to contain gold. The fourth is a pan of *gravel* that I did not notice in range when the picture was taken, and shows how easy it would be to take a picture of a panful of sand

A $5000 CLEAN-UP

and call it "gold." The clean-up was also a small one —about $5000.

George Wilson showed me his note-book, with the records of the pannings made during the winter on Swiftwater Bill's "lay," of which he was half-owner. The "pay" was already located, and they simply panned to keep upon the "streak." The first pan was taken October 19, 1897, and the last March 11, 1898, and about two pans a day were taken. The total was $6584.50, an average of $50 to the pan! On many claims on Bonanza and Eldorado pans of $3 to $8 were so common that they failed to cause special comment. Still, to show how misleading single high pans are, a pan of $150 was found on a certain claim which on the clean-up hardly paid the wages of the men. The pay-streak on No. 3 Eldorado was not located until late in March, and several of the "laymen" had quit work in discouragement. When the "pay" was found, the first fourteen pans went $2200. Two nuggets, weighing respectively $312 and $400, were found during the summer on No. 36 Eldorado.

The question is often asked, What was the largest amount of gold taken in a single pan? One of about $1700 was reported on Eldorado, but was probably a "picked" pan—that is, taken a little here and a little there—and therefore not representative. On No. 36 Eldorado, in August, the shovellers were handling dirt which any one could see at a glance was very rich. One of the workmen threw a shovelful out on a flat rock to show the boss, and another was added so as to make a full pan. Mr. Styles panned the dirt out, and it went $690 (figuring $17 to the ounce). A second pan went over $500. These were not "picked," but "shovelled square." I asked Mr. Styles to estimate the product of a single "box-length." He said that from a space 15 × 12 feet he had taken $17,000. His "pay" being two feet thick, a richness is indicated of $1.20 to the pan.

The "Dick Lowe Fraction," probably the richest ground in Klondike, carries the pay-streak of Bonanza and that of Eldorado and the "wash" of Shookum Gulch. The foreman, out of whom a corkscrew couldn't pull any information of the amount of his clean-ups, confessed to have taken four pans containing forty ounces, or $680, each, and that had he desired he could have "picked" a pan of a hundred ounces. A man told me he saw a "cupful" of gold panned out of a single shovelful of dirt. Those who saw the first clean-up from this strip of ground say that it was all two men could do to carry off the gold in two pans from the clean-ups of the dumps. A "panful" of gold is not by any means a "pan full." A mining-pan will bear only so much weight without "buckling" when lifted by the rim, but it holds safely seventy-five pounds. This year it was estimated that forty days' sluicing off the dumps turned out $60,000. Summer work, "ground-sluicing," began about the end of July. Half a dozen men were working. At the end of three weeks seven panfuls of gold were carried away to the cabin—about 300 pounds, or $75,000. In the next six days $68,000 was cleaned up, making a total for the year of about $200,000. These estimates are only approximate, but made by careful on-lookers who reported what they saw. Leaving a wide margin for inaccuracy, and assuming that a whole 500-foot claim ran as evenly as the 78-foot strip, it would represent over $1,300,000; and if authorities are right who say that by the present crude methods of mining not more than *one-fourth* of the whole amount of gold in the ground is taken out, the possible richness of Klondike ground is bewildering to contemplate. The creeks are, however, left in such shape that it does not pay to work over the ground the second time by present methods, the only hope being cheaper labor and some kind of hydraulicking on a large scale.

Charley Anderson, who was "buncoed" into buying No. 29 Eldorado, has taken out $300,000 for his two years' work. He gave a "lay" to a man who had befriended him before he went to the Yukon. This "lay-man" expected to clean up $130,000.

Last November two men applied to Picotte & Hall, No. 17 Eldorado, for work. They were given a supposed valueless "lay," 60 × 40 feet, sunk to bed-rock, and in the first pan scraped up $400. Two months later Hall offered them $50,000 to leave their work, but they refused. Their clean-up is not known, but they stated that their "prospect" pannings for the winter lacked just $150 of being an even $10,000.

The benches continued the wonder of the camp. The hill-sides for eight miles below and four miles above Discovery, on Bonanza Creek, were spotted with dumps, encircling spots like French Hill and Lancaster's "Gold Hill" like a fillet of gold at a nearly uniform level. All day long was heard the *swish*, *swish* of hundreds of rockers. "Bed-rock" of the benches is a stiff, clay-like, decomposed mica-schist, extending from the so-called "rim," nearly level into the hill. The best workings were at the "rim," where the gold was covered by only a few inches of dirt. As the miners dug into the hill the depth of pay increased from a few inches to several feet. Those on the second tier were obliged to sink shafts. Five or six tiers back holes were sunk by the slow process of burning over one hundred feet. I was at Staley's after he had worked about twenty feet into the face of the hill, and the gold could be plainly seen in the strip of dark earth and gravel about a foot thick. Every panful of dirt then going into their single rocker was worth $5. Two claims northward of Staley's a man named David-son rocked out ten pounds of gold for three consecutive days! I happened to be at Lancaster's one day at noon, just after a clean-up of seventy-six ounces. In the afternoon fifty more ounces were rocked out, or $2142 for the day, the Klondike bench record for one rocker. One hundred dollars a day was common in several places. There were claims one hundred feet square worth probably $50,000, yet there were others in the most favorable locations that did not yield a single dollar from edge to edge of the claim.

Rich bench discoveries were made on Bear and Quartz creeks, and on Dominion; the latter, however, being at lower levels than on Bonanza.

The gold was carried down on the backs of men, mules, and dogs. It was nothing unusual to see twelve or sixteen men along the trail loaded with gold from a single claim. The amount of gold a man can carry for a long distance is much less than one might suppose. Gold is one of the most concentrated substances known, and there is scarcely any way of equalizing the weight so it will bear evenly upon the back. One 500, 600, or 800 ounce moose-hide sack full of the dust makes an ample load for a man. The sack is wrapped in cloths, then put into the pack-strap; but many a sack, especially those belonging to the smaller miners, was carried down in blankets, partly to make the load carry more softly, and partly to avoid suspicion, although whenever one observed a blanket dragging hard on the straps, one could be pretty sure there was gold inside. Horses and mules brought down the greater part of the clean-up. The amount actually carried by a single horse has been somewhat exaggerated. The packers, returning "light," preferred to divide the gold equally among all the horses, and so two sacks of gold, weighing one hundred and twenty-five to one hundred and thirty pounds, worth $25,000 or more, was the usual load for one horse. The sacks for horseback packing were wrapped in about a dozen thicknesses of canvas, and then lashed each side of an ordinary pack-saddle, or else dropped into the capacious side-pouches of the leathern *arapejo*. When carried in the latter way several hundred thousand dollars might pass by unnoticed. No extraordinary precautions seem to have been taken against robbers. Bartlett's train of a dozen mules, which brought down more gold than any other, was simply in charge of two men, who rode one at each end of the string with a shot-gun resting over the pommel of the saddle. Notwithstanding the opportunities presented, there were but one or two cases of highway robbery, and those only for small amounts. Much more gold was stolen by miners from their partners or employers. There rarely was an opportunity for a common workman to steal, unless in charge of the clean-up.

It was a pretty sight to see, as one could almost any day, a train of eighteen dogs working between Dawson and the mines in charge of one man, who led one dog while the rest followed or walked ahead. Once, when coming down creek with twenty to thirty pounds of gold each, one of the dogs, in attempting to walk a foot-log over the creek, slipped and fell in. Fortunately for the dog, his load slipped off and he swam ashore. The gold was afterwards fished out and saved.

The total output of the Klondike amounted to between ten and eleven millions, or a weight of about twenty-five tons. Earlier estimates of the probable amount gave $15,000,000 to $20,000,000. But on the clean-up the winter dumps did not turn out as expected. An immense amount of work on Lower Bonanza produced small results, the laymen on several claims consenting to remain only upon receiving seventy-five per cent. On the other hand, upper Bonanza and Eldorado washed-up better than "prospects" indicated. The output was divided among the creeks about as follows :

Eldorado, \$4,000,000 to \$5,000,000 ; Bonanza, \$3,000,000 to \$4,000,000 ; Hunker and Bear, \$1,000,000 ; Dominion, Sulphur, and other creeks, \$1,000,000. The amount re-

DOG PACK-TRAIN LEAVING DAWSON FOR THE MINES

ceived by refiners and the United States Mint, chiefly at Seattle and San Francisco, amounted, between July 1 and November 1, 1898, to \$10,055,270.*

If the number of men directly engaged in the production of this sum may be considered as 2000 (and it

* Samuel C. Dunham, Report of U. S. Department of Labor.

is nearly twice the number estimated by one excellent authority), this output represents an average production per man of over $5000.

Upon reaching Dawson the gold was taken either to the warehouses of the commercial companies or to the "vaults" of two newly arrived banks — the Canadian Bank of Commerce and the Bank of British North America—where it was packed in strong, square, iron-bound boxes for shipment by steamer to Seattle and San Francisco.

A complete assaying office was established, where miners could have their gold assayed at about the same cost as "outside," *plus* freight and insurance, and received drafts or bank-notes for the full value. No lot of less than fifty ounces was received for assay. The gold came from the smelter in ingots weighing forty to one hundred ounces, of the shape and size of chocolate cakes.

The gold from the different creeks varies greatly in fineness, as is shown by the following table supplied by the assay office :

Lower Bonanza	$15.75 to $16.35 to the ounce.
Upper Bonanza	$16.75 to $18.50.
Eldorado (Creek)	$16.50.
French Hill	$15 to $16.50.
Mouth of Skookum	$15 (much quartz in the gold).
Dominion, nearly	$17.
Hunker, sometimes	$17.50.
Bear	$15 to $16.
Forty - Mile and Birch Creeks (American Ter.), nearly . . .	$17.50.
Minook (American Ter.), about .	$18.

The different kinds are distinguishable to the trained

eye. Eldorado gold, having the largest alloy of silver, tin, etc., has a distinct brassy color as compared with upper Bonanza or Dominion gold.

"Trade" gold, the dust in ordinary circulation, had been rated at $17 per ounce, but Klondike gold proving to be of less value than that in the American territory, where the standard had been originally fixed, the banks, soon after their arrival, in June, reduced the price to $16, which amount, according to the assay office, is nearly 50 cents more than its actual value, because of the dirt and black sand usually left in it. This magnetic sand is readily removed with a strong magnet, and in some transactions it is required to be done. The Bank of Commerce had arrived in a scow, and found temporary quarters in a small warehouse, about fifteen by eighteen feet in dimensions, with no windows and a single door, in front of which a counter was built, leaving sufficient space inside for customers to stand. Within the room was a table and chairs, and the agent, Mr. Wills, assisted by one or two clerks, received gold-dust, which he weighed in a pair of immense scales, issuing paper money or drafts in return. The "vaults" were two wooden tin-lined boxes, four feet long, three feet wide, and three feet deep, with a lid. Upon one occasion I saw these half full of gold sacks, also five boxes of gold packed for shipment, each holding from 500 to 800 pounds of gold-dust —close to a million dollars in all. On the table in front of the agent was a stack of notes a foot high, though the door was wide open, and there was not a weapon or a guard in sight. Afterwards they removed to a large building next to the barracks. Being under government auspices, each shipment of gold was accompanied by a mounted policeman armed with a Winchester rifle. The first quarters of the Bank of British North America was even more crude—only a frame of scantling covered with canvas.

"*Chechahko* money," as currency is called, rapidly superseded gold-dust. The Bank of Commerce alone issued nearly a million dollars in bank-notes during the summer. The new-comers also brought in much small change, with the result that by the end of summer about half the retail business was conducted in currency. The use of currency was further encouraged by an important decision of the court, which declared that gold-dust could not be forced in payment of indebtedness unless expressly stipulated.

There have been curious checks presented to cashiers of banks, as when Jay Gould purchased a railroad and drew a check in payment on the back of an old envelope; but probably there never was one more unique than a check presented at the Bank of Commerce in Dawson. It was written on a piece of spruce lumber about six inches square with a wire nail "toe-nailed" into its upper edge. It read:

"CANADIAN BANK OF COMMERCE.

"*Gentlemen,*—Please pay W. F. Foster $3.00 for services rendered.   J. C. HORNE & CO.

"BY B.

"DAWSON CITY, *August* 4, 1898."

The check was duly endorsed "W. F. Foster," and stamped "Paid." The cashier was in doubt what the nail had been driven in for, until Mr. Foster suggested that it might be for "filing" the check.

From the moment it was understood that the richness of Klondike was locked in frozen ground, the brains of inventors had been busy trying to devise a quicker and cheaper way of getting at the gold than burning. One of the most practical of these, and the only one I saw in operation, was a machine consisting of a hollow auger having a diameter of nine inches with a length of twelve inches, and a hollow stem connecting with a generator, through which steam was forced, thawing the ground as the stem was turned, and the stem being lengthened as the depth increased. When stones were reached too large to pass, the auger and various drills and picks were

LOADING BOXES OF GOLD UPON THE STEAMER FOR SHIPMENT OUT

used to loosen them, or else blasting was resorted to. It was successfully tried on the flat at Dawson, and a nineteen-foot hole was put down for $330 that would have cost $700 to sink in the old way. The inventor charged $15 per foot for the first ten feet, and $20 per foot for each succeeding foot. This price, while high, was about half the cost of burning. By such means a claim can be punched full of holes until the pay-stream is located, when it can be worked in the old way. Patent "riffles," for saving the fine gold lost at present, were brought in, but not yet tried. The only other labor-saving machinery used was a common road-scraper operated by a steel cable passing over a drum run by a small steam-engine, used for removing the top dirt in summer diggings. Dredging-machines, of which much was expected, and of which several arrived, have not up to the present been successful, their sanguine promoters apparently being unaware that the gold does not lie on the bottom of the frozen rivers, but many feet below, in frozen gravel.

Of all the fortunes in Klondike, Alexander McDonald is generally credited with having the largest. He is a Scotchman born, who came into the Yukon in 1895, after varied success as a miner in Colorado. At the time of the Klondike strike he was in the employ of the Alaska Commercial Company at Forty-Mile, where he showed good judgment in buying mining properties.

In the stampede from there, McDonald was obliged to join or be left alone, and reached the new diggings in September, 1896. Being too late to stake in the rich ground, he used what money he had in buying-in at the low prices which prevailed at that time. His first interest was No. 30 Eldorado. Although he thought so little of it that he put men to work on a "lay," while he went to work on another claim, there is no doubt that he was among the first to rightly apprehend the richness of Klondike mines. By mortgaging his claims (payable at the clean-up on "bed-rock") he purchased other claims, with few errors in judgment. He is only half or quarter owner in the richest claims that are credited to him, but he now owns upwards of forty interests and full claims. In appearance he is a large, brawny, swarthy man, canny and close of mouth, with a curious habit of slowly rubbing his chin whenever a new proposition is presented to him. He makes it a rule to first say "No" to every proposal, however alluring, thus gaining time to think it over. At one time

PACK-TEAM, LOADED WITH GOLD, GOING DOWN BONANZA CREEK

in the camp whatever "Big Alec McDonald" approved of in mines was "all right." His fortune has been estimated at $5,000,000, and may be more than that. While that much gold and more may be in his ground, it is hard to say what he is actually worth. To-day, however, he is popularly known as "King of the Klondike."

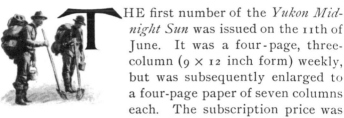

T HE first number of the *Yukon Midnight Sun* was issued on the 11th of
June. It was a four-page, three-
column (9 × 12 inch form) weekly,
but was subsequently enlarged to
a four-page paper of seven columns
each. The subscription price was
50 cents per copy, or $15 per year. Its first Yukon num-
ber was published in the late winter at Caribou Crossing, its single issue there being the *Caribou Sun.* On
the 16th of June appeared the *Klondike Nugget*, a particularly well-printed, four-page, four-column folio, issued semi-weekly, at 50 cents per copy, or $16 a year.
Early in September appeared *The Klondike Miner*, a
weekly.

The startling news of the blowing-up of the *Maine* in
Havana Harbor was brought in late in the spring by the
" Montana Kid," a sporting gentleman who, in his haste
to get out of Dawson the fall before, had borrowed a
team of dogs without the owner's permission. There
were indefinite rumors of war. About June 1 a new-
comer brought word that some one had told him he had
seen a bulletin at Seattle of a big battle with the Spanish

fleet. No one credited it. Representatives of outside newspapers planned for public readings of the first definite news, and stationed a man at Klondike City to intercept any newspapers that arrived. On the 6th of June word was passed along the street that a paper had been found, and every one was told to be at the "A. C."

YUKON
MIDNIGHT SUN

VOL. I   DAWSON. NORTHWEST TERRITORY, SATURDAY JUNE 11TH, 1898.   NO. I.

GOLD OUTPUT FOR THE YEAR

TWENTY MILLIONS.

That is the Amount Which the Klondike Will Produce This Year.

much lower. Not more than twenty-five claims on Eldorado have been extensively worked. During the winter, while drifting was going on, very little thorough prospecting for the purpose of determining the value of the gravel was done. The dumps have not been sampled, and as a result very few mine owners or managers had any definite idea before they

which is expected to leave on the 18th inst. Their departure, while ostensibly only for a temporary stay, may be permanent. There is hardly one of the old timers who does not express regret that the good old Captain and the worthy "first lady of the Yukon" are to take their departure, probably for good. The MIDNIGHT SUN will have more to say of the good work Captain Constantine has done in the Yukon country. Certainly the departure of no people from this country has ever caused so

store at eight that evening. Long before the appointed time the crowd began to secure places around a goods box that had been placed in the middle of the street. By eight o'clock fully five hundred people had gathered. Promptly at the hour the New York *Times* man and "Judge" Miller, a lawyer from San Francisco, came down the street with another crowd at their heels, and pushed inside the ring. The Judge, who had been chosen as having a good voice, wearing a cowboy hat, mounted the box. There was a breathless silence as, after making one or two opening remarks to make himself feel at home, the Judge opened the paper—

THE KLONDIKE NUGGET.

VOL. I. No. 1. DAWSON, N. W. T., THURSDAY, JUNE 16, 1898 PRICE 5^{cts} CENTS

THE LATEST NEWS FROM THE WAR.

A Succinct Review of the Situation as It Now Stands.

will be furnished with the news promptly and accurately

Latest, Outside War News.

On the steamer Bellingham, from Bennett, came Charles Eschwege and son Michael. Mr. Eschwege is an Englishman, and has spent a number of years as a mining broker in the great gold fields of Johannesburg, and will open a like business here. His son has just re-

had retired, but a sufficient number remained to welcome her in true Yukon style.

As the gang plank was being lowered the good natured crowd interviewed the few employes aboard asking for news, and in imitation of hotel runners could be heard, "Free 'bus to the Astor House!" "All aboard for the Brewery Hotel!!" "Hotel, sir?" "An ounce a day at the Klondike Hotel!" with the proper emphasis.

The Victoria carried no passengers and her cargo of about 85 tons consisted mainly of provisions and hardware.

WHAT THE DIGGINGS WILL YIELD.

Opinions Vary But All Agree That the Output Will Be Very Large.

a Seattle daily of two weeks previous. Clear and distinct came the words: "Dewey's Great Victory. The Spanish Fleet Annihilated!" There was a moment's silence, when a cheer broke out from five hundred throats, and arms and hats were waved in the air. When the reader could begin again, and read something about the English captain telling the German admiral "Hands off!" the enthusiasm of the crowd knew no bounds.

They cheered and cheered, demanding every item of news relating to our preparations for the war that evidently was on. That night hardly anything else was talked about. Next day another paper was found, and as soon as it was known a crowd started down the street for the Alaska Commercial Company's store like a lot of schoolboys, calling out "Miller! Miller!" Now for the first time we heard of the preliminary movements of the Atlantic fleets; our unpreparedness for the war; the bombardment of San Juan; the sad mishap to the *Winslow*. A third paper gave us details of the fight at Manila. Again and again the reader paused for the cheers of the crowd as the graphic story

424

of the battle was told. When that part was reached where the Spanish captain nailed his colors to the mast and his brave men kept firing as the ship sank beneath the waves, there was a dead silence. Then several low voices said, "They were all right! They were all right!" There was not a man in the crowd but whose heart was touched, and it would not have been hard just then to have raised a cheer for the men who could fight like that.

Immediately after this the two newspaper plants were in operation, and there were no more public readings until the 22d of July, when papers arrived with accounts of the destruction of Cervera's fleet on July 3.

The first newspapers with war news brought whatever was asked. As it was known the news was for public reading, their owners did not make exorbitant demands, the highest price I knew of being $1. In April sixteen hundred newspapers, all several months old, were brought in by dog teams and sold for $1 each. The new-comers brought boatloads of all the prominent daily, weekly, and monthly periodicals; magazines sold for $1 and newspapers for 25 cents.

It sounded strangely out of place, in this erstwhile wilderness, to hear the newsboy, walking up and down the street, with a bunch of papers in his arms, shouting at the top of his voice, " Springfield *Republican*, Detroit *Free Press*, Chicago *Times-Herald*, Omaha *Bee*, Kansas City *Star*—all the daily papers!" even though they were from three weeks to a month old.

The Americans, who comprised the bulk of the population, felt proud of Dewey's victory; but hardly any one was prepared for what happened at just one minute past twelve on the morning of July 4th. At that time night and day were so near alike that half of Dawson was awake and up. At one minute past midnight a rifle cracked out on the hill-side. Within the next minute a dozen shots followed, here and there over the camp. In five minutes five thousand guns and revolvers were making a steady roar—bang! bang! bang! Everybody else then remembered that it was the Fourth of July—and what an uproar! The street was soon filled with men whooping and emptying revolvers, shot-guns, and rifles. The dogs, in alarm at the uproar, began running with ears straight back and tails between their legs, as if distracted. They ran into people, or into each other, until, with the jumping, howling, yelling, and shooting, it looked and sounded as if pandemonium were let loose. The police at the barracks sprang out of bed, and I afterwards heard one of them laughingly say he didn't know but that the Americans had begun to carry out their one-time threat of rebelling. However, when they remembered it was the national holiday, the cornet-bugler gave "Yankee Doodle," "America," and the "Star-Spangled Banner." In the afternoon the local town band, made up of theatre orchestras, returned the compliment by a serenade. The dogs kept on running whichever way they happened to be started. Several plunged into the Yukon, and it was days before their owners got many of them back.

During midsummer four variety theatres were running, with the usual adjuncts of bars and gambling lay-outs. They were respectively the "Pavilion," "Monte Carlo," "Mascot," and "Combination." The last named was a wooden building, but the rest were simply tents. The entrance to all was through the bar-room, but at the Monte Carlo there was an additional bar inside the theatre for the greater convenience of the patrons. The stage was commodious, and in some there was real painted scenery, but in others the "scenery" consisted solely of a screen of striped bed-ticking or similar goods, which was also used abundantly for wall coverings. The audience were seated on boards placed on stools; but "Eldorado kings," government officials, and other "dead game sports" "spending their

THE "COMBINATION" THEATRE AND DANCE-HALL

money," occupied "boxes" on one or both sides of the pit, and raised sufficiently to allow the occupants, who sat upon hand-made board stools, to see over the heads of the common herd. The price of admission was 50 cents (including cigar or drink) in all but the "Combination," where it was $1. For the boxes there was no extra fixed charge, but occupants of such were expected to receive female members of the troupe, or any lady friends they themselves might choose to bring in, to help them dispose of champagne, which varied in price from $40 a quart to $40 a pint. At the opening of the "Monte Carlo" one man spent $1700 for wine during one

427

night. The same evening two girls opened forty-eight
bottles of wine, receiving $4 commission on each bottle.
The orchestra consisted usually of piano, violin, trom-
bone, and cornet, and musicians were each paid $20 a
day. The actors and actresses received various salaries,
$150 a week prevailing. At the "Monte Carlo" girls for
the "grand balls" after each night's performance were
specially employed at $50 per week and commissions.
The running expenses of the latter place were $500 a day.

The show was a succession of vaudeville parts, inter-
spersed with impromptu local sketches, which were
changed each week. Some of the performers, who came
out of English and American concert-halls, gave a fairly good performance ; while their impromptu jibes and
horse-pranks would convulse the audience, who were
never over-critical, for whom the humor could not be
too broad for them to relish, and who never tired of the
same performances night after night. Many of the songs
turned on something of local interest, as "Christmas in
the Klondike," or "The Klondike Millionaire," and when
sung by Freddy Breen, "the Irish Comedian," sounded
not badly, but when committed to paper were the veriest
doggerel. Of the female vocalists, with one or two ex-
ceptions, the less said the better. Untrained, never even
second rate, at times they sadly tried even the patient
Klondike audience. As the old pirate at the *Admiral
Benbow* used to sing :

> "Sixteen men on a dead man's chest,
> Yo ho, ho, and a bottle of rum.
> Drink and the devil had done for the rest,
> Yo ho, ho, and a bottle of rum."

Besides the Jesuits already spoken of, several religious
bodies established missions for work among the miners.

RELIGIOUS WORK

The Presbyterians, under Rev. Hall Young, built a church in the fall of 1897, the upper story of which was cut into rooms and rented to lodgers, but it was destroyed early in the winter by fire. The Church of England, under Rev. R. G. Bowen, built a church in the summer of 1898. The Christian-Endeavorers and the familiar Salvation Army held daily meetings in the open during the summer. The attendance at the missions seemed so small in so large a population as that of Dawson as to incline one to the prevailing opinion that among miners of the class of whom prospectors are made religious work finds not much place, unless accompanied by work for their physical as well as moral well-being.

The benevolent societies, such as the Masons, Odd-Fellows, etc., were organized by Colonel O. V. Davis, of Tacoma, Washington, and the government presented them with a plot of ground upon which they built a 40 × 40-foot "Society Hall" of logs. Many destitute men were cared for by these societies. One case particularly drew my attention, for it was a fair sample of what straits a man might be in who had property outside, but was "broke" or without friends here. He was an old man, a Mason, worth $20,000 in property outside, yet absolutely penniless. The Masons paid his way home.

As had been predicted, the town was in a terrible sanitary condition. There was no drainage, and, except by giving warning about cesspools, the government did nothing but provide *two* public conveniences, entirely inadequate for a town of nearly 20,000. Fortunately good drinking-water was had at several springs. Still, as could not be otherwise in a city built upon a bog, by midsummer the hospital was filled to overflowing, men were lying on the floor, and there were many in cabins, suffering from typhoid fever, typhoid-malaria, and dysentery. The number of deaths were three to four a day, in one day reaching a total of nine. At this juncture, when the amount of sickness had become a cause for general alarm, the Canadian doctors, who were greatly outnumbered by American, began prosecutions against the latter, and several of the highest standing, but who had come unprovided with licenses to practise in Canada, were haled before the magistrate, jailed, and fined. While Americans should have expected this, it was admitted by most persons that a more unfortunate moment for the prosecutions could hardly have been chosen. The American physicians continued practising, however, without signs or asking fees. In all there were about seventy physicians in the camp, only a few of whom, however, found lucrative practice. In August another hospital, "The Good Samaritan," was established, with a local board of directors, the government contributing $5000 towards its maintenance.

I jotted into my note-book, among odd items, that the first cat and kittens in the Yukon arrived in August, and the kittens sold for $5 to $10 each. About a dozen horses, brought up from Forty-Mile and Circle, had wintered, being kept in stove-warmed tents and fed chiefly upon native hay that cost $500 to $1200 per ton. Several hundred more horses and mules came in on scows, until they became too common to notice particularly. Many beeves, including one herd of a thousand, were driven in over the Dalton Trail; but the arrival of the first milch cow, however, that ever came into the Yukon, and her first milking, were duly recorded as follows in the *Nugget* of July 8th:

"THIRTY DOLLARS A GALLON

" The first milk cow ever in Dawson arrived on Wednesday. She is not very well pleased with her surroundings and did not give much milk, but that first milking brought in just $30 in Klondike dust. She will be treated to the best that Dawson affords—flour and packing-case hay—and is expected to do better as the days grow shorter. One hundred dollars a milking is not too much to expect of her, as she comes of good family and will not do anything to make her ancestors turn over in their graves —or, more properly speaking, in the stomachs of their patrons. H. I. Miller is the man who brought her in along with 19 male companions. The gentleman is more favorably known as "Cow" Miller, and as Cow Miller let him be known from this on."

Before the newspapers started, and even afterwards, notices of buying and selling, meetings, and lost and found, were posted upon the bulletin - boards at the Alaska Commercial Company's store. Of the curious signs that appeared there from time to time the following is remarkable, as showing an unusual confidence in human honesty:

"NOTICE

Lost

June 24 1898 about 11 at night a gold sack containing all a poor woman had : between old man Buck (Choquette) cabin and small board House selling Lemonade upon bank of the Troandike River any person finding same will confer a verry great favor a poor woman who is sick and must go out. she made Her Dust by washing and mending a Liberal reward will be paid by Enquiring at Ferry Beer Saloon at Lousetown Bridge."

CHAPTER XXI

Government in the Klondike—Mining Laws—Incompetence and Corruption of Officials—The Royalty Tax—Collecting the Royalties—Investigation of Charges—An Orderly Mining Camp

D URING the winter of 1897–8 only ten per cent. of the population of Dawson were Canadians; a considerable percentage were of English birth, but the overwhelming majority were Americans, or foreigners who had lingered in the United States long enough to imbibe American ideas. In the crowd which poured in later the percentage of Canadian citizens, or British subjects, was probably still smaller. These people under United States law would have had the making of their own laws, subject only to broad statutory limitations. Indeed, with reference to Alaska, non-interference with liberty by the central government has been but another name for neglect.

In the Klondike, those who best knew the country's needs had no voice whatever in its government; all laws were made at Ottawa, and those sent out to enforce them were responsible only to the home government, or to the officials to whom they owed their appointment. Dawson was an "alien" camp, where, if the position of the majority of the residents was different from the "Ouitlander" at Johannesburg, it was only that the laws were

432

in intent more liberal. Distant weeks and months from the seat of responsibility, it is not difficult to understand how, even if government intended well, the condition of the miner might be scarcely better than that of his unfortunate *confrère* in the Boer republic. In fact, conditions which actually prevailed at Dawson were likened by British citizens direct from the Transvaal as even worse than what they left.

The natural difficulties that stood in the way of putting into immediate operation an effective government were so great that one should not judge the Klondikers too harshly. On the other hand, if there were not serious disorders it was due less to the quality of government than to the orderly character of the population, and to the fact that men were there enduring the privations of an Arctic climate to make their fortunes and get away, not to help set in order the political households of their Canadian friends.

The mounted police, both officers and men, in their capacity as preservers of order and as individuals, commanded the respect of every miner. Captain Constantine, upon his departure from Dawson, received a testimonial in the form of two thousand dollars' worth of nuggets, which were subsequently made up in their natural form into a beautiful loving-cup, to show how the miners felt at a time when almost every branch of the public service had forfeited their confidence. It seems! to be a well-ordered Canadian's belief that an "official," whether a policeman or a land-surveyor, is qualified, by reason of being an official, to fill any post under government.

The police, instead of trained mail-clerks, were given the work of handling the mails. Provoking slowness in the transmission and delivery resulted from their inex-

perience and lack of system. Often it required a week
to sort a mail. Those who had money to spare preferred
to pay $1 a letter to a policeman to get his mail after
hours, or else employed women, who, being gallantly admitted, at once could get it for them.

GOVERNMENT BUILDINGS, DAWSON—RECORDING CLAIMS

The size of creek claims, at the time of the Klondike
strike, was five hundred feet long by the width of the
valley; all other claims being one hundred feet square.
The miner was required to mark each corner of his claim
with a stake four feet high, squaring not less than four
inches, and upon one face of each stake to write the
number of the claim and the words: "I claim five hundred (or fewer) feet up (or down) stream for mining
purposes. (Signed) John Smith." After making affi-
davit of discovery of gold, and paying $15 to the Gold
Commissioner, he received a lease for one year, renew-
able each subsequent year at an annual rental of $100.

All disputes were settled by this officer, who was account-
able only to the Minister of the Interior, and possessed
arbitrary powers without appeal. At first the laws and
the manner of enforcement, although necessitating long
journeys to the seat of the recorder, gave general satisfaction to the small, scattered mining population. But
when the news of the discovery of Bonanza Creek reached
Ottawa, the Dominion cabinet, in ignorance of the true
conditions, passed an "Order in Council" reducing the
size of all new creek claims to one hundred feet, reserv-
ing each alternate claim for the crown, and imposing a
royalty of twenty per cent. on the gross output of claims
producing over $500 per day, and ten per cent. on all
claims producing less than that amount. When news
of this measure, only equalled by the recent war-tax of
the Boers, reached Dawson, a mass-meeting of the miners
was held, and a committee of three, consisting of Messrs.
M. Landreville, a miner; Edward J. Livernash, a lawyer,
and Dr. E. A. Wills, a surgeon in the mounted police,
was appointed to carry to Ottawa a petition for the re-
duction or abolition of the royalty.

So great was the outcry in Canada, however, that before the committee reached Ottawa the cabinet made
haste to remedy its blunder, and by "Order in Council,"
approved January 18, 1898, reduced the royalty to ten
per cent., deducting the sum of $2500 (a ridiculous
amount) from the gross output to cover the cost of
working! Creek claims were increased to two hundred
and fifty feet in length, to be staked in blocks of ten
claims each, alternate blocks of ten being reserved for
the crown. Bench claims adjoining creek claims were
made two hundred and fifty feet wide by one thousand
feet deep, all other claims being two hundred and fifty
feet square. Before a miner could stake a claim or

perform any work in connection with mining, except buying stock in stock companies, he was required to take out a " free miner's " license at a cost of $10. If a discovery distant more than one hundred miles from the seat of the recorder was made by five or more persons,

DATE OF ISSUE 7ᵗʰ Apl 98   No. 2611

DOMINION ᵒᶠ CANADA

FREE MINER'S CERTIFICATE.

PLACE OF ISSUE Dawson   NON-TRANSFERABLE.   VALID FOR ONE YEAR ONLY.

This is to Certify that Tappan Adney of Dawson has paid me this day the sum of Ten dollars and is entitled to all the rights and privileges of a Free Miner, under any Mining Regulations of the Government of Canada, for one year from the 7th day of Apl 1898

This Certificate shall also grant to the holder thereof the privilege of Fishing and Shooting, subject to the provisions of any Act which has been passed, or which may hereafter be passed for the protection of game and fish; also the privilege of Cutting Timber for actual necessities, for building houses, boats, and for general mining operations; such timber, however, to be for the exclusive use of the miner himself, but such permission shall not extend to timber which may have been heretofore or which may hereafter be granted to other persons or corporations.

Countersigned,

To be Countersigned by the Gold Commissioner, Mining Recorder, or by an Officer or Agent of the Department of Interior.   *Deputy of the Minister of the Interior.*

FREE MINER'S LICENSE

they might appoint a temporary recorder among their own number. While the law required the "gum-boot" miner to stake *in person*, so-called "dredging permits," in five-mile blocks, were granted over fifteen hundred miles of Klondike and Yukon streams to men who, for the most part, had never seen, nor intended to see, the Yukon. Such, in brief, are the regulations now in force, which further provide for the sale of timber-berths to private parties, whereby miners are virtually prevented from cutting wood, even for their own use, except on such terms as the monopolists concede. The tendency of the new legislation is against the "gum-boot" miner, the man whose enterprise, labors, and hardships have made for Canada all that is worth while in the Klondike to-day. This is always the inevitable trend, but never in any camp has so much been done in so short a time in that direction as in the Canadian camp. The Gold Commissioner, Mr. Thomas Fawcett, came in for some censure for what his superiors were alone to blame for. Yet a position calling for judicial, legislative, and executive qualities of a high order should have been filled by a man possessing other qualifications than personal honesty and fair ability as a topographical surveyor.

The commissioner arrived at Dawson in the summer of 1897, and established an office in a small cabin with a single room, and with two assistants began receiving applications for claims. The rush to record became so great that, in order to comply with the law limiting the time in which a miner had to record after staking, the whole staff were kept busy during office hours, which were strictly from 9 A.M. to 5 P.M. The registry books, or copies thereof, which elsewhere in Canada are considered public property, were not accessible to the public, and the clerks were quick to take advantage of this state of affairs to begin a "side-door" business, selling to individuals, for cash or interests in claims, information of unrecorded claims. Afterwards, emboldened by the impotency of the commissioner to correct these abuses, favored ones began to be admitted during office-hours, upon passes, and recorded claims ahead of men who had been waiting often for days in line outside. It became recognized by every one who was obliged to deal with the office that the only way of getting even what belonged to him was to bribe an official. Appeal to the Gold Commissioner was as likely as not met with dismissal in an arbitrary, unjust, or illegal manner. During the greater part of the rush there was no one to verify measurements of claims (only survey by Dominion land surveyors being recognized officially). The commissioner was in ignorance of the location and identity of creeks; he would give two different names to the same creek, not knowing them to be the same; he would grant the same claim to different men, and yet refuse, when the fact was proven, to refund the record fee to one of them; he allowed *two* discoveries on one creek, and claims became so mixed, in consequence of overlapping between discoveries, that he was obliged to close the creek, to the great loss of miners, who were not allowed to record (pending arrival of official surveyors), and who were holding the claims in person, in compliance with the mining law. Thus, between the incompetency of the commissioner and the corruption of his clerks, legitimate business came almost to a standstill. The general law of Canada, providing that no person should suffer from the incompetency of an official, was of no effect to the poor miner, who had neither money nor time to obtain the remedy.

In February two " Inspectors of Mines," a Crown Prosecuting Attorney, and Lands Agent (the last two in one person), and a judge of the Supreme Court of the Northwest Territories, arrived in Dawson. The judge, the Hon. Thomas H. McGuire, entered upon his duties at once, largely relieving the police magistrates, and performed his duties to the satisfaction of the entire camp. Concerning the rest, so much can hardly be said. The Crown Attorney, a "Pooh-Bah" in fact, leased the waterfront to private parties, by whom he was employed in a private capacity as legal adviser; and by various acts as Crown Attorney, Lands Agent, private practitioner, and by his overbearing and threatening conduct towards his critics, aroused a general belief that he was using his official powers to further his private interests. The mining inspectors had only such previous experience in mining as they may have acquired as a horse dealer and an uncertificated master of a whaling vessel, respectively.

Major Walsh, the governor or administrator of the "Provisional District of the Yukon," as the territory was officially known, did not arrive until summer. Finally, mass-meetings of outraged and indignant citizens were held in the streets, under the leadership of Englishmen and Canadians, to protest against the mining laws and officials.

The Miners' Association, organized for self-protection, with George T. Armstrong and Dr. Percy McDougal, both British citizens, respectively as chairman and secretary, appealed to Ottawa for a parliamentary investigation of affairs in the Yukon. Meanwhile, on May 27th, the "Yukon Territory" had been created, with the Hon. William Ogilvie as Governor, and a council of six. The appeal went out late in the fall; six months later a Royal Commission was despatched, naming Mr. Ogilvie as Commissioner. The guileless miners, who looked for a clear investigation from top to bottom, were sadly disappointed. The investigation was one of accused officials by themselves. Although conducted with impartiality, the miners found simply a court before which they were litigants. The investigation was limited to specific charges mentioned in the appeal, and to none others. Many of the officials and witnesses had left, and the miners were not permitted to bring into court cases (they were daily happening) that occurred *after* the sending of the petition. Adequate protection was not granted witnesses, nor was there any provision to pay the expenses of those who, working many miles off in the mines, could not lose days or weeks of time in Dawson to testisy during the investigation without some compensation. The miners, perceiving that the investigation could not accomplish their purpose, virtually gave up the fight. The accused officials were exonerated, except certain persons connected with the Gold Commissioner's Office, who were proven to have taken bribes and deprived rightful owners of their claims.

Mr. Ogilvie, who is regarded as a conscientious man, and of whom much was expected in remedying the abuses, succeeded only to a small extent. When the matter of incorporating the town was raised, those who were entitled to vote in Canada were unanimously against the officials, and could not agree on certain important points, so Dawson remains a city where citizens have practically no voice in the local government.

The police control of the country was as nearly perfect as one could expect. Thefts and misdemeanors were numerous, and effectively dealt with, and one or two murder cases were tried. The saloons were closed on Sunday, nor was any labor permitted on that day. A man sawing wood, for his own use, and another engaged in fishing were arrested. No city on the continent presented a more orderly appearance.

To appease the miners, who had threatened to make trouble if a policeman should be detailed to watch their clean-ups when collecting the royalty, a mining inspector simply accepted the affidavits of miners as to their outputs. In cases where the tax bore heavily, the royalty was lowered or payment was temporarily suspended.

Among those so relieved was Alec McDonald, the "King of the Klondike." Without doubt much gold was withheld, although the penalty for so doing was confiscation of the claim. A singular fact regarding the royalty collection is that in no case was the amount paid as royalty specified on the receipt. The same was true of custom receipts on the trail. About $500,000 was received in royalties. The total revenue derived from the Yukon was $1,530,000. The expenditure was $647,000, leaving a balance of $883,000 paid by the miners of the Yukon into the treasury of Canada, or a *net profit* of about $20 upon every man, woman, and child who entered Canadian territory.

CHAPTER XXII

Vegetation and Agricultural Possibilities—Animal Life—Birds—Fish—
Mosquitoes—Native Tribes

THE great territory of Alaska and the Yukon is divided into parts, differing radically in general features of climate and vegetable and animal life. Along the Pacific coast both rain and snow fall are great, vegetation is luxurious, and the air so mild that in summer even the tender humming-bird finds its way as far north as Juneau. The interior, however —comprising the valley of the Yukon and tributaries, with its more than 330,000 square miles of area—is dry; the rainfall is small and the temperature hot in summer; in winter the air is dry and excessively cold, and the snowfall is light. Vegetation is confined mainly to a moss which covers the ground to a varying thickness, and to three varieties of trees—spruce, white birch, and cottonwood. These are found abundantly from the lowest valleys to the tops of all but the highest mountains. In the flat valleys of the streams, exposed to the rays of the sun and with plenty of water, the spruce grow as thickly as anywhere in the world, some attaining a diameter of two feet, while trees a foot in diameter are common. On the sides of hills, however, the trees become suddenly stunted in appearance, the spruce rarely exceeding a few inches in thickness, but the rings of growth being as thin and close as the leaves of a book. The white birch, not less beautiful here than southward, rarely exceeds eight inches in thickness ; the cottonwood attains to a foot in diameter. Willow bushes and alder trees are found in the moist places, and berries of several ground and bog growing species are found often in great profusion, and there are not a few species of wild flowers, among which the most common and readily recognized is a golden-rod about six inches in height. Towards the mouth of the Yukon the temperature becomes milder, and grasses grow luxuriantly ; but the trees grow smaller, until the characteristic tree-clad landscape of the Yukon merges into a bare, rolling *tundra*, or frozen morass, skirting the shores of Behring Sea. In consequence of the long hours of sunshine, garden vegetables, when planted on hill - sides exposed to the sun, spring with great rapidity out of the fertile soil. Potatoes are grown to a weight of seven or eight pounds, turnips sixteen pounds, while cabbages, radishes, etc., are readily raised. The larger vegetables, however, are coarse in texture. The agricultural possibilities of the Yukon are greater than has been generally supposed, but the short summer probably will not allow the raising of cereals or fruits that require a long season to ripen, and it will hardly support an independent agricultural population. Several small vegetable gardens at Dawson were a source of large revenue to their owners. A bunch of about six radishes, each no larger than the end of one's thumb, readily brought $1 in the restaurants.

Animal life in the Yukon valley is not so varied as farther south, but its species are important, and in places exceedingly abundant. Easily first is the moose. This, the grandest of the deer family, is found in the whole region of trees, and is very abundant on the Klon-dike—undoubtedly much more plentiful than in any part of its more familiar range to the extreme south and eastward. Of the stature of the tallest horse, it wanders at will from valley to mountain-top, in winter browsing upon the tender twigs of the willow and white birch, the light snow not impeding its movements and causing it to "yard," as farther south. In summer it is hunted by lying in wait for it at paths leading to certain lakes. During the winter of 1897–8 probably one hundred and fifty were killed around Dawson by Indians and white men. A few years ago moose-hams could be purchased for $3 each; now they bring $1 to $1.50 per pound, the hides being worth $25 to $30 each for moccasins and the larger gold-sacks. The moose of the extreme west of Alaska has lately been found to be of a new species, distinguished chiefly for its great size, and has been given the name of *Alces gigas*. The moose of the Klondike, when specimens have been examined by naturalists, will probably be found different both from the latter and from the common moose, *Alces americana*. A pair of antlers, respectively 4 feet 7 inches and 4 feet 5 inches, evidently locked together in mortal combat, were found on Stewart River in July, 1898. These, though not large for Alaskan moose, sufficiently indicate what a struggle of giants had taken place before they died of exhaustion or were pulled down by wolves.

The woodland caribou roams as far north as Big Salmon River, where it is known by the Takish Indians as "Mut-siq." North of there, and ranging to the shores of the Arctic Ocean and Behring Sea, is the barren-ground caribou, or wild reindeer, found often in immense bands, which migrate each year in search of a peculiar gray moss which constitutes their food. The

headwaters of Forty-Mile and of Klondike are two cen-
tres of great abundance. Several years ago three hundred were killed in Forty-Mile town. Early the past fall
two white men on the upper Klondike killed forty-seven,
and several hunters independently reported the herd,
which was then changing its feeding-grounds, as numbering from ten to twenty thousand. Ten years ago deer
were regarded as not occurring east of the coast moun-

INTERLOCKED MOOSE-HORNS FOUND ON STEWART RIVER

tains; but at the Canyon, at Lake Labarge, and near Big
Salmon I saw numerous unmistakable "deer" tracks in
the mud and light snow that could hardly have been any
but those of the Sitka deer.

The white goat is found in the Chilkoot Mountains
and northward to Lake Labarge. A species of mountain sheep, differing from the Rocky Mountain bighorn
in its pelt being woollier and of a dirty white color (probably "Dall's sheep"), has been killed at Fort Reliance.

"Stone's sheep," another variety of the bighorn, discovered in 1896 on the Stikeen River, may also be found in the Yukon Valley.

Bears are plentiful and of two kinds in the Yukon : a so-called "grizzly," or "silver tip," and the black bear, both the black and "cinnamon" phases being found together. The caches of the lonely prospector are occasionally broken into by grizzlies, and on the upper Klondike a miner was killed by one. In the early summer, after their winter's sleep, black bears frequent the exposed hill-sides, digging for roots and old berries. A party on Stewart River, in descending that river forty miles on a small raft in 1898, killed five.

The gray or timber wolf is found in scattered bands. They feed upon the moose and caribou, and seldom attack miners. Sometimes they attain great size and weight. Mr. J. B. Burnham, of *Forest and Stream*, captured one near Fort Selkirk that weighed upwards of 120 pounds. A hunter on the upper Klondike killed one, and obtained from the carcase nearly a *quart* of oil, it being the only wolf, the hunter told me, he ever saw that had any fat at all. I saw the spot on the Klondike where the band to which this belonged had attacked, killed, and devoured a moose only a few days before. Two apparently distinct kinds are met with, recognized as the "gray" and the "black," but they are regarded by scientists as individual variations of the same species. The red fox, the valuable black or silver-gray fox, the white or Arctic fox, the cross fox, and the blue or stone fox are found in places plentifully, the last three being confined to the shores of Behring Sea.

The furs from the Klondike are of the most beautiful description, rather pale in color, but exceedingly fine. Beaver, formerly more plentiful than now, are taken by the Indians with a harpoon through a hole in the ice, the spot being baited with willow twigs, or else by means of a peculiar dead-fall of poles built on the bank near their homes. Muskrat are plentiful. The wolverine (not a "wolf" of any sort, but the largest of the weasels) roams everywhere, and is taken in dead-falls. Its coarse brown and black fur has small market value, but is in great demand for the trimming of the winter garments of the miner. The sable, ermine, mink, and otter are found everywhere, the last two not being plentiful. The varying hare, or "rabbit," is exceedingly plentiful in some years, rare in others. It is taken in sinew snares by the Indians, and its white coat is cut into strips, plaited, and sewed into coats, mittens, and robes, the fur being the lightest and warmest known, except the Arctic hare, a species with longer fur found near the Behring Sea.

The Canada lynx, or "bob-cat," comes and goes with the rabbits, upon which it feeds. Its fur makes one of the best robes. A species of marmot, or large "ground-hog," found in the Chilkoots and along the coast, is taken in snares for its fur, which makes warm and serviceable robes. A kind of ground squirrel is found, whose pelts make the lightest and best *parkas*, and a small mouse (probably "Dawson's mouse") frequents the cabins of the miners after provender ; but the most familiar of all the small animals is the red squirrel, the same saucy, chattering, scolding, cone-tearing, snow-burrowing little beast on Bonanza Creek as in the New England States.

Bird life is both abundant and interesting. There never was an hour of the day in winter when the chipper of birds was not to be heard, and as spring approached the woods seemed alive with flocks of small cone-eating, red-polled linnets and white-winged crossbills, and there was no visitor more welcome to the cabins of the miners than the Canada jay, or moose-bird, the same fearless, confiding, mysterious camp-thief as in the woods of Maine. But the most striking feature of the Klondike landscape is the raven, whose hollow "klonk" is heard everywhere, haunting the cabins in winter for whatever may be thrown out, feasting on the leavings of hunters and wolves, in summer nesting on the inaccessible cliffs of the Yukon. No traveller down the river has failed to notice the thousands of holes in the tall sand-banks on the upper Yukon, the nesting-place of the bank swallow, which, with its much less common relatives, the violet-green swallow and the common eave or cliff swallow, which nest in the crags, are only summer visitors to these regions.

Whoever imagines that there are no birds in Klondike should have stood with me at my cabin one day early in May, after the spring migration had begun. He would have thought a bird-shop had been there turned loose among the evergreens and birches. He would have heard the cheery song of the western robin, the "tsillip" of the red-shafted flicker, the soft murmur of the beautiful and rare Bohemian waxwing, the jangling notes of the graceful rusty grackle walking the margins of the creek, the lisping "tsip" of the yellow-rumped warbler, the chipper of white-crowned sparrows and slate-colored juncos, mingled with the melodious love-songs of white-winged cross-bills, and the twittering of innumerable red-polls feeding in the birches. Game birds, however, were not plentiful. I shot two ruffed grouse, several Canada grouse, and one blue grouse—all I saw. Flocks of small ptarmigan were frequently met with on the wind-swept tops of the hills. Geese and ducks nest sparingly along the larger watercourses.

Among the inhabitants of the water the lake trout

grows to great size in the upper lakes, being taken weighing 24 pounds. The grayling is taken in spring with hook and line, with either a bait or a fly, it being said to rise readily to the "coachman," "brown hackle," and "raven." The burbot, or fresh-water cusk, is taken on set lines in spring. The pike is taken in great numbers at Medicine Lake, on the trail to Birch Creek, weighing 15 to 18 pounds. The sucker occurs on the authority of Dr. Dawson. The whitefish is taken in the lakes and in the Yukon at Dawson, weighing as high as 40 pounds. But the fish of fish is the salmon, of which there are several species or varieties. The salmon is a salt-water fish, which resorts to fresh water every few years to spawn. The "king" salmon reaches Dawson between the 10th and 15th of June, and is taken, weighing as high as 51 pounds, in weirs by the Indians and by the white men with drift-nets 150 to 250 feet long. Salmon of 80 pounds' weight have been reported at Fort Reliance. A few king salmon ascend the rapids and canyon as far as the foot of Marsh Lake, but it is not probable that many, after their exhausting journey of nearly two thousand miles, almost or quite without food, ever reach the sea alive again. By August the biggest of the king salmon have passed up river. The "silver" salmon is the next run, and weighs not over 30 pounds. After the silver is the third and most plentiful "run" of all, the dog salmon, so called either from the resemblance of its teeth to those canines, or to the fact of its being the staple article of dog-food.

The price of salmon on June 15, 1898, was $2 a pound, by midsummer 25 cents a pound. One party of white men in the height of the king "run" in one day caught seven fish, weighing 150 pounds, for which they received $75.

2 F   449

A wrong impression generally prevails concerning the Yukon mosquito. The statement will hardly be credited that during the whole summer on the flat at Dawson I did not see a single one! On the islands in the river, in new creeks not yet cleared of trees, however, they were exceedingly numerous. On Bonanza Creek, which was cleared partially, they were hardly more annoying than in a certain town less than a thousand miles from New York city where these words are being written. Undoubtedly, as one approaches the mouth of the Yukon the mosquitoes grow more deadly, until one can quite believe the returned missionary who said that at his station the mosquitoes were so thick that when a man wanted to tell the time of day he had to throw a stick into the air so as to be able to see the sun! At the mouth of the Tanana River a horse was killed in a single night, and men in the woods without protection have been so blinded by their stings that they have lost their way. Even smoke sometimes fails to repel their attacks altogether. When one is travelling it is necessary to tie a bit of netting over the hat-brim, and when sleeping out-of-doors the face must be covered with netting, and even then the sound of their singing as they try to get through will keep a nervous person awake.

The natives of the Yukon Valley are a hunting race, subsisting in winter upon the moose and caribou, and in summer upon fish. Out of the skins of the former they make their clothes and the coverings of their winter houses; and, until it became more profitable to sell meat to the increasing number of white men, they trapped quantities of furs, which they sold to the traders, receiving in return blankets, guns, ammunition, flour, tea, sugar, and tobacco. From Pelly River down the tribes are of the "Athapaskan" branch of the Tinné-Apache family of North American Indians, but towards the mouth of the Yukon the Indians are replaced by Eskimos, whose villages continue at short intervals to Behring Sea.

INDIANS' WINTER ENCAMPMENT ON THE KLONDIKE RIVER

The Indians of the Klondike River, numbering about seventy souls, are known to themselves as " Tro-chu-tin," and their river as the " Tron-duk," of which the miners' " Klondike " is a corruption.

In their summer costume, these Indians affect "store" clothes, the men imitating the miners, even to their broad, gray, cow-boy hats; while the women imitate their white sisters to a corresponding degree in dresses and jackets from the well-filled stores of the trader.   In winter, however, when hunting, one sees them in their former wild picturesqueness.   The men wear legging-trousers with moccasins, made in one garment, of caribou skin with hair inside, and worn next to the skin ; a shirt of the same or rabbit skin, or of blanket-stuff, which in vividness and variety of color rivals the spectrum ; a sable or beaver cap, and large pocket-like mittens of rabbit or caribou skin, with hair inside, or moosehide lined with lynx fur.

The house-dress of the women is made of calico or cloth. Over this, when travelling, they wear a voluminous dress reaching half-way from the knees to the ground, with a large hood, which can be pulled over the head, but is used more often as a receptacle for the baby; while a kerchief of fancy cotton or silk is tied around the head. The children dress entirely in furs, the

KLONDIKE INDIANS GOING AFTER FALLEN MOOSE WITH TOBOGGANS

boys wearing legging-trousers and deerskin shirts, or *parkas* provided with hoods, the mittens of the very smallest being sewed fast to the sleeves; while the girls wear garments like those of their mothers. When so rigged they roll about in the snow at play as unmindful of cold as

polar bears. Every Indian village has a plentiful assortment of native " wolf " or Eskimo dogs. These are mainly
employed to haul their toboggans of birch-wood, on which

INTERIOR OF INDIAN SKIN-HOUSE

are placed all their goods, including even the babies and
small pups, when they travel from place to place in pursuit of the moose and caribou. The winter's hunt lasts
several months, and the whole village, including old men,
women, and nursing babes, accompany the hunters. The
winter houses are made of caribou skins sewed together
to make a rounded cover and hauled over a dome-shaped
frame of bent poles set into a ridge of snow banked up
in the form of an ellipse eighteen feet long by twelve
feet wide, the ground inside being covered with spruce
boughs. A large hole is left overhead for the smoke of
the camp-fire to ascend. The hunters go ahead upon

snow-shoes, while the women follow with the camp equipment to a designated spot, generally six or seven miles distant, where they make camp. The moose is surrounded in its feeding-ground by a band of eight or more hunters, who are generally able to secure a quick shot as it runs, although some of the best hunters prefer to stalk and shoot the moose as it lies in its bed in the snow. The meat is hauled to camp by dogs, and the hides dressed by the women. The traders supply them with modern repeating rifles, which they use with a success that is not remarkable when one considers that only a few years ago they had no more effective weapons than bows and arrows and stout spears. The snow-shoes are long and narrow, with upturned toes, the frame being of white birch, filled with caribou-skin webbing.

Their canoes are made of birch-bark, but in construction are less like the birch canoe of the East than the Eskimo *kyak*, or skin‑boat. They are slender and graceful in appearance, with high, upturned ends, the forward part being decked over with bark for about five feet. Like the *kyak*, a man's canoe usually carries but one grown person ; the women's or family canoe is not decked over and is somewhat larger. The occupant sits in the middle of the canoe and propels it skilfully by means of a single-bladed paddle deftly dipped from side to side. When going up‑stream in shallow water the canoe-man uses two slender poles, one in each hand, with which he digs his way along.

CHAPTER XXIII

ON the 16th day of September ice was making in the gulches, and what was thought to be the last steamboat which could reach St. Michael and connect with the ocean vessel for home before navigation closed left Dawson with a million and a half in gold-dust and a goodly number of passengers, who chose the longer route by Behring Sea to the now quicker route by which we had entered the Yukon a year before. Our journey—the ten days by river on the *John Cudahy*, fastest of river-boats, the grand scenery, the native villages and settlements of historic interest along the Yukon, the ten days of waiting at bleak St. Michael for an ocean steamer to appear, the incidents on shipboard, the brief stay amid the incomparable glacier-topped mountains and land-locked inlets of Unalaska, with its sea-birds, Aleuts, and smoking volcanoes, the six-day ocean voyage to Seattle, and the final adieus to friends and companions in hunger and plenty, in misery and good-fortune—all these were a fitting close to sixteen months of an experience that none of us can hope to see repeated in a lifetime. A life of freedom and adventure has a fascination which grows rather than diminishes, and yet the privations that every person who went into Klondike endured taught him better to separate the good from the bad, the essential from the non-essential, and to recognize the real blessings and comforts of civilization. This imperfect story of what I saw of one of the most remarkable movements of people in the history of the world cannot come to a close without more particular reference to what has been taking place, not only in Klondike proper, but in our own American territory. It has been shown that the great "mineral belt," rich not only in gold, but in copper, silver, coal, and other minerals, continues westward to the very sands of the beaches of Behring Sea, embracing a vast territory, which, together with that of the unexplored rivers of the Canadian Yukon, will, it is safe to predict, furnish a field for prospecting during the life of this generation.

During the winter of 1897–98, Forty-Mile, Birch Creek, and other streams on the American side of the 141st meridian, were relocated by new men, chiefly in claims of 1320 feet, or twenty acres, the extreme limit allowed under the United States law. Not much work has yet been done, the creeks, on account of the lower-grade earth, being regarded as "company," or hydraulicking, "propositions." The International Boundary crosses Forty-Mile River twenty-three miles above its mouth, and has been clearly cut out by Mr. Ogilvie to a point on the Yukon forty miles below Forty-Mile. The Canadian Forty-Mile mining district includes the head of Sixty-Mile. Nothing startlingly large was found on Forty-Mile until Miller Creek, Sixty-Mile, was discovered by O. C., otherwise "Kink," Miller, in 1892, from which the next year eighty men took out $100,000. In 1896 a German-Swiss, Johnnie Müller, took $12,000 out of No. 17 below Discovery, so that he was able to deposit at San Francisco 286 pounds of gold, for which he received $54,639, besides paying about $13,000 in wages; while Charlie Anderson and another took out $17,000 more. The output of Forty-Mile in 1896 was $460,000. The present town contains about two hundred cabins, and probably fewer persons.

Fifty miles below Forty-Mile, at the mouth of Mission Creek, on tributaries of which gold was first found in 1895, a town was laid off by twenty-eight miners on the 28th of May, 1898, and named "Eagle City." Cabin-sites were allotted by drawing numbered slips of paper out of a hat. About a thousand persons wintered there, and it has been selected as a United States military post.

Thirty miles below Mission Creek, at the mouth of Seventy-Mile Creek, a stream 150 miles long, that in 1888 paid $50 per day to men with rockers, a town-site was laid off, in the winter of 1897–98, and called "Star City." In the spring it was flooded, so another town was started two miles above on the Yukon, called "Seventy-Mile City," with a population of two or three hundred.

Two hundred and fifteen miles below Dawson the Yukon enters the "Yukon Flats," an ancient lake-bed a hundred miles in width and about two hundred and fifty miles long, through which the river courses, spreading out in a maze of channels to an extreme width of ten miles. Seven miles beyond the head of the Flats, straggling for two miles along a low bluff, is Circle City, a town of about three hundred cabins, including the stores of the two old companies, office of the United States Commissioner, a government school, an Episcopal mission, and a miners' association, with a library of one thousand volumes. Government is represented by the Commissioner, two customs officers, a deputy internal revenue collector, a deputy marshal, and a postmaster. The first Commissioner, Hon. John B. Crane, entered upon his duties on October 2, 1897. The Birch Creek diggings, lying from thirty to eighty miles back of Circle City, were discovered in 1892 by two Russian half-breeds, Pitka and Sorresco. Next year Henry Lewis, John McLeod, and Gus Williams worked "Pitka's Bar" with such results that when the news reached Forty-Mile, where the season had not been an encouraging one, eighty men, or about half the population, were given outfits on credit by McQuesten, and descended to a point on the Yukon twelve miles above the present Circle City, and established a town, which they named "Circle City," from its supposed proximity to the Arctic Circle (it was really somewhat to the southward). The spring following several cabins were washed away, so the town was moved to its present site. That winter Mammoth, Mastodon, Hog'em, Greenhorn, and Independence creeks were prospected, yielding $9000. Other creeks were added, and, in 1895, the output was $400,000, with a population of 700. In 1896 the output was $900,000, for a total population of 900. Regarding the future of this district, abandoned for Klondike, Samuel C. Dunham, United States Labor Statistician, who spent the winter of 1897–98 in Circle City, makes this remarkable report:

"The prediction is here made, based on authentic information, that the ten miles of ground on Mastodon and Mammoth (which are one creek except in designation) already prospected, will eventually produce as much gold as any successive ten miles on Bonanza, while the ten claims on Mastodon, from 4 below to 5 above Discovery, inclusive, will without doubt prove as productive as any ten claims on Eldorado, taken in their numerical order. Furthermore, on account of the even distribution of gold in the Birch Creek district, the output here, extending over a longer period of time and employing larger numbers of men, will be of incalculably greater economic benefit to the community than the more phenomenal production of the creeks in the Klondike district."

LITTLE MINOOK

Less than a thousand wintered in 1898–99 at Circle City.

At Fort Hamlin, an Alaska Commercial Company post, the river enters the mountains, or "Lower Ramparts." Fifty miles farther, at the mouth of Minook Creek, is "Rampart City," established in the fall of 1897 chiefly by a number of intending miners, who had started for Klondike on various regular and specially chartered steamers, and were frozen in and staked a number of creeks tributary to and in the neighborhood of Minook Creek, a stream on which fine gold had been found in 1882. In 1893 John Minook, a Russian half-breed, found the first coarse gold on Little Minook, a tributary of Big Minook. In 1896 there were seven men at work ; in the spring of 1897 thirteen men cleaned up 122 ounces of gold. Of the three hundred and fifty "stranded" men who wintered there in 1897–98, only eighty-five did any prospecting or work, and that was mainly on five claims on Little Minook, which cleaned up about $110,000, of which $43,000 came from No. 6 above Discovery. In April, 1898, an Idaho miner, named Range, discovered bench-diggings of value on a hill between two tributaries of Minook, naming it "Idaho Bar," and other " bars " were subsequently discovered in similar situations. During the winter of 1898–99, a large part of the population, then numbering about a thousand, stampeded to the headwaters of the Koyukuk River, where a number of parties had gone the fall before. But nothing important appears to have resulted.

The most significant discovery was made on the Neukluk River, a tributary thirty miles from the mouth of Fish River—a stream 150 miles long and navigable for steamboats — which enters Golovin Bay, Behring Sea, one hundred miles north of St. Michael. In 1895 traces

of coarse gold were discovered on the Neukluk by one
Johansen, a miner who was "grub-staked" by Edwin
Englestad, a trader of Unalaklik and St. Michael. In
the winter of 1897–98, several parties, consisting mainly
of some miners who had reached St. Michael on vessels
of too deep draught to enter the Yukon, prospected and
found gold. W. F. Melsing, of San Francisco, made the
first discovery of importance, in March, at the mouth
of "Melsing Creek," and A. P. Mordaunt, of the same
city, found even better diggings on "Ophir Creek" and
its tributaries, "Dutch" and "Sweetcake" creeks. Ophir
Creek showed $2 to the pan, the diggings being shallow.
Three men, with a rocker built out of baking-powder
packing-cases, rocked out $1500 in eleven or twelve days,
and $70 in two days. During the summer about two
hundred persons outfitted at St. Michael for the new
diggings, and located other tributaries of the Neukluk.
"Council City," eighteen miles up the Neukluk, was the
centre of the new diggings, and consisted, in May, 1898,
of two dwellings—a log cabin and a tent. Not much
work was done until the following winter, when a number of claims were opened up. In the spring the first
steamer arriving at Seattle from St. Michael brought reports of large clean-ups at Council City, but these were
accompanied by other news of so sensational a character
that in the published reports Golovin Bay and Fish River
were lost sight of. This was no less than the discovery
during the winter of immensely rich gold deposits on
Snake River, eighty miles west of Golovin Bay, followed
by the discovery of gold *in the beach sand* of Behring Sea
at Cape Nome. The most reliable account of the discovery appears to be as follows :

In September, 1898, H. L. Blake, partner of W. F.
Melsing, learned through an Eskimo of gold at Cape

Nome, and in company with Rev. J. O. Hultberg, a Swedish evangelical missionary from Golovin Bay, Christopher Kimber, and Frank Porter, went up Snake River, and on "Anvil Creek" discovered gold that ran $4 to the pan, but did not stake, intending to keep their discovery secret and return in the spring with provisions and out-

ROCKING GOLD ON SHORES OF BEHRING SEA, AT CAPE NOME, OCT. 3, 1899

fits. The Rev. Mr. Hultberg gave the information to a fellow-missionary named Anderson, who immediately organized a party of seven, and, braving the storms of that season, set out for Cape Nome, and found on Anvil Creek even richer diggings than Blake's, staked claims, returned to Council City, and claimed the honor of discovery. The secret being out, there was a stampede from all the region around about. Four hundred men reached Nome by January, where they lived in tents till spring. The sufferings of the miners, some of whom had come two hundred miles overland from Kotzebue Sound, were intense. Many tributaries of Snake River were staked, and a city known as " Anvil City " laid out at the mouth of Snake River. In June or July, 1899, gold was discovered in the sand of the beach. When the news reached Dawson eight thousand men left that place inside of a week. On October 1st Anvil City, or " Nome City," at the mouth of Snake River, was a town of eight thousand souls, with warehouses, saloons, thea- tres, tents, and cabins extending for four miles along the beach. Many miles of creeks and the beach for thirteen miles were staked in claims, the beach gold being secured with rockers. The output of the whole region, includ- ing Fish River, for the summer is estimated at $2,000,000 —much more than the Klondike for its first year ; and if the diggings prove as extensive as supposed Klondike will be surpassed. In the spring it is expected that not less than thirty or forty thousand persons will reach the new diggings, which are comparatively easy of access.

A final glance at the upper Yukon. Diggings promis- ing some richness were discovered in the summer of 1898 at Atlin Lake, a connection of the Taku Arm of Tagish Lake. This field, only seventy-five miles from Skagway, is in British Columbia, and that province immediately passed an "alien" law, to prevent any but Canadians from holding claims there. There was no Gold Commis- sioner at the start, records became hopelessly confused, and finally a special commission had to be appointed to try to straighten the affairs out.

As this goes to press, the output for the third clean-up at Klondike is reported at twenty millions, taken almost wholly from the creeks previously described. Dawson has a population of ten thousand, with brick houses, an electric tramway under way up Bonanza Creek, and a telegraph line to Skagway. The railroad is being extended towards White Horse Rapids, where a lode of copper has been reported. A few days after the Cape Nome stampede, cabins that had previously been valued at $500 or more were to be had for the taking. The town has been much improved in appearance, and there are many desirable features of social life—such as clubs —that did not exist before. At the present moment the life of Dawson, as an important mining camp, is limited by that of the half-dozen creeks that have been herein described, unless rich quartz ledges have meanwhile been discovered and developed.

The time by single dog team from Dawson to Skagway has been reduced to ten days. By relays of dogs between the police stations the mounted police have carried letters in nine days. "Jack" Carr, the United States mail carrier, referring to the wonderful change that has taken place in these years, is reported to have said: "If any one had told me a person could make the trip in winter from Dawson to Skagway without lighting a match I couldn't have believed it."

APPENDIX

I

A TYPICAL ONE‑YEAR OUTFIT FOR ONE MAN, SUPPLIED BY THE ALASKA COMMERCIAL COMPANY AT DAWSON, IN JUNE, 1897

ARTICLES	PRICE
500 pounds flour, $6 per sack of 50 pounds	$60.00
80 " beans	10.00
25 " pease	6.25
25 " rolled oats	6.25
15 " corn-meal	3.75
1 case condensed milk, 4 dozen 1-pound cans	24.00
1 " cabbage, 2 dozen 2-pound cans	12.00
1 " roast beef, 1 dozen 2-pound cans	9.00
1 " corned beef, 1 dozen 2-pound cans	9.00
1 " sausage meat, 2 dozen 2-pound cans	18.00
1 " turkey, 2 dozen 2-pound cans	12.00
1 " tomatoes, 2 dozen 2½-pound cans	10.00
1 " string beans, 2 dozen 2-pound cans	12.00
75 pounds bacon	30.00
50 " ham	22.50
25 " dried apples	6.25
25 " dried prunes	6.25
25 " dried peaches	7.50
25 " dried apricots	8.75
25 " raisins or grapes	6.25
100 " granulated sugar	30.00
1 keg pickles, 5 gallons	5.00
1 " sauerkraut, 5 gallons	5.00
5 gallons maple-syrup	15.00
25 pounds evaporated potatoes	12.50
15 " cheese	7.50
20 " coffee	10.00

2 G   465

APPENDIX

ARTICLES	PRICE
5 pounds black tea	$6.25
5 " chocolate	3.75
2 bottles lime-juice	4.00
6 " Worcestershire sauce	4.50
30 pounds lard	9.00
1 box macaroni, 12 pounds	2.00
12 pounds mince-meat	12.00
2 pairs rubber boots	18.00
1 tin assorted cakes, 36 pounds	10.00
4 boxes candles, 120 to the box	24.00
1 case baking powder, 2 dozen $\frac{1}{2}$-pound cans	12.00
6 bars washing-soap	1.00
5 " toilet soap	1.00
15 pounds salt	1.50
1 case coal-oil, 10 gallons	12.00
2 lamp chimneys	.50
100 feet rope, three-fourths or seven-eighths inch	18.00
1 five-foot bull-saw	6.00
2 bull-saw files	1.50
1 pair Arctic overshoes	4.50
2 pairs felt shoes	5.00
4 " woollen socks	4.00
2 " moccasins	5.00
2 " seal water-boots, or mukluks	5.00
6 " skin mittens	15.00
Total	$550.25

PRICES PAID FOR GOODS AT DAWSON, OUTSIDE OF THE STORES OF THE TWO PRINCIPAL TRADING COMPANIES DURING WINTER OF 1897–98

Candles, $1 each ; $40 per box of 120 ; Kerosene, $40 per gallon.
Yukon sheet-steel stoves, with three joints pipe, $40 to $75.
Yukon sled, $40 ; basket sleigh, $75.
Dogs, up to $400 each.
Horses, $3400 per pair ; native hay, $500 to $1200 per ton.
Moccasins, moose-hide, native-made, $7 ; formerly 50 cents per pair.
Moccasins, Canadian moose-hide, $12 per pair.
Mittens, native moose-hide, $6 to $10 per pair.

APPENDIX

Flour, $100 to $120 per sack of 50 pounds in October, 1897; $25 to $50 per sack in January, 1898; $12.50 per sack in May; $3 per sack in June, 1898.

Oysters, about 1-pound tin, $18 to $25 each.

Men's deer-skin "parkas," $50 to $100; ladies' mink-skin "parkas," $100; ladies' tailor-made cloth jackets, $65; men's suit clothes, custom-made, $135 to $150; trousers, not less than $30 per pair; mink or marten caps, $20; drill "parkas," with fox-tail around hood, $7 for making; fur robes, $150 to $400 each; snow-shoes, $30 per pair.

Washing, 50 cents per piece; white shirts, $1.50 each.

Tobacco, smoking, $7.50 per pound; cigarettes, 50 cents per pack.

Fresh mutton, $1.50 per pound; beef, $1 per pound; moose, $1 to $1.75 per pound.

Firewood, $35 to $75 per cord.

Copy of Shakespeare, $50.

SOME STORE PRICES DURING WINTER OF 1897–98

Alcohol, $40 to $83.25 per gallon.

Nails, $500 per keg of 500 pounds.

Blue denim, 28-inch, 75 cents per yard; white muslin, 25 cents to 50 cents per yard.

Pencils, needles, thread, etc., 25 cents each.

12-pound blankets, $25.

Repeating-rifles, $45 each; cartridges for same, 10 cents each.

WAGES AT DAWSON IN WINTER AND SUMMER OF 1897–98

Ordinary miners, $1 to $1.50 an hour.

Foremen in mines, $15 and upward per day of ten hours.

Ordinary labor other than mining, $1 per hour.

Tin-smiths, $1.50 an hour; skilled wood-workers, $17 per day of ten hours; tailors' workmen, $1.50 an hour.

Bartenders, $15 per day; book-keepers, $17.50 per day; faro-dealers, $20 per day; musicians, $17.50 to $20 per day.

Typewriters, 50 cents per folio.

Services of man and two-horse team, $10 per hour; drivers, $300 per month and board.

Typesetters, $1.50 per hour, or $2 per thousand ems.

Cooks in restaurants, $100 per week and board; men waiters, $50 per week and board; women waiters, $100 per month and board.

Barbers, 65 per cent. of receipts of chair, $15 to $40 per day.

During summer of 1898 common wages fell to 60 cents an hour; winter contracts, 1898–99, for ordinary labor in mines, $100 per month with board.

APPENDIX

PRICES OF COMMODITIES AT DAWSON IN SUMMER OF 1898

Oranges and lemons, 50 cents to $1.50 each.

Watermelons, $25 each.

Apples, 25 cents to $1 each.

Champagne, $20 to $40 per pint; sherry, $15 per pint; claret, $15 per pint, $25 per quart; ale, $5 per bottle; mineral water, $3 per bottle.

Shave, $1; hair-cutting, $1.50; bath, $2.50.

II

TABLE OF DISTANCES

	MILES
San Francisco to Dawson *via* St. Michael.........4408 to 4629	
Seattle to Dawson " " ....4018 to 4239	
" " Dyea " "	1000
" " Skagway (steamboat route)................	1012
Juneau to Skagway................................	106
Skagway to Dyea.................................	4
Skagway to Lake Bennett *via* White Pass and Yukon R'w'y	40

DISTANCES ACCORDING TO MR. WILLIAM OGILVIE'S SURVEY

	MILES
Dyea to Summit of Chilkoot......................	14.76
" " Lake Lindeman.........................	23.06
" " Lake Bennett (head of navigation on the Yukon)	28.09
" " Foot of Tagish Lake (Canadian Custom-House)	73.25
" " Head of Miles Canyon...... ⎫ Tramway ⎧	122.94
" " Foot of Miles Canyon....... ⎪ operated ⎪	123.56
" " Head of White-Horse Rapids ⎪ by ⎪	124.95
" " Foot of White-Horse Rapids. ⎭ Horses ⎩	125.33
" " Head of Lake Labarge....................	153.07
" " Foot of Lake Labarge.....................	184.22
" " Hootalinqua, or Teslinto, River............	215.88
" " Big Salmon River.......................	249.33
" " Little Salmon River.....................	285.54
" " Five-Finger Rapids......................	344.83
" " Pelly River (Fort Selkirk).................	403.29
" " Stewart River...........................	508.91
" " Sixty-Mile River (Town-site of Ogilvie)......	530.41
" " Dawson City (Mouth of the Klondike River)..	575.70
Dawson City to Forty-Mile River...................	51.38
" " " International Boundary on the Yukon..	91.73

APPENDIX

III

TABLE OF TEMPERATURES OBSERVED BY MR. WILLIAM OGILVIE AT FORTY-MILE, FROM DECEMBER, 1895, TO NOVEMBER, 1896. FAHRENHEIT DEGREES

	Dec.	Jan.	Feb.	Mar.	Apr.	May	June	July	Aug.	S'pt.	Oct.	Nov.
Lowest....................	−55	−68	−64	−37	−38	−5	30	33	27	5	1	−38
Highest....................	− 6	6	32	40	49	62	80	81	76	63	51	22

TABLES OF TEMPERATURES, FROM SPECIAL REPORT OF THE UNITED STATES GEOLOGICAL SURVEY. FAHRENHEIT DEGREES

LOWEST TEMPERATURES

Station	Jan.	Feb.	Mar.	Apr.	May	June	July	Aug.	S'pt.	Oct.	Nov.	Dec.
St. Michael.................	−47	−55	−39	−27	−2	22	33	31	18	3	−24	−43
Fort Reliance (near Dawson)	−80	−72	−36	10	16	..	..	..	18	−11	−50	−69

HIGHEST TEMPERATURES

Station	Jan.	Feb.	Mar.	Apr.	May	June	July	Aug.	S'pt.	Oct.	Nov.	Dec.
St. Michael.................	44	41	43	46	57	75	75	69	69	54	42	45
Fort Reliance (near Dawson)	20	27	45	59	76	..	..	..	67	55	36	34

PRECIPITATION (RAIN AND SNOW) IN INCHES

Station	Jan.	Feb.	Mar.	Apr.	May	June	July	Aug.	S'pt.	Oct.	Nov.	Dec.
Juneau...................	10.17	4.98	7.20	4.49	10.28	5.45	6.41	7.14	7.82	6.26	7.95	7.28
Ft. Reliance (nr. Dawson)	7.40	1.26	1.13	0.08	0.69	..	..	..	5.30	0.79	2.93	1.78

APPENDIX

	Oct.	Nov.	Dec.
	°	°	°
Highest, at 8 A.M.	30	20	26
Lowest	18	—40	—34
Mean......................	8	—7	—6

IV

UNITED STATES MILITARY IN ALASKA

On October 29, 1897, by order of the Secretary of War, all the
land and islands within a radius of one hundred miles from St.
Michael Island was declared a military reservation and named
"Fort St. Michael." Other military posts have been established
at Tanana, Circle City, Eagle City, Dyea, and Wrangell.

V

THE BOUNDARY DISPUTE

In 1867 the United States acquired by purchase the territory
held by the Russians in North America. The boundary between
Russian America and the British Possessions had previously been
defined in a treaty between Great Britain and Russia, naming the
141st meridian, from the Arctic Ocean to Mount St. Elias, thence
southward along the summit of a range of mountains. The first
attempt by the United States to locate the boundary was made
in 1869, when Captain Raymond, U. S. A., ascended the Yukon to
the Porcupine River, and by rough observations discovered Fort
Yukon, a Hudson's Bay Co.'s post, to be in American territory. No
further attempt was made by any one until Lieutenant Schwatka,
in 1883, roughly located the line at "Boundary Butte," at the mouth
of Mission Creek. In 1887 the Canadian government sent a party
of exploration into the Yukon, and instructed Mr. William Ogilvie to make astronomical observations and locate the boundary.
In the winter of 1887–88 Mr, Ogilvie built an observatory on the
Yukon, below Forty-Mile, and located the line nine miles to the
eastward of Schwatka's line. To verify this, the United States,

APPENDIX

in 1889, sent two members of the Coast and Geodetic Survey, Messrs. Turner and Magrath, who located the line to the westward of Ogilvie, but a revision of Magrath's figures showed the line to be *east* of Ogilvie's. Meanwhile Forty-Mile Creek, which lay on both sides of the supposed boundary, was attaining such importance that the Canadian government entered into correspondence with the United States government with a view to the appointment of commissioners to meet and finally decide upon the line. In 1896, Mr. Ogilvie, the Canadian commissioner, proceeded to the Yukon, expecting to meet a commissioner from the United States, but, none appearing, he alone cut out the present line, which has been accepted by the miners as final. As respects the southern coast of Alaska, however, the wording of the treaty is not so clear. The line laid down upon all maps followed the crest of a range of mountains parallel with the coast-line, some distance inland, and is shown as crossing Lake Lindeman. Neither the United States nor Canada seems to have considered the exact location of this part of the line of much importance until the discovery of the Klondike, when it became desirable for Canada to obtain a port by which she could enter the Yukon without crossing American territory. Upon the failure of her various attempts to put through a feasible " all - Canadian " route into the Yukon, Canada vigorously asserted her right, by interpretation of the treaty, to the possession of Dyea and Skagway, at the head of Lynn Canal, claiming that the canals or fjords which indent the coast of Alaska merely cut into but do not break the " continuous range of mountains " designated as the boundary, and forthwith demanding arbitration. The American contention is that there is no continuous range of mountains along the coast, although numerous high peaks ; that the canals or fjords effectually break the continuity of any range that might exist, and, besides, they cannot consent to arbitrate territory that has been in undisputed possession of the United States and of Russia. A *modus vivendi* has been agreed upon whereby Canada remains in possession of her posts at the Chilkoot and White Pass and Chilkat summits pending a final settlement.

THE END